Women Directors and Their Films

Women Directors and Their Films

Mary G. Hurd

PRAEGER

Westport, Connecticut
London

Library of Congress Cataloging-in-Publication Data

Hurd, Mary G.
    Women directors and their films / Mary G. Hurd.
      p. cm.
    Includes bibliographical references and index.
    ISBN 0–275–98578–4 (alk. paper)
    1. Women motion picture producers and directors–Biography.   I. Title.
PN1998.2.H86   2007
791.43023'30922–dc22   2006029526
   [B]

British Library Cataloguing in Publication Data is available.

Copyright © 2007 by Mary G. Hurd

Library of Congress Catalog Card Number: 2006029526
ISBN: 0–275–98578–4

First published in 2007

Praeger Publishers, 88 Post Road West, Westport, CT 06881
An imprint of Greenwood Publishing Group, Inc.
www.praeger.com

Printed in the United States of America

The paper used in this book complies with the
Permanent Paper Standard issued by the National
Information Standards Organization (Z39.48–1984).

10 9 8 7 6 5 4 3 2 1

Contents

Contents

Introduction

The reader of this book will be introduced to basic biographical and critical information about selected women directors. Although it is primarily offered to those who want to know more about women directors, film students or enthusiasts may also find something of interest here. The women included in this discussion were chosen on the basis of their contributions to filmmaking in the United States or because their films are widely known in the United States. Owing to limited space, the women presented in each category, with the exception of Arzner and Lupino, are merely representative and not exhaustive. Many others deserve recognition and appreciation and should be the subjects of future volumes.

The book progresses in a somewhat chronological fashion, beginning with Dorothy Arzner and Ida Lupino, the only two mainstream women directors in America until 1971, when Elaine May became the first woman to write, direct, and perform in her own film. The mainstream success of Nora Ephron in the 1980s and Nancy Meyers in 2001 and 2003 hinged on their facility with the romantic comedy genre. Both Amy Heckerling and Martha Coolidge found mainstream success with high-school teen comedy, whereas Mimi Leder and Kathryn Bigelow were singularly noted for their action and special effects.

The burden on mainstream directors to make money for the studios—more rigorous for women and usually dependent upon formula films—has led most women to consider independent films as a means of expressing their personal visions of women's lives and experiences. Lizzie Borden, who promotes radical feminist views, saw documentaries as a primary means of disseminating her beliefs regarding the responsibility of women to choose their own images, whereas Mary Harron's lifelong interest in popular culture led to her intense studies of deranged characters. Other filmmakers representing specific ethnic or social backgrounds—Dash, Savoca, Anders, Spheeris—have been very vocal about their desires to communicate meaningful experiences for other women with similar backgrounds.

The goal of Barbara Kopple in her documentaries of struggling workers has always been to provide a voice for those who had none.

The international directors included in this volume, while reflecting interesting historical trends and social conditions in their respective countries, are also noteworthy in that, with the exception of Riefenstahl, all are continuing to make films. Each of the four talented, young newcomers, has made a large impact on the cinema world with her interpretations of women's experiences, and perhaps provides indications for the future of women's films. Of the four directors who gained access to directing by virtue of their acting experience, May and Marshall have not made films exclusively about women.

I must express my gratitude to students who have responded to the study of women directors and who have shared my frustration with the limited opportunities for women directors. I appreciate the tireless efforts of research assistants Wilson Onstott, Paul Ludwig, and especially Reg Ivory. Also, I am indebted to my family for their patience and encouragement.

1

Pioneers

In the early years of film, opportunities for women were plentiful, ranging from positions as typists, assistants, writers, editors, actresses, with some women gaining chances to direct, and a few creating their own companies. Pioneering woman director, Alice Guy Blache, secretary of Leon Gaumont of Gaumont Studios in France, directed in 1896, *La Fee aux Choux* (*The Cabbage Fairy*), arguably the first fictional film. Between 1896 and 1907, she directed around 400 films (*Silent*, Slide viii). She and her husband came to the United States and she set up her own studio in New Jersey, where she turned out an additional 354 films (Slide viii). America's "first native woman film director" (Slide viii), Lois Weber, who also began writing and directing at the American branch of Gaumont Studios, was one of the most important and highly paid American filmmakers in the 1910s (Corrigan and White 384). A true auteur, Weber wrote the films she directed and, early on, starred in them, using them as a medium for her ideas and philosophy (Slide viii). Screenwriter Frances Marion started with Weber and went on to write screenplays for more than 150 films in her career (Corrigan and White 384). Mrs. Wallace Reid, a former actress, returned to directing and producing after her husband's death and made numerous melodramas. Slide has noted that between 1911 and 1920, women were directing films "as often and as well as their male counterparts" (iv), although the exact number of these women, many of whom were uncredited or whose films have been lost, may never be known.

By the 1920s, most women, other than editors and screenwriters, encountered difficulties as the movies became big business. Owing to the production costs in the 1930s, the growing departmentalization of filmmaking, and the reluctance of studio executives to trust a director of silent films with talkies, the number of women declined sharply after the coming of sound in the late 1920s. Many notable women and male silent film directors were shuttled aside for stage directors, mostly male, and from New York. In the 1930s, unions and guilds were firmly established in Hollywood, with predominantly male membership, and few women occupied prominent positions in any of them. Women were essentially barred from directing until the 1960s and 1970s, and then their contributions were linked primarily with alternative filmmaking.

DOROTHY ARZNER

Although Dorothy Arzner was not the first woman director, or possibly even the best, she was the only woman director to survive the transition between the silent and sound films and to sustain a career in filmmaking for thirty years. From 1927 to 1943, Arzner directed seventeen films, four silent and thirteen with sound, that testify to her talent and perseverance, and to the inspiration she became to succeeding film directors.

Dorothy Arzner was born January 3, 1897(?), in San Francisco, to restaurateur parents who moved to Los Angeles and opened the Hoffman Café, famous for its German food and its locus as a meeting place for film luminaries. Arzner attended The University of California for two years studying medicine, but, after working in a doctor's office for a year, she abandoned the idea of becoming a doctor. In 1919, convinced that film production was the career for her and that she should learn everything about it, she began typing scripts for fifteen dollars a week at Famous Players–Lasky Studios. She soon worked her way up to script girl, and later to editor, where she acquired most of her knowledge about film. Her mentor, editor James Cruze, was so appreciative of her editing abilities in *Blood and Sand* (1922), the famous Rudolph Valentino vehicle, that he hired her to edit his enormously popular *The Covered Wagon* and additional films (Arzner 21). She had begun writing scripts for various studios and made it known that she would like to direct them. In 1927, Paramount, sensing her imminent departure, offered her an opportunity to direct.

Reflecting on her beginning in film directing, Arzner indicated she had watched other directors at work, but that she had not directed anything before *Fashions for Women*, her first film (Arzner 23). Despite mixed reviews, it was successful, leading to a long-term contract with Paramount. *Ten Modern Commandments* and *Get Your Man* followed in 1927 and *Manhattan Cocktail* in 1928. This time, Arzner gained a reputation as "star maker" directing female actors, who in many ways epitomized "modern" women—those who sought careers and financial independence in roles that emphasized their unique talents and mirrored the complications inherent in being ambitious American women.

Arzner's first talking picture was *The Wild Party* (1929), starring Clara Bow and Frederic March, the first of the seven films she made at Paramount: *Sarah and Son* (1930), *Anybody's Woman* (1930), *Paramount on Parade* (a sequence, 1930), *Honor Among Lovers* (1931), *Working Girls* (1931), and *Merrily We Go To Hell* (1932). She then decided to freelance, directing *Christopher Strong* (1933) at RKO; *Nana* (1934), MGM; *Craig's Wife* (1936), Columbia; *The Bride Wore Red* (1937), MGM; *Dance, Girl, Dance* (1940), RKO; and *First Comes*

Courage (1943), Columbia. Arzner also codirected or contributed to *Behind the Makeup* (1930), Paramount; *Charming Sinners* (1930), Paramount; and *The Last of Mrs. Cheyney* (1937), MGM.

Following a bout with pneumonia, Arzner retired from the screen in 1943, continuing to film Women's Army Corps training films during World War II and Pepsi commercials for her friend Joan Crawford, later teaching at UCLA, where one of her pupils was future director Francis Ford Coppola. She produced plays, often for Billie Burke (Glenda, the Good Witch in *The Wizard of Oz*), one of her favorite actresses (Geller 2). In her directing career, she met Marion Morgan, a choreographer, and the two women shared a Hollywood Hills home, remaining partners until Morgan's death in 1971. The Director's Guild of America paid tribute to her in 1975, but at the end of her life, she was essentially forgotten. Dorothy Arzner died in 1979 at her home near Palm Springs.

Although the films of Dorothy Arzner were primarily unearthed and reconsidered as a part of feminist studies designed to establish a feminine aesthetic of film unmistakably different from the male, this approach systematically reduces the significance of Arzner's accomplishments. To some, Arzner's standing for posterity rests not on her ability to work within the studio system and turn out one impressive film after another, but on how well she challenged the patriarchal or male-dominated system. Arzner was not a feminist by today's standards, although she devoted much effort to the advancement of women. She did not want to be known as a woman's director or a director of women's films; she viewed herself as a Hollywood director. In Hollywood, she was seen as a first-rate director.

Despite the fact that she had written action screenplays for adventure and western films as well as scripts for and about women, most of the films Arzner directed fall into the category of Women's Melodrama. She performed the duties of directing films about women, their lives and relationships—probably what the studio wanted—using her skills and talents in collaboration with both women and men in the film industry. Speaking about her working relationships, she has said: "No one gave me trouble because I was a woman. Men were more helpful than women" (Arzner 23). She worked frequently with noted actresses, displaying their talents to their best advantage, and was instrumental in advancing the careers of Katharine Hepburn, Rosalind Russell, and Lucille Ball. In her anomalous position as the only woman director with a career in Hollywood, she wore masculine clothing as she assumed the persona of a typical Hollywood director, thereby making her role as a director of women's films even more enigmatic.

Known for her grasp of feminine psychology and her remarkable ability to get along with women, Arzner frequently achieved success when she and her scriptwriters, in this case, Zoe Akins, worked closely together to develop a dimension not in the original storyline. In *Christopher Strong*, Arzner begins with a sentimental novel by Gilbert Frankau about a fated relationship between aviatrix Cynthia Darrington and Christopher Strong, a Member of Parliament, and ends with a film that subtly raises questions about love and marriage. Cynthia (Katharine Hepburn) falls in love with Strong (Colin Clive), a man old enough to be her father and becomes pregnant. An independent woman hoping to set a record altitude flight, she is requested by Strong to cancel her flight; but realizing the depth of his ties with his family, she proceeds with the flight and commits suicide. While Arzner has gone on record saying that Cynthia took her own life because she could not face the future with an illegitimate child (Arzner 26), the inclusion of additional dialogue and scenes in the film not present in the book suggests a more complex motivation. In the bedroom scene, when Cynthia and Strong have made love for the first time, the camera records the entire scene by focusing on Cynthia's outstretched arm. The couple's voices are offscreen. Strong has presented her with a bracelet and asks her to give up flying, for him. Cynthia, with her hand extended into the frame to turn on the light, says, in voiceover, "I love my bracelet. . . . Now I'm shackled." Cynthia agrees to give up her altitude flight.

Women critics have commented on this famous scene, and some unfavorably. Judith Mayne sees Strong's request during "this supposed moment of afterglow" an exertion of his authority; she cites this scene as his "conquest, so to speak, of Cynthia" (Mayne, 1999, 118) by Strong. Film reviewer Pauline Kael insists that Cynthia's "acquiescence destroyed her." Kael continues that the word for what Strong did to Cynthia is "'emasculation,' [and] it was perfectly well understood in 1933 that her full possibilities as a woman, as a person, were being destroyed" (Kael 341). Interestingly enough, a similar scene shows Lady Strong at her dressing table removing her bracelets, a gesture that suggests a connection of fetters with love and marriage, but Cynthia, "shackled" to a man she loves, whose child she carries, whom she cannot marry, cannot bear the loss of her independence and chooses suicide.

Arzner's very successful *Craig's Wife*, based on George Kelly's Pulitzer Prize–winning play and Broadway hit, that features a self-centered woman who foolishly prizes her elegant house above her husband becomes, in the hands of Arzner and Mary C. McCall, her scriptwriter, a character study of a woman who contemplates the institution of marriage. Harriet (Rosalind Russell) is characterized as a cold woman who refuses connections with other people, obsessively exerts control of her house, and succeeds in driving off everyone around her. She considers her marriage to Walter Craig as a bargain—her role of wife to him for the security of a house. She is frequently seen posed by the mantle, bordered by Greek sculptures, suggesting that her wifely role consists in playing a part for Walter. Harriet's niece is appalled to hear Harriet describe marriage as a "bargain" and insists that her romantic feelings for her fiancé are honest. Harriet reflects upon the "honest" basis of marriage, considering the "honesty" of the recent murder-suicide of a local couple (the husband discovered his wife's adultery), and upon the "honesty" involved in her own mother's being abandoned by her husband for a younger woman, leading to her mother's destitution. Harriet recalls her mother's loss of her home and eventual death "of a broken heart" as evidence of the perils of entering into a marriage contract "honestly" or perhaps naively. Of course, Harriet's "honest" appraisal of the limitations placed upon women in marriage is deemed dishonest by everyone who knows her, and one by one, they exit her and she is left alone in the house. At this point, Harriet receives word of her sister's death and breaks down over that loss—not because everyone else has walked away. When the neighbor, Mrs. Frazier (Billie Burke), changed within the script from a bitter widow to an outgoing grandmother, comes to sympathize briefly with Harriet, she is asked to stay longer. We remember that she did not ask Walter to stay, and ponder the implication that perhaps Arzner is suggesting that Harriet is more comfortable with the "honesty" of a relationship with a good friend rather than one which seems to be a "bargain" (Geller 4-5).

Reviews of the film in 1936 were surprisingly favorable, praising Arzner and raising Russell to star status. A review from *Hollywood Reporter* applauds Arzner for a "well-directed, well-acted, handsomely produced ... deviation from the run-of-the-mill stuff" (Sept. 11, 1936, p. 3), and the *Motion Picture Daily*, noting the departure from the usual formula, insists, "It is a woman's picture" (Sept. 12, 1936, p. 2). The cinema column in *Time* magazine announces that the vitriolic Mrs. Craig "loses her husband through psychopathic selfishness" (Oct. 12, 1936, p. 32), and neglects to take into account the regeneration of Harriet that Arzner labored to accomplish. Of this, Arzner says:

> there was a crucial moment when Rosalind Russell was left alone with *her house*. The audience hated her up to that point, and I had only one close-up left with which to turn their emotion to sympathy. Russell did it so perfectly that many women cried as they moved up the aisle. (Rosen quoting from private correspondence with Arzner, 376)

Of the more contemporary critics, Rosen observes that despite Arzner's need to conform with the studio system, she "utilized her authority to effect subtle ... nuances open to interpretation as 'feminine sensibilities'" (Rosen 376).

Of Arzner's last three films, *Dance, Girl, Dance*, whose reception was lukewarm in 1940, is now considered one of her most successful and one most relevant to feminist film studies. The story concerns two women, both dancers and from different economic backgrounds. Judy (Maureen O'Hara), an aspiring ballerina, and Bubbles (Lucille Ball), a burlesque dancer interested in rich men, are both friends and rivals, and are members of a dance troupe led by Madame Basilova (Maria Ouspenskaya). Judy is a more refined student of ballet, whereas brash and vulgar Bubbles is out for all she can get, positing artistic expression against exploitation. Basilova, on her way with her protégé, Judy, to an audition, is run down by a car and killed. Bubbles, who is in demand, announces to Judy that she got her a job in burlesque at $25 a week. The job entails performing as a classical dancer in the middle of Bubbles's act (while the men jeer) to make the audience desire Bubbles even more. Judy understands that she was hired as a stooge. Bubbles also goes after Judy's married boyfriend, Jimmy, when she discovers he is rich.

The film considers the two women from the point of class as it affects their success in terms of social status and sexuality. The scene where Judy watches the American Ballet company and, to her shock and surprise, sees a ballet set in an urban area with dancers dressed as office workers and street vendors, is an apparent attempt to challenge the boundary between vaudeville and ballet and between Bubbles and Judy (Mayne 140). The film, which seems like a lament for the crass, crude society that elevates money above aesthetic sensibility seems to favor Bubbles. Judy, who is depicted as less sure of herself than Bubbles, reaches a breaking point when she learns Bubbles has married Jimmy. She moves to the front of the stage, faces her audience and delivers a strong reprimand:

> Go ahead and stare. I'm not ashamed. . . . Get your money's worth. . . . I know you want me to tear my clothes off so's you can look your fifty cents worth. Fifty cents for the privilege of staring at a girl the way your wives won't let you. What do you suppose we think of you up here—with your silly smirks your mothers would ashamed of? And we know it's the thing of the moment for the dress suits to come and laugh at us too. We'd laugh right back at the lot of you, only we're paid to let you sit there and roll your eyes and make your screamingly clever remarks. What's it for? So's you can go home when the show's over and strut before your wives and sweethearts and play at being the stronger sex for a minute? I'm sure they see through you just like we do.

After the speech and the applause, Bubbles comes out and starts a fight with Judy, to the delight of the audience. Carted off to night court, Judy is fined $50, who admits she wanted to kill Bubbles. Jimmy, who has awakened to discover he has married Bubbles, is told by his ex-wife that she can get him an annulment, at which point, Bubbles demands $50,000. Steve Adams (Ralph Bellamy), the modern dance instructor whom Judy and Basilova were on their ill-fated journey to see, is in the audience during Judy's angry speech. He pays her fine and agrees to instruct her.

Arzner was given *Dance, Girl, Dance* to direct by producer Erich Pommer, former head of UFA Studios in Germany, who replaced the original director with her after one week of filming. Arzner revised the script to focus on the conflict "between the artistic, spiritual aspirations of Maureen O'Hara and the commercial huckster gold-digging of Lucille Ball" (Arzner 18). In this film, the famous "Arzner Touch," a reference to the new image of women in her films, seems most apparent. Her female characters tend to be strong-willed, self-determined women who are not stereotypical female film characters, and whereas her male characters tend to lack depth, or attempt to make the women with whom they are involved to yield to their demands, her women are complex, multidimensional and fiercely independent. And, of course, "the overriding mood of Arzner's films is sympathetic to the women characters who struggle to advance their own ambitions even as the men in their lives oppose or destroy them," adds Louise Heck-Rabi (81).

Arzner's work ethic in her early years seemed a blend of a desire to learn and an absence of false pride. "When I went to work in a studio, I took my pride and made a nice little ball of it and threw it right out the window" (Arzner,

St. John 24), Arzner has said. She has attributed her own independent stance to her longevity as a director. Not needing to work for a living, she could have stepped aside at any time had she been unhappy. While she worked, she paid extreme attention to details, and brought in her films under budget and on time to maintain fellowship with the male directors. And, she kept her eye on the box office. Asked why she stopped directing films, Arzner replied, "Because pictures left me, really.... And ... I had had enough. Twenty years of directing is, I think, about enough" (Margulies 18).

IDA LUPINO

Ida Lupino is viewed as the Dorothy Arzner of the 1950s because she was the only woman director during that time, and, like Arzner, is catnip to feminist film critics who continue to reexamine her films for evidence of feminism. There are more comparisons: both initially preferred careers other than directing; both began directing as substitutes for male directors who had fallen ill; both worked their ways up through the film industry, ending their careers in television; and both survived in the male-dominated studio system through skill and tact. They were feminists in the sense that both attempted to depict the reality of women's lives, specifically with regard to their limited opportunities in marriage and society.

Ida Lupino was born in London, England, on February 4; her birth year, usually given as 1918, is listed variously as 1914 and 1917. Born into a theatrical family dating back to seventeenth-century Italy, Lupino was the first of two daughters born to Stanley Lupino, a music hall comedian, and Connie Emerald, an actress. As a mature-looking thirteen-year-old, Lupino enrolled in the prestigious Royal Academy of Dramatic Arts and was soon given a part auditioned for by her mother.

Her First Affaire (Allen Dwan, 1933) was the first of many films that cast Lupino in roles for women older than herself. She made five more films in the U.K. and then signed with Paramount, appearing in a string of comedies over a four-year period. Her first big break came with the starring role in *The Light That Failed* (William Wellman, 1939), which introduced Lupino's famous cynical, outwardly tough persona; and, while at Warner Brothers, she starred in *They Drive by Night* (Raoul Walsh, 1940), *High Sierra* (Raoul Walsh, 1941), *The Hard Way* (Vincent Sherman, 1943), and *Deep Valley* (Jean Negulesco, 1947).

As a talented, rising actress, Lupino resented the limitations placed on her career by studios and determined to exert some control over her own professional life. Having divorced Louis Hayward, Lupino, in 1948, married Collier Young, her second husband, became a U.S. citizen and founded with Young and Anson Ford an independent company called (for her mother) Emerald Productions. In 1950, the company became The Filmmakers, whose objectives were to make low-cost, high-quality films, frequently about provocative topics that provided work for a group of aspiring young actors.

Between 1949 and 1954, The Filmmakers produced twelve feature films. Of these, Lupino directed or codirected six, scripted or coscripted five, coproduced one, and acted in three. Lupino first moved into the director's chair for the film, *Not Wanted* (1949) (though she took no credit for it), when director Elmer Clifton became ill three days into the film. Other films she directed are *Never Fear* (1950), *Outrage* (1950), *Hard, Fast and Beautiful* (1951), *The Hitch-Hiker* (1953), *The Bigamist* (1953), and *The Trouble With Angels* (1966). Also, during these years, Lupino appeared in four films for companies other than hers, divorced Collier Young, married Howard Duff, and gave birth to their daughter, Bridget, in 1952.

In 1953, Lupino, along with actors Dick Powell, Charles Boyer, and David Niven, founded Four-Star Productions, the originator of CBS Television's esteemed drama series, *Four-Star Playhouse* (1953–1956). From 1956 to 1958, she starred with Duff in *Mr. Adams and Eve*, a series produced by their own company, Bridget Productions. Lupino devoted the rest of her career to television, having directed about fifty television program and series episodes, the majority made between the late 1950s and the 1970s. She specialized in action, mystery dramas and westerns, directing episodes of *Alfred Hitchcock Presents* (1955–1962), *Have Gun Will Travel* (1957–1962), *Dr. Kildare* (1961–1963), *The Virginian* (1962–1971), *Thriller* (1960–1962), *The Fugitive* (1963–1967), *Gilligan's Island* (1964–1967), *Daniel Boone* (1963–1967), *Bewitched* (1964–1972), *The Big Valley* (1965–1969), *The Bill Cosby Show* (1969–1971), and many others.

Of the films that Lupino directed, she either wrote or cowrote the scripts; and for the characters she created in them, she drew upon the same seemingly tough, cynical, independent women she had portrayed so well in her own film roles. Sensuous, ambitious, and vulnerable, these women appear passive or victimized, and are frequently entangled in situations that were cinematically unacceptable or off limits. Her first film, *Not Wanted*, which she took over as director because she had cowritten the screenplay, depicts the distressing plight of an unmarried girl with an unwanted pregnancy. This film is indicative of the general pattern of Lupino's narratives, in that it begins with a brief view of the character's "normal" life, proceeds to a "sudden, traumatic interruption" of that life, followed by an "overwhelming sense of alienation and disorientation," and a brief period of time in a shelter or community hostel, and ends with a "reversal of trauma" and a start toward a new life (Scheib 217).

Not Wanted, publicized as a daring look at the appalling plight of an unwed mother, actually portrays a girl ill-equipped for life. Sally (Sally Forrest), is unhappy living in a drab, small town. She meets Steve (Leo Penn), an itinerant piano player, falls for him and follows him to the next town. On the way, she meets Drew (Keefe Brasselle) who owns a gaseteria in the town she's going to. He provides her with a room and a job as a waitress in his establishment. Drew, who lost a leg in World War II, is eager to share his life with Sally; she is ignored by Steve, who moves on to the next town. Sally almost accepts Drew's proposal of marriage only to discover she is pregnant with Steve's child. She leaves home, purposeless, a dazed wanderer, who doubts she could ever return. Lupino shows lengthy sequences of Sally walking silently through the streets, emphasizing her realistic documentary-like treatment of social problems. Sally enters a home for unwed mothers, a haven from the day-to-day world, and lives there, performing domestic chores until her baby is born. But, back in the real world, her inability to earn a living and care for the child forces her to give up her baby. The painful decision to offer her child for adoption is depicted as a very real option in Sally's socioeconomic situation. Regretting her decision bitterly, she kidnaps a baby to replace her lost child. The scene showing Sally sitting in jail—the one that actually begins the film, with the foregoing action shown in flashback— among the half-crazed women, suggests Lupino sees Sally as almost insane (Scheib 218).

The boldness of Lupino's venture in this film "of a sociological nature that challenged contemporary norms" (Georgakas 33) is only faintly perceived today. In portraying an unwed mother as a person worth caring about, Lupino chose unknowns for the acting and often referred to her films as being documentary in nature. She favored straightforward narratives shot on location in the film noir style seen in many low-budget films of the era. Film noir, literally meaning "black film," refers to a stylistic trend in post–World War II films that relies on light and shadows to suggest unknowable depths in human nature, and is accompanied by feelings of anxiety, cynicism, paranoia, and a questioning of traditional values or methods, including those represented, in this case, in cinema. Film historian, David A. Cook, writes, "However briefly ... film noir held up a dark mirror to postwar America and reflected its moral anarchy" (Cook 380). Opting to leave the studio to shoot urban films on location became Lupino's trademark, occasioned partly by budgetary constraints, but more so by her desire to attain sociological realism. She was interested in fitting into the film noir style the sensibilities and characteristics of the typical working-class women whom she had played to perfection as an actor (Georgakas 34).

Not Wanted gives attention to the problem of being young, pregnant, and unwed in 1940s America. When Lupino took over direction after Clifton's heart attack, she was faced with the presumption that a woman filmmaker would ruin the film's prospects, and particularly those of a film containing volatile subject matter. Lupino rewrote the script shifting the emphasis from a seduction to a scenario that clearly showed a consensual sexual encounter. Sally is depicted as a sexually active woman entrapped in dire circumstances; the title *Not Wanted* was Lupino's own choice that referred to both the mother and the child. But to gain script approval by the Production Code Administration (PCA), which was essential for theatrical distribution, Lupino was forced to make concessions that were, by today's standards, ridiculous. She was not allowed to use the word "pregnant" in the film, nor was she allowed to show women of various ethnic backgrounds in the home for unwed mothers. Lupino was forced to show Sally's parents as more supportive than she had intended and was compelled to stress the unlawful nature of Sally's sexual life (Georgakas 35).

The reviews were mixed. *Newsweek* (August 1, 1949) noted, "the story is told with a lack of moral indignation," and *The New York Times Film Reviews* believed the film "may be classed as a solemn, good-intentioned object lesson which falls short of making the grade as satisfactory entertainment" (July 25, 1949). However, Lupino was invited to discuss *Not Wanted* on a national radio program hosted by Eleanor Roosevelt, and her appearance resulted in largely favorable responses.

Keefe Brasselle and Sally Forrest, two unknowns in *Not Wanted*, whose careers began with the film, appear in Lupino's next film, *Never Fear*, the story of an active woman forced into a disfigured form of womanhood. The film addresses the hysteria then surrounding polio, which, unlike AIDS of a future generation, struck all ages, classes, and regions, unrelated to any social behavior. The opening scenes feature Carol (Forrest) and her partner/choreographer/fiancé, Guy (Brasselle), enacting a fencing mime in a provocative dance score that celebrates and symbolizes their engagement. In the number, Lupino's camera dwells on Carol's sinuous, responsive body, her "surrender" of her heart, body, and sword to her partner and lingers on the couple's duality. Lupino depicts the onset of polio in a sharply etched scene in which Guy is working on a new routine and is unaware of Carol silently clinging to the ropes behind him, undone by the calamity that has befallen her. Lupino, who had recovered from an attack of polio in 1934, perhaps included many of her own experiences into the script. Carol is seen undergoing therapy to regain the use of her legs, and after many weeks of exercises, she wills herself to walk, but falls. She pounds the floor with her fist. Carol and Guy drift from each other, Carol seeking the companionship of another patient while Guy is drawn to a secretary where he works. The film, introduced by the statement that this is a true story, does not show how Carol resolves her situation.

In her third film, Lupino tackles another volatile issue—rape—at a time when the word "rape" was not even used. *Outrage* tells the story of Ann (Mala Powers) and the brutal attack upon her that changed everything about her life. Leaving work late one night, she starts toward home. A man closing up a coffee stand begins to follow her, and a lengthy chase takes place in a truck yard. As he closes in on her, she trips and falls, and he emerges out of the shadows toward her. Lupino's camera moves up and away from the two figures toward a nearby building where a man looks out an upstairs window, and seeing nothing, closes it. The film dwells largely on the dreadful psychological consequences of Ann's rape, beginning with her alienation from everyone. Lupino's two previous films depicted a difference in gender perception of the victimized person: Sally forms a brief sisterhood with the other women in the home for unwed mothers, while the male authorities lecture her severely, and Carol receives mute sympathy from other women when she becomes deformed as doctors and other male officials continue to insist on a cure. But, in Ann's case, the rape brought about immediate polarization. Her father and the police captain are helpless and embarrassed, but Ann's mother and a policewoman hover over Ann's bed upstairs. Guilt becomes transferred: Ann's father says, "They look at me as if I had done something"; and Ann is perceived as "damaged goods." Women are usually empathetic, but male family members and friends are ill at ease in her presence.

The second part of *Outrage* shifts dramatically from the city to the country, in another polarization. After Ann has left home, she is discovered unconscious in a farmland area, and taken by a local minister to the home of a couple who sell fruit. Ann begins to lose her feelings of alienation in the country, away from the threatening looks of the people back in her town, and seems to be recovering under the watchful care of the young minister, Doc. Once at a picnic, she is pursued by a local lothario insisting on a kiss; confusing him with the rapist, she pounds him with a wrench. At her hearing, aided by Doc's plea, she is absolved of any crime and sent back to her family, her fiancé, and psychiatric care (Scheib 222–223).

These films appear like a trilogy in that they all depict women who have reason to anticipate the direction their lives will take when they are truncated early on in the films. In *Never Fear* and *Outrage*, both women celebrate their prospects for a life. Carol dances the commitment dance with Guy and plans their future together, and Ann has accepted the proposal of her fiancé and waits for her father's approval. The traumatic events that devastate these women and blast their lives are presented on screen as journeys they are forced to take to escape from their situations for a while, and then accept their destiny. The physical journey reflects an emotional, psychological journey the women take that is depicted stylistically as film noir. Lupino presents documentary-like accounts of the lives and difficulties of the women in these films that challenge taboo subjects and function as forerunners of the independent films of women in the present day. She chose topics vital to women and proceeded to reflect in the films the claustrophobic atmosphere of the 1950s. Conservative opinion held that subjects such as sex, unwanted pregnancy, illegitimate children, or rape were not fit subject matter for film.

Hard, Fast and Beautiful (1951) serves as a kind of turning point for Lupino's films. In telling the story of Florence, a tennis player whose social mobility occurs through her association with the country club, Lupino also tells the story of Florence's ruthlessly ambitious mother, Millie, who exploits her daughter to achieve her lifelong economic and social aspirations. Florence's ill father, whom Florence adores and for whom she plays tennis, is no match for Millie and Florence's coach in their manipulation of Florence, but Florence and her father share a deep emotional bond. Florence's fiancé and Millie also have conflicting demands on Florence as Millie wants "greater and greater glory" and he grows less indulgent of waiting for Florence to marry him (Scheib 225). Florence, who seems to have no idea of economic realities, is the only Lupino heroine who does not work. When she finally discovers the extent of her exploitation, she visits her ill father in California, and returns the next day to win the match and to reject all that her mother represents and to renounce tennis. She marries her fiancé and moves from her former entrapment into the "passivity" (Scheib 225) of marriage.

Her most successful film, as well as her personal favorite, was *The Hitch-Hiker*. In it, she directs an all-male cast in a thriller, depicting the dire straits of two friends on a fishing trip who pick up a hitch-hiker who turns out to be a wanted murderer. The friends, Gilbert (Frank Lovejoy) and Roy (Edmond O'Brien), from El Centro, California, embark upon a long-awaited fishing trip in Mexico, but encounter instead Emmett Myers (William Talman). The killer commandeers the vehicle, journeying toward Mexico by day and camping by night in secluded areas, where he seems, by reason of an eyelid deformity, to sleep with one eye open, eerily watching them every moment. Lupino's interest in noir is evident here as she skillfully parallels the dry, barren desert expanse with the shadowy depths of darkness to suggest the contradictory, unfathomable aspects of human nature. Her depiction of the two fishing buddies is very sympathetic, and her approach to the serial killer as an outcast of society is reminiscent of her earlier films about characters who were unwanted. The character of Myers is based on William Edward Cook Jr., an ex-convict from Missouri who killed a family of five and a traveling salesman while hitch-hiking in December 1950. He was captured by Mexican police at Santa Rosalia (the same site of capture in this film) and executed in California in 1952. When Cook was five, his father abandoned him and his seven brothers and sisters in a mine cave, and, although his siblings were placed with foster parents, no one wanted the small, ugly kid with a deformed right eyelid ("Young Man With a Gun," *Time*, January 22, 1951, 19–20). Like Cook, Myers was rejected by his own family after "they took a look at this puss of mine and they told me to get lost" and has traveled south to Baja, California, with plans to escape to Mexico.

In this film, Lupino includes no femme fatale, usually included in more traditional noir films, whose job it is to provide fateful encounters with male characters, but relies upon a kind of dislocation to produce the vision of hell depicted. The evil in Myers is seen as a consequence of his ejection by his family and/or his violent treatment of the couple at the film's beginning (Oliver, Trigo 222). The two friends, in direct contrast with Myers, are also in contrast with each other. Gil, a draftsman, and Roy, a mechanic, respond differently to their absence from their families; Roy is interested in stopping at a bar with women, but Gil is asleep. After they pick up Myers, the distinction between the two becomes even more apparent, when Myers who has learned their occupations, says to Gil: "That makes you smarter, or does it?" Gil remains silent, trying to avoid provoking Myers and looking for an opportunity to make a move. On the desolate and hostile landscape, Roy becomes increasingly frustrated and edgy as Myers's taunts worsen. When Myers makes Roy change clothes with him, the exchange identifies Roy as someone more deeply unsatisfied and violent than Gil—in fact, closer to Myers (Rabinovitz in *Queen of the B's*, 97-99). The film ends after the police arrest Myers, and the two friends follow a policeman to the station for the investigation. Gil comforts Roy, and says, "It's all right."

Lupino's 1954 film *The Bigamist*, sympathetically depicts Edmond O'Brien in the role of Harry, who has a wife in San Francisco and another wife and child in

Los Angeles. Harry, resentful of Eve (Joan Fontaine), his ambitious, emotionally distant wife, has formed a relationship with Phyllis (Ida Lupino), a poor, exhausted waitress struggling to survive. Lupino turns traditional typecasting upside down by showing neither woman as a manipulative, scheming femme fatale; both are good wives— each blissfully ignorant of the existence of the other—whose positions are the result of Harry's emotional and communicative needs. Lupino's melodramatic story is filmed with film noir techniques whose lighting and camera angles usually indicate entrapment and despair brought about by a deceptive, deadly female. In this film, lighting is used primarily to indicate the difference between Harry and Eve's posh apartment in a well-to-do area, as opposed to the seedy area where Harry, Phyllis, and the child live. Also, whereas in traditional noir films, the treacherous female dallies with two men, this film is the story of a man, whose intolerable situation with two women is the result of his inability to resolve his dilemma.

Although studios had limited Lupino to noir and western films in order to benefit from her tough, action-oriented direction, she had longed for years to direct different genres of film. Finally, in 1966, after a thirteen-year hiatus in television, she directed *The Trouble With Angels* for Columbia, whose action occurs during three years in the lives of Mary (Hayley Mills) and her friend Rachel, at a convent school for girls under the direction of the Reverend Mother (Rosalind Russell). Essentially, the story follows the girls, who were sent there as a preparation for their lives; at graduation, Rachel is ready for the world, whereas Mary plans to join the order as a novice.

Although Lupino was only allowed to direct "B" movies, and eventually worked largely as a director of various television series, she left her mark as a female director within the studio system. She always pointed out that had she not owned her own company, it would have been difficult for her to direct. She also disagreed that her films show a special feminine sensibility: "They were not only about women's problems, they were definitely about men's too. I certainly wasn't about to crash the man's world because I had no idea of wanting to be a director." She appeared to not regard her successful directing career as "fulfilling," insisting that it was all an economic necessity. She always maintained, "I would like to be quietly and happily married and be able to stay home and write" (Heck-Rabi 246).

2

The Mainstream

Emanuel Levy has observed "That the entire contribution of women to mainstream cinema from the 1930s to the 1960s could be summed up in terms of two sustained, though not terribly long, careers is truly depressing" (Levy, 1999, 351). Despite the accomplishments of Arzner and Lupino, and many other women writers, editors, and producers, the primary placement of women for decades in American cinema was in acting. Moreover, the course of women actors through the studio system was a strange odyssey, as the representation of women on the screen shifted with various manifestations of undercurrents in American society. One of the more successful group of films was the women's films, and of these, *Blonde Venus* (1932), *Camille* (1936), *Dark Victory* (1939), and *Mildred Pierce* (1945) have become classics. These films, all helmed by "women's directors"—Josef von Sternberg, George Cukor, Edmund Goulding, and Michael Curtiz—elevated women's anguish to new pinnacles, inviting women in the audience to participate in the suffering in these melodramatic vehicles that wrung from Marlene Dietrich, Greta Garbo, Bette Davis, and Joan Crawford the performances of their lives. Women fared better in other genres, more obviously in romantic comedy, but also in screwball comedy, in which the talents of Carole Lombard, Irene Dunne, Katharine Hepburn, and Claudette Colbert were carefully guided by male directors into successful, money-making performances aimed at distracting the depression era audiences from their miseries. Child star Shirley Temple and Ginger Rogers, as Fred Astaire's dancing partner, were also entertainment mainstays of this time period.

Following World War II, however, women bore the brunt of society's anxiety concerning the displacement of women from the roles of wife and mother to members of the workforce through their depiction in Hollywood's noir films as essentially unknowable creatures. Dark passionate women who manipulate men through lust and greed, and become "spider women" who mate and kill, are contrasted with pale, fair specimens of femininity whose goals are to be wife and mother, reflecting an almost schizophrenic view of women by the men in charge. The two feminist periods in the United States—the 1920s and the 1960s—have had no real effects upon the major studios or the structure of mainstream films. The major accomplishment of the 1960s feminist movement, having ridden in on the wave of massive social change, is in the vast amount of writing and interest in the feminist criticism it generated and continues to generate to this day. The demands of the feminists, however, were felt to be abrasive and, as such, were relegated to the fringe.

The small percentage of women who direct or have directed mainstream films are not radical feminists, but are women who have struck a compromise between the stories they might want to tell and those that would appeal to a wider audience, thus making money for the studio and possibly insuring studio backing for a sequel, or another film altogether. Robin Wood's thoughts concerning the difficulty of women directors attempting to work within the system are interesting:

> What possibilities exist for a female (not necessarily feminist) discourse to be articulated within a patriarchal industry through narrative conventions and genres by and for a male-dominated culture? The closure of classical narrative (of which the Hollywood happy ending is a typical form) enacts the restoration of patriarchal order; the transgressing woman is either forgiven and subordinated to that order, or punished, usually by death (Wood, 1986, 209).

The mainstream women directors considered in this chapter, who are seeking some form of expression of the lives and experiences of women, have managed to create a niche for themselves by writing and/or directing romantic comedies, teen or coming-of-age films, remakes of popular television shows, family comedies, disaster films, or action films, thereby possibly attracting a larger audience. Most of these women have worked or continue to work in television.

NORA EPHRON

The eldest of four daughters of husband-and-wife screenwriting team Henry and Phoebe Ephron, Nora Ephron was born May 19, 1941, in New York City. Soon afterward, the family moved to Los Angeles, California, where Nora graduated from Beverly High School. In 1962, she earned a journalism degree from Wellesley College and became a reporter for the *New York Post*, later becoming an editor of *Esquire* and a contributing editor of *New York Magazine*. During the 1970s, Ephron became a masterful satiric essayist, skewering self-important people and writing at length about feminism and male oppression.

Ephron had never intended to become a screenwriter, having been a witness to her parents' devastating professional and personal ups and downs, but finding herself twice divorced with two small children, the convenience of working at home was a blessing. Her coauthored (with Alice Arlen) screenplay for

Silkwood (1983), nominated for an Academy Award, centered on Karen Silkwood, nuclear plant whistleblower, whose mysterious fatal car wreck has prompted much speculation. *Silkwood* was filmed by Mike Nichols, who also filmed Ephron's *Heartburn* (1986), an autobiographical novel about her marriage breakup with *Washington Post* reporter Carl Bernstein.

In 1989, Ephron wrote the screenplay for Rob Reiner's fifth directorial effort *When Harry Met Sally*, which won the BAFTA award for screenwriting and marked the beginning of her long foray into romantic comedy. She collaborated again with Alice Arlen to write *Cookie* (1990), directed by Susan Seidelman, and authored *My Blue Heaven* (1992), featuring Steve Martin as a Mafia snitch, directed by Herbert Ross.

Ephron's directing debut came with *This Is My Life* (1992), cowritten by Ephron and her sister, Delia, a film that explores the effects of a woman's professional success on her family. Dottie Ingels (Julie Kavner, the voice of Marge on *The Simpsons*), an aspiring comedienne, wears polka dots, lives with her two girls, Ericka (Samantha Mathis) and Opal (Gaby Hoffmann), and uses material from their lives in her act. She finally gets an agent (Dan Ackroyd) who gets her big break, so she leaves the girls at home, to be looked after by members of a comedy troupe, and heads for Las Vegas. When Dottie stays longer than expected and continues to use the family's personal experiences in her acts, the girls become resentful. Ericka attempts an unsuccessful affair, and the girls search for their runaway dad.

The title of the film refers to the conflict between Dottie and her girls about the needs of each of them. Dottie feels like her time has finally arrived, and the girls, who were glad for her at first now are angry because they seem unimportant at present to their mother. The witty film zeroes in on the agonizing difficulty single parents experience while trying to sustain a career and give love and affection to their children. Ephron shows the demands of both sides.

The following year, Ephron's second film, the romantic comedy *Sleepless in Seattle*, a loose remake of Leo McCarey's *An Affair to Remember* (1957), became enormously successful, grossing over $200 million worldwide. The story concerns Sam Baldwin (Tom Hanks), a successful architect who has lost his wife to cancer eighteen months previously. His son, Jonah (Ross Malinger), who is eight and is worried about his dad's loneliness, calls a national radio program on Christmas seeking help for his father. Angrily, Sam talks with the psychiatrist about his dead wife. Meanwhile, in Baltimore, Annie Reed (Meg Ryan), a *Baltimore Sun* reporter is driving to Washington, DC, while listening to the program, and finds Sam's voice strangely appealing. Her letter to Sam is read by Jonah, who thinks she is the one for his father, and proceeds to bring them together.

The scriptwriters for the film, Ephron, David S. Ward, and Jeff Arch, drew inspiration from a story by Arch paying tribute to the great romantic comedies of the 1940s and 1950s. Ephron seems to emphasize the differences in the time period and the fact that life is much more complex in the 1990s than it was then. Although she borrows from *An Affair* and appropriates the lovers' proposed meeting atop the Empire State Building in New York, *Sleepless* is a romance for the 1990s. In entwining the two films, Ephron also contrasts the audience of 1957, where women wept uncontrollably upon seeing McCarey's film, with audiences of the 1990s, who, when faced with Sam's grief, found something in the film for women as well as men.

But, Ephron does not see *Sleepless* as a movie about love. She says, "It's a movie about love in the movies, and how that screws up our expectations about love in our own lives" (quoted by Gerosa 33). Ephron believes the 1990s audiences crave fantasy just as the characters in *Sleepless* long for the unrealistic romance of the 1957 *An Affair to Remember*. So, Ephron endeavored to make a modern-day romantic-comedy classic. To capture a "timeless" sensibility, Ephron enumerated the following standards:

> *First*: Sex is out, and abstinence is in. On this point, Ephron says, "I have a theory that the romantic comedy was killed by sex. Romantic comedies flourished in a period when you couldn't put sex in a movie. The way people flirted was by going 'blah blah blah' to one another. Suddenly when you could have sex it wasn't necessary to talk anymore."

> *Second*: Product placement was out. Ephron: "I wanted this to be a movie that when you look at it, you would not know quite when it was made. So that means there are a huge number of things that people can't wear and can't have in their homes. Plastic was banned from the set."

> *Third*: Every 1990s reference is balanced with an allusion to vintage Hollywood films. The characters' mention of *Fatal Attraction* (Adrian Lyne, 1987) and AT&T phone commercials are offset with a soundtrack including Louis Armstrong and Jimmy Durante, and the final scene atop the Art-Deco Empire State Building (Gerosa 33).

Ephron's next film, *Mixed Nuts* (1994), is a film about a suicide prevention hot-line whose counselor, Philip (Steve Martin), and his coworkers, Mrs. Munchnik (Madeline Kahn) and Catherine O'Shaughnessey (Rita Wilson), have recently been notified by their landlord, Stanley Tannenbaum (Garry Shandling), that they are being evicted from the apartment. Philip, who must find money for the rent, becomes entangled with a hugely pregnant Gracie (Juliette Lewis) and her boyfriend (Anthony La Paglia), a veterinarian (Rob Reiner), two tenants in the building, played by Robert Klein and Adam Sandler, Stephen Wright on the verge of suicide, and unemployed Santas. The script, written by Ephron and her sister, Delia, is unfunny and depressing.

Michael (1996), written by Pete Dexter, Jim Quinlan, and the Ephron sisters, features three tabloid writers sent by their editor (Bob Hoskins) to Iowa to investigate a report received that a lady there (Jean Stapleton) is living in a motel with an angel. The writers on that mission are Frank Quinlan (William Hurt); Dorothy Winters (Andie McDowell), the angel expert; Huey Driscoll (Robert Pastorelli); and his dog, Sparky. They arrive to find an overweight, hairy angel, Michael (John Travolta), wearing boxer shorts and drinking beer. He quotes the

Beatles instead of the Bible and insists, "You can never have too much sugar." Michael has huge wings that trail on the floor and are hidden under a trenchcoat when he goes out.

After casting Lucifer out of heaven, Archangel Michael has visited earth several times, but as this is his last visit (they are numbered), he is interested in sightseeing. During one of his trips here, he recalls, "I invented standing in line." Learning his visitors are writers, Michael says "I'm a writer, too." When asked what he wrote, he replies, "Psalm 85. They weren't numbered then." Michael's primary mission on this trip is to help Quinlan rediscover his heart, which is accomplished by Quinlan and Dorothy falling in love. Also a romantic comedy of sorts, *Michael* is fascinating because of Travolta's performance as Archangel Michael, who loves food, drink, sugar, and women on his farewell tour to Earth.

You've Got Mail (1998), the third remake of Ernst Lubitsch's *The Shop Around the Corner* (1940), is Ephron's fifth film, and another popular romantic comedy. Written by Ephron and her sister, Delia, the script concerns a couple who detest each other in real life but unwittingly establish an intimate relationship online. Re-pairing Tom Hanks (as Joe Fox) and Meg Ryan (as Kathleen Kelly), presumably America's most lovable couple, guaranteed audiences would flock to theaters just to see them together. The plot offers Joe as the heir to the giant Fox's Books, who has just opened another superstore around the corner from Kathleen's small children's book shop, appropriately named The Shop Around the Corner. Joe, who delights in swallowing up smaller shops with his mega-company, arrogantly dismisses Kathleen's complaint that he is stealing all her customers. Despite the fact that she has a boyfriend (Greg Kinnear), she turns to her friend, who of course is Fox, for consolation, and he, ignorant of her identity, gives her advice about how to fight the huge corporation. Fox also has a girlfriend (Parker Posey), but he seems drawn to his chats online with Shopgirl. Eventually, the truth is out, and each is horrified to discover that the other is a detested enemy. The problem is solved when Kathleen's employees are hired by Joe's megastore, and audiences are delighted to see Joe and Kathleen finally together.

You've Got Mail is reminiscent of *Sleepless in Seattle* in that it has been adapted from an earlier film and fashioned into a modern romantic comedy. Updated to fit the electronic age, *You've Got Mail* advances the possibility that two people could develop an intimate, loving relationship online, and yet pass on the street unaware of one another. The fantasy in this situation seems less fanciful than that in *Sleepless*, because the couple recognize themselves earlier in the film and, therefore, spend more time together on screen. Ephron again adheres to her rules regarding romantic comedy, specifically the absence of any sexual encounter between the principals, thus encouraging talk as a means of knowing one another. The use of a laptop in bed, which connects reading with romance, suggests the unlikelihood of real romance measuring up to the kind depicted in books, as the idealized film *An Affair to Remember* remains the fantasy to which the society in *Sleepless* aspires, and largely fails.

Lucky Numbers (2000), Ephron's sixth film, is about Russ (John Travolta), a weatherman in Harrisburg, Pennsylvania, who is going bankrupt and needs money desperately. After a botched robbery, he cooks up a plot to rig the state lottery with the help of his friend Gig (Tim Roth) that sounds workable because Russ has access to all the lottery balls, and he is having an affair with Crystal (Lisa Kudrow), the Lottery Girl. But Gig is also having an affair with Crystal, hence more and more characters become aware of the plot and the payoff diminishes drastically with each new person in the plan. Written by Adam Resnick, the script seems to waffle between slapstick comedy and black comedy, never actually getting its bearings. The film was disastrous at the box office, returning only $10 million of the $65 million budget.

About this time, Ephron began reinventing herself, a process that she claims occurs about every ten years (DeVries 1), as she has segued from biting essayist, to novelist, to screenwriter, to director, and now to playwright. Extending her career to Broadway from Hollywood, Ephron wrote her first play, *Imaginary Friends*, about the rivalry between writers Lillian Hellman and Mary McCarthy. Ephron pursued writing for the theater after the failure of *Lucky Numbers* made directing another film unlikely for a while.

Ephron's seventh film, *Bewitched*, which opened June 2005, is her effort to pay tribute to the famous television series of the 1960s, *Bewitched*, without just redoing the same story. Written by Ephron and Delia, the script follows the misadventures of Jack Wyatt (Will Ferrell), hammered by a series of film flops and a greedy wife who reconsiders divorce when she learns he has been cast in a potentially lucrative part, who worms his way into the part of Darren in a remake of *Bewitched*. Demanding to use an unknown actress in the role of Samantha and to choose her himself, Wyatt runs across Isabel Bigelow (Nicole Kidman) in a book store and is captivated by how perfectly she can wrinkle her nose. But Isabel is no ordinary female. She is a witch who, sick of being one, wants very much to give it up and become a mere mortal. "I want to experience being thwarted," she tells her warlock father, Nigel (Michael Caine). More prophetic words are rarely uttered. Attracted to Wyatt, who seems to be "such a mess," she takes the part, only later realizing his real intentions, which are to elevate himself to the main part (unlike the real program) at her expense. Stepping on her lines and ignoring her, he is an egotistical lout who throws his weight around both on the set and off. "Guys, make 200 cappuccinos, and bring me the best one," he roars. The tide begins to turn when Isabel, incensed to the point of using her magic against him, makes him appear more ridiculous than he really is. Also, the test results come in, indicating a 90 percent approval rating for her and a mere 30 percent for him. At this point he becomes a bit more accommodating, and gets even nicer when they fall in love.

As a romantic comedy, which is Ephron's real forte, *Bewitched* does not fare as well as either *Sleepless in Seattle* or *You've Got Mail*, primarily because of Will Ferrell's character. As the film deals with power and the use of it, the struggle for it—even with Isabel's use of magic, fulfilling the fantasy part in Ephron's previous romantic comedies—points to the lack of character meshing between Kidman and Ferrell. The film becomes more of a comedy than a romance. At the box office—the ultimate test of "success" for a mainstream film, especially a woman-directed mainstream film—*Bewitched* recouped $62 million against an $85 million budget.

Ephron maintains that with all the choices and advantages available to women, there is no excuse for failure. Consequently, when adversity befell Ephron, she, much like her mother when confronted with hardship, used her own misery as a source for her screenplays. One of her greatest successes was *Heartburn*, which dealt with Bernstein's extramarital affair and their subsequent divorce; telling the story her way helped her gain control of her life again. Her desire for control has extended into filmmaking, in order to avoid having to accommodate a director by changing her script or perhaps suffering the "misdirection" of it. Ironically, although Ephron became a director to retain control over her scripts, only one of her directorial efforts has surpassed the success of *When Harry Met Sally*.

Ephron searches for the right balance of romance, comedy, superb acting, and lightness of touch (and a well-crafted script) in a cinematic world whose criteria for survival is hard, cold cash.

NANCY MEYERS

Much like Nora Ephron, Nancy Meyers also began in screenwriting, a profession in which she had excelled long before she tried directing. Born December 8, 1949, in Philadelphia, Pennsylvania, to a businessman and a designer, Meyers graduated from American University in 1971 and then worked as a story editor in Hollywood. In 1976, she met Charles Shyer, a writer for *All in the Family* and *The Odd Couple* on television, who had also written film scripts. Meyers and Shyer began a working relationship, and soon they were living together. They had two children but did not marry until twenty years after they began a relationship. "Being a wife is not something I perceive as enviable," said Meyers to Paul Rosenfeld in 1987 (*LA Times p.4*), while she continued to work with Shyer on scripts about marriage. Their first hit was *Private Benjamin* (1980), written for Meyers's college friend Goldie Hawn. The success of that film allowed them more control over their next script, *Irreconcilable Differences* (1984), a well-received film. Meyers and Shyer followed up with *Protocol* (1984), another Goldie Hawn vehicle; *Baby Boom* (1987); *Father of the Bride* (1991); *Father of the Bride Part II* (1995); and *I Love Trouble* (1994).

Meyers's directing debut came in 1998 with *The Parent Trap*, updated from the 1961 Disney film. Myers and Shyer tinkered very little with the plot, merely changing the residences of the parents. Dennis Quaid and Natasha Richardson portray the parents of twin daughters who divorce, each taking a daughter. Quaid, a winemaker in Napa, California, and Richardson, a dress designer in London, never speak of the other child, raising each as an only child. Strangely enough, at a camp in Maine, the girls meet, learn they are sisters, and set about trying to get their parents back together. The film was praised as family entertainment; as a sort of romantic comedy, it maintains a light tone throughout.

After the filming of *The Parent Trap*, Meyers separated from her longtime partner, Shyer, and began filming *What Women Want* (2000). The film received mixed reviews, but was popular with viewers, grossing $183 million. *What Women Want* casts Mel Gibson as Nick Marshall, an ambitious womanizer, who is passed over for a promotion to creative director of an ad agency in Chicago because his boss (Alan Alda) realizes the potential of women buyers, and promotes instead Darcy (Helen Hunt) to lead the push for female-inspired marketing. Stunned, Marshall decides he needs to "try to think like a broad." He reads women's magazines, buys women's products, paints his toenails, and, in the process of struggling with panty hose, falls into the tub and nearly electrocutes himself. Miraculously, he gains the unique ability to hear what women think, which, at first, is an overwhelming jumble of comments. He finds out that most women do not like him, but his real intent is to use his newfound talent to benefit himself. He steals ideas from Darcy and uses them in an attempt to have her removed from the office. However, Marshall begins to empathize with women, which benefits his adolescent daughter, the suicidal female messenger at work, but not Lola (Marisa Tomei), his former girlfriend. He also realizes he has feelings for Darcy.

Meyers has entered the territory pioneered by Ephron and directed her own version of a romantic comedy. While her film is more comedy than romance and lacks Ephron's light touch, specifically with the fantastical element of being privy to women's thoughts, Meyers appeals to both genders with the casting of Mel Gibson. Gibson, with whom men identify and about whom women fantasize, runs the gamut from arrogant sexist, by way of his antics with women's products, to a somewhat chastened, if not redeemed, sexy man. Despite condescending to women practically throughout the film, audiences understand Marshall and Darcy are meant to be together.

Something's Gotta Give, Meyers's 2003 film continues the pattern of casting a famous male actor whose character undergoes an attitude adjustment regarding women. Harry Sanborn (Jack Nicholson), a wealthy recording executive, who will date no women under the age of thirty, is pursuing Marin Barry (Amanda Peet), who takes him to her home in the Hamptons for a weekend. There, they discover that Amanda's mother, playwright Erica Barry (Diane Keaton), and her sister Zoe (Frances McDormand) have also come up for the weekend. Harry suffers a mild heart attack, and is forced to stay at Erica's house to recover. Marin and Zoe return to New York, and the remainder of the film is dedicated to fulfilling the expectation that Harry and Erica belong together.

Obviously a romantic comedy, the film also has a message for both Hollywood and film viewers that women over forty, or even fifty, are still attractive, interesting, and sexy. It was not easy for Meyers to interest studios in the film because of the presumption that American audiences would not watch a film about middle-aged people. The film's popularity was boosted by superstar Jack Nicholson and the fact that much of his dialogue refers to Nicholson himself, as well as Harry. The same could be said of Keaton, who seems to draw from her previous acting roles. In the film, we see Nicholson's rear, and we see a brief nude shot of Keaton, and we see a sexual scene between a sixty-three-year-old man and a fifty-seven-year-old woman. Harry's brush with mortality has evoked a need to talk with someone who understands his anxieties, and the emotionally withdrawn Erica does just that. The flies in the ointment are that Harry is a commitment-phobe, and the young doctor, Julian (Keanu Reaves), who is half Erica's age, is smitten with her. Naturally, the obstacles are overcome, and the happy pair is reunited, in a validation of middle-aged romance.

AMY HECKERLING

The daughter of an accountant, Amy Heckerling, was born May 7, 1954, in Bronx, New York. She attended the High School of Art and Design and graduated from New York University in 1975 with a BA degree in film and television. In 1973, while she was a student, she saw Martin Scorsese's film *Mean Streets*, and was so taken with it that it changed her view of film: "Suddenly, there was this movie where I could understand what everybody was saying. I understood their motives, and there was music and energy, and the shooting was cuckoo, and I was going, 'Wow, movies are for me now'" (Cohen 53). Consequently, Heckerling applied to and received a fellowship from the prestigious American Film Institute, where she earned an MA in filmmaking and in the process made a short comedy, *Getting It Over With*, about the attempts of a nineteen-year-old to lose her virginity. Impressed with her film, Metro-Goldwyn-Mayer Studios offered her a contract for her first feature, but all plans came to naught with the actors' strike in 1980.

In 1981, on the strength of her second-year film at AFI, *Getting it Over With*, Heckerling at Universal Studios was shown the book, *Fast Times at Ridgemont High*, and given the job of directing it. Based on the best-selling book by Cameron Crowe, a journalist in his twenties who attended high school undercover to glean information about the "real" goings on there, the film transformation promised to be a raunchy view of sex, drugs, and rock'n roll in a California high school. But, despite its obvious representation of 1980s contemporary culture, Heckerling and Crowe worked together to achieve a more universal appeal in the story of highs and lows (mostly lows) during a year in high school. Heckerling's first film, it established comedy as her area of interest, if not expertise, and began for her a career in formulaic teen comedy.

The film includes an ensemble cast and afforded several now-major actors and actresses their start. Jennifer Jason Leigh, never before in a major film, plays Stacy, sister of Judge Reinhold and friend of Linda (Phoebe Cates); but the focus is on Sean Penn, as Jeff Picoli, the California surfer who has been stoned since third grade. One of the plot lines follows the misadventures of two girls: Stacy, fifteen and anxious to lose her virginity, is under the tutelage of Linda, who, despite claiming to be more experienced about such matters, seems to have very little real understanding of them. Stacy meets an older salesman and on the first date go to "the point" to engage in sex. Heckerling specifically shows this event as a humiliating and painful encounter. She has recounted her battle to depict the scene in such a manner, saying, "The first time a young person has sex, it's not 'Yahoo! We'll all rip our clothes off and know exactly what we're doing'" (Heckerling Film School 101).

Linda, of course, encourages Stacy to continue with the sexual activity that "doesn't mean anything," insisting that "it gets better." Meanwhile, Mark Ratner has eyes for Stacy, but being shy, turns for advice to Mike, the ticket scalper, who is then pursued by Stacy, who becomes pregnant with Mike's child. After her abortion, Stacy comes to realize what she really wants is a relationship and manages to have one with Mark, the male virgin. The audience is assured at the film's end that he and Stacy "are having a passionate love affair but still haven't 'gone all the way.'"

Another story line features the efforts of Stacy's brother, Brad (Judge Reinhold), to move up in the "business" world, going from All-American Burger to a 7-11, where, by virtue of foiling a robbery attempt, he becomes a manager. Most of the fun is from Spicoli, surfer dude, who, consistently late for class, literally falls out of his smoke-filled van on the parking lot, orders pizza to be delivered in class, and barks at his history teacher, the infamous Mr. Hand (Ray Walston), "You dick!"

The appeal of the film is its emphasis on sex, masturbation, abortion, and drugs within the high school crowd. Scenes that are remembered fondly include the one in the school cafeteria where Linda, wielding a carrot, instructs Stacy in the finer techniques of fellatio, and Brad's fantasy of Linda removing the top of her bathing suit at the pool. But, behind the sensational scenes are few happy moments; most of the characters end the year with a sense of loss. Robin Wood considers the film within the cycle of '80s high school films—actually beginning in 1973 with George Lucas's *American Graffiti*—and notes that Heckerling's film is the first of these to present adolescent sexual encounters from the female's perspective. In fact, he contends that her "unobtrusive critique of male positions" depends not on skewing the narrative, but on her explicit shots of girls eyeing boys as boys eye girls, and shots such as the row of rears clad in tight jeans scanned by the camera that turn out to be boys' rears. Heckerling also allows the girls desire and moments of contemplation of the male body; besides the aforementioned carrot scene between Linda and Stacy, at another point, Linda asks Stacy, "Did you see his cute little butt?" Wood contends that Heckerling "manages the extremely difficult feat of constructing a tenable position for the female spectator without threatening the male" (Wood 219–20). Heckerling echoes the trends in other 1980s teen comedies—students whose lives seem to revolve around sex; the absence of parents in their lives; the addition of several main characters to increase the range of identification with the youth audience; and the exclusion of no minority group altogether (Wood 215–16). Within the conventions of teen comedy, Heckerling poses no radical challenge, but instead skillfully displays the current attitudes and, at the same time, reaps box office success. She was immediately propelled into another studio contract, making her one of the very few American women to direct mainstream films.

Heckerling's next film, *Johnny Dangerously*, a parody of 1930s gangster films, met with critics' disapproval and failed at the box office. Written primarily by Harry Colomby and Jeff Harris, the script offers Heckerling a great opportunity to assemble another great cast for which she should be envied. The main character, Johnny (Michael O'Keefe), who owns a pet store, nabs a kid trying to steal a puppy and recounts to him the story of his rise in crime and his ultimate escape from it. It seems that in Johnny Kelly's youth, he becomes a paper boy to make money for his Ma (Maureen Stapleton), a hypochondriac, who continually finds new ailments that require surgeries. While Johnny's brother (Griffin Dunne) goes to school, Johnny runs errands for Jock Dundee (Peter Boyle), the local mob boss. When Johnny saves Dundee's life in a disastrous raid on a hotel owned by a rival mob boss, he ingratiates himself forever to Dundee, who hires him and changes his name to Johnny Dangerously. Johnny moves up in the world of crime rapidly while trying to steer clear of the newest member of the mob, Danny Vermin (Joe Piscopo). Meanwhile, his brother graduates from law school and becomes assistant district attorney to a corrupt district attorney (Danny de Vito). Tommy gets rid of the DA and comes after Johnny, who manages to get out of the mob, get rid of the rival mob and go straight. The film is loaded with sight gags, one liners, numerous sexual jokes, and puns. While the slight plot relies on the humor of the characters to sustain it, many critics thought the film silly and sophomoric. And, although it did not do well at the box office, Heckerling came back the next year (1985) with *National Lampoon's European Vacation*, a comedy starring Chevy Chase and Beverly D'Angelo and more successful than *Johnny Dangerously*, as it reputedly earned $12.3 million its first weekend out in the world.

National Lampoon's European Vacation, the second in a series begun by *National Lampoon's Vacation* (1983, Harold Ramis), received some unkind reviews, but many were supportive, and audiences enjoyed the burlesque of the American family on vacation in Europe. Accidentally winning the trip on a TV game show, the bumbling Griswolds proceed to cut a swath across Europe and endear themselves to no one along the way. The same year the film came out, Heckerling and her husband, Neal Israel, became the parents of a daughter, Mollie Sara, who inadvertently exerted an enormous influence upon Heckerling's future film direction. While watching her, they began to imagine words or phrases to fit her expressions—all of which provided the inspiration for Heckerling's next film, *Look Who's Talking* (1989).

Scoring big at the box office, this film has a very simple plot. Mollie (Kirstie Alley), an accountant, falls in love with one of her clients, Albert (George Segal), and becomes pregnant with his child. But Albert is married and, for a variety of excuses, will not leave his wife. Unhappily, Mollie resigns herself to being a single parent. When she goes into labor unexpectedly, she calls a taxi to take her to the hospital; the driver, James (John Travolta), takes her there at breakneck speed, stays with her through the delivery, and offers his future services for baby-sitting. Mollie determines to find a good father for her son (Mikey), casting her net far and wide and overlooking the perfect choice right in front of her—James.

But the film is a comedy, and an irreverent one at that, filled with wisecracks from the sperm (Mikey's voice is Bruce Willis) trying, along with all the other racing sperm, to attach itself to the ovum. He succeeds, and continues from then until he is two years old, a series of more wisecracks, jokes, reactionary jibes at the world, and attempts to direct his mother toward James. There are gags galore, the funniest ones occurring when Mikey is thirsty (he yanks on the umbilical cord, and yells, "How about a little apple juice down here?") and when he is born (trying to resist the push toward birth, he kicks and screams "Put me back in! Put me back in!"). Before birth, the camera focuses upon the baby in the womb as Willis's voice matches up with the baby's actions or expressions; after Mikey's birth, we see Mikey and James bonding as father and son for everyone to see except Mollie. The best scenes in the film are of James dancing with Mikey and later when the two are asleep together on the couch. There are humorous incidents in Mollie's succession of dates with men who are being scrutinized as possible husband prospects, and in her general ditziness in regard to her situation, but the heart of the film is the warmth and closeness of James and Mikey.

Look Who's Talking Too (1990) was rushed into production to capitalize on the success of the first film, and, in it, Heckerling as writer (with Neal Israel) and director continue the saga of James and Mollie, now married and having another baby, daughter Julie (voice of Roseanne Barr). Problems arise when Mollie's brother, Stuart (Elias Koteas), arrives to live with them a while and Mikey and Julie experience sibling rivalry. Roseanne's voice adds a new slant to the narrative, but she is less funny than Willis. Most of the jokes refer to potty training; Mel Brooks's voice is Mr. Potty, the talking toilet. Damon Wayans' voice becomes Eddie, a child who tells stories among the children, who comment on the lives and behaviors of adults. The film relies on the gags of the talking babies, sperm zooming toward the ovum, and Mikey's efforts to succeed at potty training to carry it through a somewhat flimsy plot.

Heckerling achieved the critical success of her career in 1995 with *Clueless*, a contemporary adaptation of Jane Austen's *Emma* that appeals to both teens and adults. Transplanting Emma Woodhouse, Austen's nineteenth-century match-making heroine into Beverly Hills, California, in the form of Cher Horowitz (Alicia Silverstone), a perky, privileged fifteen-year-old high school student, Heckerling returns to the teen comedy genre of her earlier success. Cher, a motherless girl, spoiled by her wealthy litigation lawyer father (Dan Hedaya), spends much time, as witnessed in the opening montage, shopping at the mall, driving her white Jeep and talking on her cellphone. When at school, she devotes time to dreaming up "projects," or helping people she sees as clueless. Her best friend, Dionne (Stacey Dash), also rich, observes, "Cher's main thrill in life is a makeover; it gives her a sense of control in a world of chaos." Designated first for a makeover is Tai (Brittany Murphy), a new student from New Jersey wearing flannel shirts and falling short of Cher's level of refinement. She is turned into a well-dressed snob. She then levels her attention on two teachers at the high school who strike her as being lonely. Maintaining that "happy teachers give better grades," Cher turns matchmaker and manipulates a relationship between Ms. Geist and Mr. Hall.

However, while Heckerling works within the teen comedy genre, she revises many of its conventions she had followed in *Fast Times at Ridgemont High*, thereby extending the limits of the genre to a fresh perspective. Whereas the six main characters in *Fast Times* seem largely without parents, Cher's father dotes on her. He tells one of her dates: "If anything happens to her, I have a .45 and a shovel, and you won't be missed." Cher fusses over him, much like a wife, reminding him to take his vitamins, and basically wrapping him around her finger. She has no need of a job, unlike most of the characters in *Fast Times*, so she can devote her time to looking fabulous and "doing good." The kids in *Fast Times* are obsessed with sexual experimentation, but Cher, aware of the horrors of AIDS, is a virgin, saving herself for her true love. Also new to *Clueless* is the addition of a gay male student, ironically named Christian, in a group of students where many, including Cher, are Jewish. The teenage angst or anxiety, usually part and parcel of teenage comedies, concerning the loss of virginity, relationships, and looming adulthood is redirected through Cher's self-absorbed contentment into a kind of introspection and a concern for others. But, the satiric point of the film is that Cher is clueless about herself, and when she finally perceives the errors in her presumptions about the world and her place in it, she sets about to perform a makeover on her own attitudes. She also comes to realize that her best prospect for a relationship is her half-brother, Josh.

Clueless is an excellent example of a postmodern film. Difficult to define, postmodernism actually operates under a variety of definitions. Frederic Jameson, author of several books on the subject, sees postmodernism beginning back around the late 1950s or early 1960s, when "a new kind of society began to emerge (variously described as . . . consumer society, media society, and so forth). New types of consumption; planned obsolescence, an ever more rapid rhythm of fashion and styling changes; the penetration of advertising, television and the media generally to a hitherto unparalleled degree throughout society" (Jameson 124) have effected change in every sphere of culture in contemporary society. In film, the modernist concern with auteur directors (those whose varied films bear the auteur's "signature"—recurring theme, preoccupation, or stylistic trait—that identify him as their "author" and lend a sense of wholeness to his body of work) fell by the wayside in the postmodern world. Various styles and techniques prevail, and the modernist emphasis upon order has been replaced by a more chaotic film that revels in fragments, inconsistencies, pastiche, references to other works of both high and low culture, and comments obliquely on the construction of its own narrative.

Clueless' attention to consumerism and technology establishes its postmodernism right away. Cher lives in a mansion among other mansions; she has unlimited money (daddy's credit card, which makes her feel in control) to purchase extravagant clothes; she has only a learner's permit, but drives her white Jeep anyway, and is seen always with her cellphone to her ear. Her computer plays a prominent role in her life, mainly in the coordination of her extensive clothing into a stylish outfit each day. Cher's voiceover introduces us early on to her references to cartoons, TV, movies, famous people. She asks if we think we are watching a Noxzema commercial; then, she announces that she's Cher and her best friend is Dionne, both of whom are named after "famous singers who now do infomercials." Between the Mentos ads and references to Starbucks and along with Cher's appreciation of *Ren and Stimpy* as "way existential," we are regaled with Californiaspeak: Cher is not just a virgin—she is "hymenally challenged"; she regularly says "as if," "majorly," or "whatever." In her English class, she settles a question, not because she knows her Shakespeare, but because she knows her Mel Gibson (star of a 1990 version of *Hamlet*). In the re-creation of Emma's story into Cher's story, Heckerling contributes to postmodernism by reworking an old story into a new one, and by following Jane Austen's narrative (while resisting script changes because the studio wanted more guys in the film) and transferring similar characters and situations from High-bury village to Beverly Hills. This film begat a television series (1996-1999) that Heckerling was not happy with, but served as its executive producer, episodic director, and writer.

Heckerling's most recent film, *Loser* (2000), is a romantic comedy that leaves high-school students and moves up to those in college. Written by Heckerling, the script concerns Paul (Jason Biggs), a high school graduate who has been awarded a scholarship to attend a prestigious New York City university. Having lived in a rural area all his life, Paul tells his father (Dan Ackroyd) he is afraid he will not fit in there. His father advises him to talk to people and listen to their stories, because "people are basically good." Paul arrives at school and becomes a joke because of his niceness, his cap with ear flaps and his need to study to keep up his scholarship. His roommates are there to have fun, as they do not have to work, and they have him expelled from the dorm. He finds a room in a veterinarian's office with the caged animals.

In class, he meets Dora (Mena Suvari of *American Beauty*), who is carrying on an affair with their European Literature professor (Greg Kinnear)—an arrogant, egotistical person who cares only about himself. For Dora, struggling to attend class, keep up with homework, work for the professor, sleep with the professor, work nights as a waitress in a topless bar, and make her commute to another borough is becoming an impossibility. She gives up the commute, staying occasionally with Paul. At a party thrown at the veterinarian's office by Paul's ex-roommates, one of them slips Rohypnol in her drink and she sinks into unconsciousness. Paul rushes her to a hospital, where it is discovered she has listed the professor as the person to be notified in case of emergency. The hospital notifies him, but he claims not to know her. The rest of the film is given over to Dora's finally extricating herself from the professor, who lands in prison after Paul's ex-roommates extort A's from him in all his classes with the threat of making his misdeeds public.

The words of Paul's father, "People are basically good," ironically ring throughout the harsh treatment of Paul and Dora, two outsiders who become enmeshed in the cruelty of others as they struggle to get a college education. Darker than her other films, the film reflects some of the painful realism of high school in *Fast Times at Ridgemont High* as these students, freshmen in college and not too far removed from high school, get a glimpse of the world outside their native habitat. Apparently, audiences unaccustomed to such a dark film from Heckerling would have preferred something genuinely funny. The film failed to recoup its budget amount.

Heckerling has been denounced by some critics for sacrificing quality for profits, but she has shrugged off such charges with a reminder that money is the bottom line in Hollywood—a perspective that may help explain her success in the male-dominated American film industry. With the drop in the average age of cinema viewers since the 1960s, making the contemporary dominant viewing age group in the 1980s between the ages of 12 and 20 (Levy 29), Hollywood's efforts to cater to the youth audience by turning out films about high school problems, sex, and drinking compel many fledgling directors including Amy Heckerling to try to tap into this market. *Fast Times* concentrates upon bodies and sexuality to the extent that it drew charges of sexism. But, it did well at the box office and allowed her to make other films, eventually those exploring female perspectives. Heckerling has always made calculated moves in her choice of films, seeming to be acutely aware that her ability to continue directing films depends on her capacity for turning out a money maker. Her timing and pacing skills, acquired in her job as a television editor, have continued to serve her well in her directing career. Her well-written scripts contain fast-paced dialogue, humor, dramatic events leading to a character's transition into self-realization—all achieved with deft insight into contemporary culture. And, despite the reliance upon formulaic narratives, Heckerling continues with classic Hollywood direction, and excellent actors.

MARTHA COOLIDGE

Martha Coolidge has also gained recognition for her direction of films for a teen audience, but after having made several independent documentaries. Following critical praise for her documentaries about women's issues, she was offered the directorship of a low-budget teen film, followed eventually by big-budget films that allowed her to deal with more serious issues. Coolidge's interests extend into acting, producing, writing, editing, working in television, and establishing networks whereby aspiring East Coast film directors find contacts to continue their work in California. In 1999, Coolidge was the recipient of the USA Film Festival's Great Director Award, becoming the first woman allowed in the ranks of male directors such as Robert Altman, Oliver Stone, George Cukor, or Frank Capra. But her most notable award was in 2002, when she became the first female president of the Director's Guild of America.

Born August 17, 1946, in New Haven, Connecticut, to a Yale University professor of architecture, who was third cousin to President Calvin Coolidge, Martha Coolidge was encouraged by her parents to become an artist. Beginning a career in folk music, which was unsuccessful, Coolidge turned her attention first to acting and then to directing. Coolidge attended the Rhode Island School of Design to study printmaking, but became interested in animation when she directed an animated film. She entered New York University Film School, where she was informed that, because of her gender, she should not pursue directing (Lane 67). Coolidge left for Canada, where she gained experience working on a children's television program, eventually returning to study at Columbia University and New York University Film School, where she was hired to direct an hour-long documentary that was aired on public television.

Coolidge began to turn out impressive personal documentaries, two of which are portraits of her family members. *David: Off and On* (1972) is a short film about her brother, and *Old-Fashioned Woman* (1974), an interview with her grandmother, is the type of film many women filmmakers pursued at the beginning of their careers as they sought role models or images of women to popularize. Coolidge talks with her father's mother about Coolidge's father, who died at the age of 40 from cancer. The camera lingers over Mable's hands, old photographs, and features of the grandmother's house, as Coolidge herself appears to view her from a different perspective. At one point, the two women remove Mable's wedding dress from a trunk, whereupon we see wedding photos and hear Mable's memories. Coolidge moves to her father's baby book, containing locks of hair and pictures, as Mable's memories and the grief of both women for their son/father act as an affirmation of familial bonds. Encouraging Mable to speak of women's goals in her day, Mable also elaborates on some of her political beliefs, specifically in support of women's suffrage, planned pregnancy, and delayed marriage. Finally, Coolidge emphasizes the number of women artists in the family, specifically Mable, who excelled in photography, and had received her first camera at the age of ten and, soon, a darkroom built for her by her father. The film establishes a reinforcement of Coolidge's status as a filmmaker in light of her grandmother's status as a photographer (Lane 70-1).

Much like *Old-Fashioned Woman*, Coolidge's next film is largely an attempt to accept the past and express what it means to be a woman. Possibly made to release some of the anger that such an action engenders, *Not a Pretty Picture* is a semi-autobiographical account of Coolidge's own rape. Coolidge presents the narrative through documentation, dramatization, and fictional narrative, and reflects the debate that was occurring at that time between feminists who praised realistic documentaries above Hollywood's glossy realism. Coolidge's experimentation includes staged episodes, interrupted by rehearsals of the episodes, the conversations of the actors and the emotional response of the director that interrupts the narrative. Influenced by 1960s and 1970s theories of the avant-garde cinema, the film mirrors the tension between reality and fiction, with Coolidge clearly intending the viewers to understand that even documentaries are artificially constructed (Lane 72-3). The film begins with these introductory comments: "This film is based on incidents in the director's life. The actress who plays Martha was also raped when she was in high school. Names and places have been changed."

The film begins with Michele, an actress who portrays Martha, discussing her own rape, and her lack of knowledge concerning her own personal safety. She maintains her role is not to act the part of a rape victim, but to instruct others about her experience, to reach additional self-understanding and to learn more about the long-term consequences of her rape. Both Michele and Coolidge say they both feel somewhat responsible for their own rapes; whereupon, Coolidge states her intention to discredit the misinformation given to her by her mother that "there's no such thing as rape," implying that women allow themselves to be raped.

The narrative begins with Curly (Jim Carrington) and his friend, West Virginia, watching Michele, as performed by Coolidge, singing a folk song. The two men, whisper to each other and shake hands, presumably hatching a rape plot. Immediately, Coolidge cuts back to the apartment in the previous scene where Michele and Martha had discussed their own rapes. Now Jim, when asked about his perceptions of the film, confesses that he is confused because some women he has known have expressed rape fantasies. Coolidge, in turn, suggests that his confusion allows him to blame women for their own victimization, and proceeds to discuss with him the difference between fantasy and reality. The narrative returns to a car where three people (a couple involved in kissing and West Virginia) are in the back, and Curly and Michele up front. Curly controls the conversation with racist, sexist outbursts; Michele is uncomfortable.

The plan between Curly and West Virginia is now unfolding: the group is going to the apartment to have drinks and relax. The camera cuts to a rehearsal scene of the events to occur in the apartment, where Coolidge provides directions to the actors in the rehearsal. In guiding this film, she relives and explores her own experiences. She also asks Michele to relate how her rapist entered her apartment, encouraging the actors to draw on personal experience in their portrayals. The two rape rehearsals—which are all that is shown of the rape—occur halfway through the film, in order to leave time for much discussion of the rape and to point up the difficulties involved in the representation of rape, even one that includes personal experience.

The plot follows Curly's luring of Michele into an isolated bedroom. In the first rehearsal, Curly starts out slowly trying to persuade Michele, but becomes very forceful. Coolidge stops the action, appearing emotionally stressed. Jim apologizes to Michele for wanting to hit her and is bewildered that he could feel so aggressive toward someone he loves. Coolidge talks with Jim about his feelings, aiming toward increasing his self-knowledge. During the second rehearsal, Jim struggles with Michele until Coolidge halts the action, unable to speak. Michele and

Coolidge share an emotional embrace. The film ends as Coolidge acknowledges her fear of men and commitment, as well as her anxieties about displaying her vulnerability. She begins to cry, the scene becoming a freeze frame as the credits roll (Lane 72-7).

Impressed by *Not a Pretty Picture*, Francis Ford Coppola invited Coolidge to direct *Photoplay*, a rock and roll romance, at Zoetrope Studios, but the financially troubled studio was forced to abandon the project two and a half years later. Coolidge returned to Canada to direct a television mini-series on Canadian Broadcasting Company and, while there, was asked to direct her first feature film, *City Girl*. But, before it was distributed, she was given the script for *Valley Girl* (1983), an independently produced film that brought her into the ranks of mainstream direction.

The film that catapulted to national prominence the "Valley Girl" culture, specifically its speech and fashion, became a cult hit because of Coolidge's deepening of female characterizations and relationships (Lane 78). The *Romeo and Juliet* scenario set in southern California, where mall-addicted Julie (Deborah Foreman) dumps her preppie boyfriend, Tommy ("It's like I'm totally not in love with you anymore, Tommy—I mean it's so boring"), spies Randy soon after and falls for him instantly. But, Randy is a punk from Hollywood and is as strongly individualistic as Julie is dependent upon her friends' approval. He is unacceptable to her friends, who threaten to drop Julie from their crowd if she does not dump Randy. Julie consults her parents, former Woodstock hippies and owners of a health-food store, who, despite the hilarity of their over-the-top performances, encourage her to be herself. Julie attends the prom with Tommy, but follows her feelings and her parents' advice, and ends up with Randy.

While Coolidge's layered, satiric romance pits hair, fashion styles, music, and speech as conflicting value statements to encourage spectator interest, her camerawork focusing on the female characters seems designed to elicit spectator identification. The film's emphasis from the beginning is on Julie, a young woman actively in pursuit of romance, and the shots of Julie from her point of view make it plain that she desires Randy. Coolidge features reaction shots from Julie, notably her aversion to Tommy, who, following their brief reunion, eats her food. Also, Coolidge follows Julie's friends, specifically as she chronicles Loryn's seduction by Tommy, who by callously refusing to be her steady boyfriend, signals he is a selfish jerk. Loryn's face registers a distinct vulnerability to Tommy's cruel insensitivity. In the continuation of her own version of the "woman's film," Coolidge includes both women's and men's issues as well as emotional reactions that would summon identification with both genders. Coolidge's episode of Randy hiding in the bathtub while he waits for Julie to eventually come to the bathroom features his privileged view of various goings-on between males and females and his disgust for their behavior. Further identification is accomplished when in the film Randy takes Julie into underground bars and music venues as she and the audience experience the vibrant, expressive punk music that is part of Randy's world. Julie's consciousness raising—a theme throughout Coolidge's films—is recorded as she moves through her friends' expectations of her, into her realization of the restrictions placed upon her, and on into her pursuit of whom she wants.

Coolidge's next film, *Real Genius* (1985), tells the story of sleazy, egotistical scientist, Dr. Jerry Hathaway (William Atherton), who recruits fifteen-year-old whiz kid Mitch Taylor (Gabe Jarret) to attend Pacific Tech, where he is to be mentored by Chris Knight (Val Kilmer) on a high-powered laser project. With the deadline approaching, Hathaway forces Taylor and Knight to labor furiously in the lab on his governmentally sponsored research for the military's Crossbow program. Ethics is an word unknown to Hathaway, who applies his defense contract money to the construction of his mansion—while conscripting the boys to complete the research—and who keeps secret the true purpose of the laser research, which is to establish the U.S. military's capacity to obliterate any human target from space. Chris, who succumbed to burn-out after three years of extreme pressure, has since turned to pranks and the aggressive pursuit of the absurd. He never attends classes; instead, he freezes nitrogen to slice for drink machine slugs, turns his dorm into a skating rink, and transforms a lecture hall into a swimming pool complete with girls in bikinis. Chris confesses to Mitch that the turning point for him was the discovery of Laszlo, a brainiac smarter than both of them, who had cracked under the pressure at Pacific Tech and retreated to living quarters in the steam tunnels that he entered through the closet in Chris's dorm room. When the two discover the true purpose of the research, they set about to perform a critical adjustment on the laser, causing it to strike the professor's house and dispense several hundred pounds of popcorn out of the windows and doors of the house.

The film is interestingly a coming-of-age story for Mitch, who is only 15 and is the target of many jokes. At a particularly trying time, Mitch phones his mother and begs to come home, a conversation recorded by his jealous classmates and played over the public address system in the dining hall. He is humiliated, but is persuaded by Chris to stay and retaliate. The pranks that Coolidge films, based on actual pranks perpetrated at the California Institute of Technology, all serve to help Mitch find a place where he feels he belongs. Mitch, who had idolized Chris, is shocked by Chris's role as a slacker, who commits himself to the laser project only when Hathaway threatens him with not graduating. Mitch eventually meets Laszlo, who researches and wins 32.6 percent of the Frito-Lay Sweepstakes. Mitch suffers a loss of innocence when he realizes the extent of duplicity of Hathaway and the true purpose of the work. He is, however, supported by his growing knowledge of who he is and the friendships he has made. He also meets Jordan Cochran (Michelle Meyrink), a pretty, hyperkinetic inventor who lives down the hall and never seems to sleep. They become friends.

When *Real Genius* was finished, Coolidge remembers, "I just knew that if I didn't get out of high school movies, I was a dead duck," and she consciously sought a different type of script (Holleran). Coolidge had read the *Rambling Rose* script and made it known she was interested in it. She began negotiating with actresses, particularly Laura Dern, and Dern's mother, Diane Ladd. She signed

Lukas Haas and Robert Duvall, who had originally declined the offer. Coolidge says, "We had a first choice cast.... I don't know how many times in one's life one gets writing like that. I've worked with some great writers, but with *Rambling Rose* (1991), every scene is so deep and literate. You can get lost in it" (Holleran).

Set in Georgia in 1935, Rambling Rose (the script beautifully written by Calder Willingham from his autobiographical novel) tells the story of a troubled girl, Rose (Dern), who comes to work for the Hillyer family. Rose, an orphan from Alabama, who has a shady past that includes poverty, abuse, and troubles with men, is rescued by Daddy Hillyer (Duvall), who manages the local hotel. The other family members are Mother (Diane Ladd, Dern's real-life mother), Buddy (Haas), who tells the story in flashback in 1971 as the adult Buddy (John Heard), and two smaller children, Waska and Doll-Baby. The family is a bit eccentric in that Mother, who is completing her MA thesis at Columbia University, is seen as a type of early feminist.

Upon her arrival, Rose immediately falls in love with Daddy and responds to his gallantry and kindness as she had to other men in her past—sexually. Abruptly, while washing dishes, she leaps into Daddy's lap and begins kissing him; Daddy rejects her, saying, "I only kiss Mrs Hillyer." Rose, confused and fearful of being mentally unbalanced, slips in to Buddy's room and into his bed, where she ponders her own nature, while he explores her body. In this delicate episode, her arousal connects with the coming of age of thirteen-year-old Buddy, who falls in love with Rose, who then leaves his room even more convinced that she's going insane.

After her fiasco with Daddy, Rose goes to town looking for other men. Soon, men are visiting her in her bedroom and fighting over her on the Hillyer grounds—situations Daddy Hillyer will not tolerate. He is of the opinion that women should control their own sexuality. Rose becomes ill and is thought to be pregnant but, instead, has an ovarian cyst resulting from teenage promiscuity and STDs, and needs surgery. The doctor, who is also in pursuit of her, appeals to Daddy Hillyer for his approval to perform a hysterectomy "for Rose's own good," of course. The operation is stopped by Mother, who delivers a stinging rebuke to the two men: "Are you human beings or are you male monsters? Is there no limit to which limit you'd go to keep your illusions about yourselves? You'd go so far as to mutilate a helpless girl who has no means of defending herself?"

For Coolidge, who prides herself on always bringing to each film the fact that she is a woman, and never allowing a stereotypical female characterization, the emphasis upon the woman's point of view in this film is no surprise. By virtue of Mother's advanced work at Columbia, her knowledge is not really contested. Although Daddy occasionally chides her gently about her strong beliefs, saying, "Now, Darling, let's not go into the fourth dimension," Mother underscores the maternal theme in the film with her notions of humanity. Mother insists that Rose behaves as she does because she needs love, not sex. At one point, Mother and rose confide to each other their history as orphans and forge a mother–daughter bond by holding hands. Mother's belief that Rose's promiscuity arises not from the lack of a man's love but the need for a mother's love is validated later in the film by Rose's final conversation with Buddy. Rose, in her final conversation with Buddy, explains that when her mother died, her father began harassing her, and she ran off to the city. The loss of her mother had begun a downward path that was corrected by Mother Hillyer; Rose tells Buddy that her mother was a saint like his. She also asks Buddy to remember that women care much more about love than sex.

But, Coolidge will not devalue the father–son theme in the film by focusing solely on the female relationships. Since the night Rose came into his bed, Buddy has loved her. Actually, Coolidge sees the theme of the film developed through that scene. She says:

> It's about higher love. That boy's ability to love for the rest of his life. He's devoted to Rose. But his interest is carnal at first. He's a thirteen-year-old boy who wants to know what she did as a prostitute—he wants all the details.... When she starts crying and he starts feeling her pain, and he starts understanding her dilemma, he's lifted above his carnal interests into his sudden identification with the girl and he loves her. He wants to protect her. It's about the boy becoming a man and a man's ability to love, as an integration of sex and love—of the mind and the body (Holleran).

In 1971 when the adult Buddy comes home to visit Daddy and hears that "Rose is at rest with Mother," he mourns Rose's death and tearfully visits the location of his last conversation with her. Although the film ends in a pairing of the two women with a sense of closure, Coolidge is very proud of the fact that "*Rambling Rose* tested in previews better with men than with women" (Lane 85). This film is illustration of her desire to express both male and female views, balancing femininity with masculinity.

Coolidge's next feature film, Neil Simon's Pulitzer-winning play, *Lost in Yonkers* (1993), deals with a dysfunctional family and various experiences of that family in Yonkers, New York, during 1942. The film is narrated by Jay (Brad Stoll) during the aftermath of his mother's death, when his father, bankrupt after paying for his wife's medical expenses and funeral, borrows $9,000 from loan sharks. Unable to repay the money by the deadline, he places Jay and his brother, Arty, with his mother, a tough-as-nails German immigrant, while he goes south for ten months to work in wartime scrap industries. Grandma (Irene Worth) owns a candy store where the boys help out, and she runs the store, as she does her life, with steely discipline and control. Also living there is Grandma's daughter, Bella (Merced Ruehl), a child-woman of 36, who longs for a life and a family of her own. Grandma's son, Louie (Richard Dreyfuss), spends several hectic days in the house, while he hides out from two rough characters.

As the narrative is told from Jay's point of view, he and Arty learn about their family's harsh taskmistress, their grandmother, the major interest throughout the film is Aunt Bella's attempt to be independent. As a refuge from her mother,

Bella goes to movies several times a week and has made the acquaintance of the theater usher, Johnny (David Strathairn), whom she wants to marry. While Bella is a little slow, Johnny has a learning disability and has been in the "home" that Grandma has threatened Bella with periodically, but their dream is to marry and open a restaurant together. Bella plans a family dinner, where she announces this to her mother, Louie, sister Gert, and her young nephews. The evening opens with a skirmish between Bella and Louie but turns into a battle royal between Bella and her mother. Bella's impassioned diatribe about her own needs in the face of her mother's oppression stuns everyone, but the entire episode crackles with the strength and will of these two hopelessly opposed women. Louie is so impressed with Bella's courage, he gives her $5,000 to open the restaurant. Grandma accuses Bella of having stolen the money from her, but despite the rift between the two women it all becomes a moot point. Johnny cannot conquer his fear of failure to even begin the venture. Eventually, Bella leaves home in search of a life of her own, and the boys are reunited with their father, who has paid the debt, and Grandma is left alone, with her candy store and her enormous reservoir of self-control.

Coolidge's film *Angie* (1994) was originally written for Madonna, but after a circuitous journey, it was offered to Geena Davis, who insisted upon Coolidge as the director. The film, about a young woman who decides to have her baby without marrying the father, has been lauded by some critics as feminist. Promoted as a "woman's film," *Angie* treads much of the same territory covered in *Rambling Rose*, in that both women, deep in familial disorder, are searching for their own identities as well as looking for ways to express their sexuality. Also, both are motherless and learn by the end of the film to reach out to another mother. Coolidge seems sensitive to themes of motherlessness in films because her father died when she was a child, and also because her son underwent surgery soon after his birth, similar to Angie's baby in the film.

The film begins with Angie (Davis) and Tina, childhood friends, who paint one another's face and plan to grow up, marry twin boys, and remain best friends always. Angie shows a faded picture of her mother, who left home when Angie was three. Angie thinks of her mother as a "free spirit." This scene morphs into a more current scene where Angie and Tina, walking to work down the same street in Bensonhurst, New York, see themselves in the children they see in the same places where they used to be. Tina, married with a child, and not quite as happy as she thought she would be, believes strongly in marriage. Angie, who works in Manhattan, still is obsessed with her mother, whom neighbors recall witnessing dancing in the snow.

Angie discovers she is pregnant, and although her fiancé, Vinnie (James Gandolfini), is delighted, Angie decides not to marry him. She meets an Irishman, Noel (Stephen Rea), whom she likes, and they begin seeing each other. Angie's baby is born with serious medical complications, in need of surgery, but Angie is determined to find her mother. Boarding a bus, she manages to find her mother in Texas and discovers that her mother left home not for a life of challenge or adventure, but because she was slowly declining from schizophrenia; moreover, she learns that not only has her father been sending her mother news about Angie on a regular basis, but had sent the mother away to protect Angie. The scene where Angie kneels at her mother's side calls to mind the scene in *Rambling Rose* where Rose and Mother tell their stories and hold one another's hands. On a long road to self-discovery, Angie reconciles herself to the reality of the condition of her mother, who burns the faded picture of the two together, thereby seeming to destroy any binding connection between them, and resolves to go home to her son and be the mother her mother never was to her.

As Coolidge allows Angie to overcome her dislike for her stepmother and reach out to her as a mother, who may very well replace Tina, whose relationship with Angie at this point is not clarified, she shows Angie unable or unwilling to marry for the sake of her son. The mother–daughter relationship, Coolidge implies, is primary for women and must be resolved before a woman can maintain a positive, nurturing environment for her child. Also, Coolidge managed to critique Hollywood's women's genre pictures, or Hollywood's proverbial happy endings, in favor of a woman who is not being punished for refusing to get married and raise a child alone.

Coolidge follows this film with another story of a woman raising her two sons alone—her pilot husband having been shot down and MIA in the Korean War. *Three Wishes* (1995) features Jeanne (Mary Elizabeth Mastrantonio), who, much like Angie, rejects two men who love her, choosing, instead, to be a single mother. The film begins with Tom (Joseph Mazello), who is down on his luck and trying to avoid losing his house. Driving one night, he glimpses a hitchhiker and his dog and is thrust into a flashback into his own childhood in 1955, when his mother, Jeanne, accidentally hits a hitchhiker, breaking his leg. Feeling guilty about the accident, she takes Jack (Patrick Swayze) to her home while he recuperates. Neighbors look askance at such behavior and question other aspects of her life: she wears shorts, also deemed inappropriate, and she continues to bring up her two sons alone, despite Tom's very obvious need for a father to help him in Little League and five-year-old Gunny's affliction with a mysterious illness. Jeanne, too, is plagued with indecision. She dislikes her job as an accountant and wants to start her own business.

Into this troubled household, Jack is a breath of fresh air. Espousing a personal philosophy that is at odds with the 1950s suburb preoccupied with conformity, he uses an unconventional approach based essentially on positive thinking to help each of them. Poised and radiating quiet strength, Jack stands out in the neighborhood. He sips tea and meditates, and it is rumored he sunbathes nude in the backyard. All are shocked when he uses a Zen approach to instruct Tom and the entire team, which begins to win games. To Tom, Jack becomes the father he does not have; Jack and his magical dog, Betty Jane, watch over Gunny (Seth Mumy) as he battles stomach cancer; and Jack urges Jeanne to follow her own instincts and not succumb to the pressure to marry the rich banker in order to provide a father for her sons.

The script for *Three Wishes*, inspired by European folklore, was originally a thirty-page outline of a story written by coproducers, Clifford and Ellen Green, and then given to Elizabeth Anderson, who had a fellowship at Sundance Writing Institute, to write the script. The story suggests that if an individual does a good deed, such as Jeanne looking after Jack after he was injured, then he or she would be repaid in kind. Coolidge, sensitive and clear thinking, resists making the film syrupy, yet clearly invokes the magical. The emphasis upon thinking for oneself, upon being the person one wants to be seem to reflect the kind of character Coolidge prefers, and the kind of character she is herself.

The film also found itself in the political sphere. Coolidge and her associates, in order to publicize the film, took out a full-page advertisement in *The Washington Post* at its release in Fall 1995, inviting President Clinton and Senator Robert Dole to the screening of the film. The ad specified that if they screen the film together, $100,000 would be donated by Rysher Entertainment to the Make-a-Wish Foundation. Aside from attempting to access advertising not usually available for independent films, Coolidge calls attention to the political nature of her earlier documentaries and her continued outspokenness about gender inequality and sexual harassment. Coolidge has worked outside and inside of Hollywood, beginning with experimental films and *Valley Girl*; *Real Genius* was a studio production; *Rambling Rose* was independently produced; but *Lost in Yonkers*, *Angie*, and *Three Wishes* were all mainstream films.

In 1997 Coolidge completed *Out to Sea*, a comedy with Walter Matthau and Jack Lemmon, who have worked together in numerous films since *The Fortune Cookie* in 1966. Resembling *Grumpy Old Men*, this film continues the humorous escapades of the aging pair. Charlie (Matthau) is a con artist who drags his brother-in-law onto a cruise ship, where he can meet rich widows to support his gambling habit. The brother-in-law, Herb (Lemmon), is still grieving for his dead wife and is not interested in rich widows. Moreover, Charlie neglects to tell him that he has signed them up as dance instructors on the cruise, in order to pay for their passage. Of course, they meet attractive widows; in fact, Herb meets Vivian (Gloria de Haven) and falls in love with her almost immediately. Charlie meets Liz (Dyan Cannon) and her feisty mother (Elaine Stritch). The two men are hilarious in the dancing sequences and so is Donald O'Connor.

Coolidge's next effort was a movie for HBO, *Introducing Dorothy Dandridge* (1999), produced by and starring Halle Berry as the first African American woman to be nominated for the Best Actress Academy Award in 1954. Both Berry and Dandridge grew up in Cleveland, Ohio, and Berry had the honor of being the first African American woman to be awarded the Best Actress Academy Award in 2001. It was Berry, in her desire to make Dandridge's life and career known to many who do not know who she was, who insisted upon Coolidge as the director. HBO supported Coolidge in her intent to show some of the less attractive aspects of Dandridge's life.

The film follows Dandridge from her start in show business with her sister and a friend billed as The Dandridge Sisters, who achieve fame as dancers and singers, and travel across the country. On tour, they meet The Nicholas Brothers (dancers), and Dorothy and Harold are married in 1942. Their only child, Harolyn (Lyn), born in 1943, is severely mentally handicapped, and Dorothy's marriage to Harold who refuses to be a father to Lyn, ends in 1951.

Dandridge's agent, Earl Miles (Brent Spiner), gets her an interview with director Otto Preminger (Klaus Maria Brandauer), who casts her in the all-Negro production of *Carmen Jones*, for which she is nominated for an Oscar. She begins an affair with Preminger which lasts for years, and when he refuses to divorce his wife and marry her, she begins a downhill slide. Bad decisions she has made on the advice of Preminger cost her a lucrative contract with Darryl F. Zanuck, head of Twentieth Century-Fox studios. She marries Jack Dennison, a white restaurant owner, who abuses her and takes her money for his own investments. After two years, she divorces him. She has some parts in movies, and she tries singing again, but she cannot perform well because of the antidepressants and alcohol she turns to for comfort. Miles, her former agent who loves her, finds singing engagements and a movie contract for her and is in the process of helping her get her life back together, when he discovers her body on September 8, 1965. She has died of a drug overdose, but it is not determined whether it is accidental or intentional. Miles believes strongly that it was accidental.

Coolidge emphasizes Dandridge's poor choices in men as well as the two violent episodes she depicts on screen. When Dandridge returns home after her first date, with Harold, she is met by Auntie (the live-in woman who takes care of the girls while their mother works, and unbeknownst to the girls is their mother's lover) who demands to know if Dandridge and Harold have engaged in sex. Ignoring Dandridge's answers and protests, Auntie, a large woman, throws a hysterical Dandridge on the couch and proceeds to examine Dandridge to her own satisfaction. The traumatic effects of that invasion is observed throughout Dandridge's life in her sexual relations with her husbands and Preminger. While Auntie's brutal beatings of the girls are hinted at but not shown onscreen, Dennison's on-screen attack on Dandridge is vicious.

Coolidge devotes much energy to the depiction of 1950s racist society's treatment of Dandridge and, by extension, all black people. In clubs where Dandridge had singing engagements, she is not allowed to use the bathroom facilities; she is given a Dixie cup. She is not allowed to eat in the restaurant or enter by the front door. In Las Vegas, she is required to enter the club by the back door, going through the kitchen to the main room, and she is denied the use of the pool. Defiantly, Dandridge sticks her toe in the water, whereupon the pool is drained and scrubbed by black workers before it can be refilled for use. As for Hollywood at that period in history, parts for African American actresses are limited to slaves, mammies, servants, or other menial workers. Black women could not be paired with white men, and as a result desirable parts for black women were very hard to come by.

Following *Introducing Dorothy Dandridge*, Coolidge directed one segment of *If These Walls Could Talk 2* (2000), a television series that focused on lesbians living in a house at three different time periods. Coolidge's segment concerns a chemistry-laden attraction between a feminist and a butch lesbian that takes place in 1972. Coolidge has directed numerous episodes in television series, including two on *Sex and the City* (2000, 2002).

Coolidge's film, *The Prince and Me* (2004), follows Coolidge's interest in female empowerment and following their dreams in the story of Paige Morgan (Julia Styles), a farm girl at The University of Wisconsin who dreams of being accepted to Johns Hopkins University and eventually joining Doctors Without Borders, and Edvard Dangaard, the restless Crown Prince of Denmark (Luke Mably), who comes to Wisconsin, lured by a video of Wisconsin girls removing their tops frequently. Eddie meets Paige at the bar where she works and asks her immediately to take her top off. She squirts him with seltzer and he is hooked. He has never approached anyone who did not know who he is. He signs up for her chemistry lab, becoming her partner, but cannot always make it to class on time. She invites him home with her for Thanksgiving holidays, and he meets her parents and he participates in a lawnmower race with her brothers. Back at school, Eddie learns that his father is ill, and he must go back to become King of Denmark. Paige follows, eventually winning the approval of his parents. Acknowledging the claim of her becoming a doctor upon her, she tells Eddie she cannot continue and returns home. But, the story is not finished. Page graduates, is accepted to Johns Hopkins University, and, at her graduation, Eddie arrives to tell her he wants her in his life, and he will do whatever is necessary; he will wait however long it takes.

In 1954, *The Student Prince* (Richard Thorpe), a film based on Sigmund Romberg's operetta of the same name, tells the story of the Prince of Karlsberg, who, while incognito and preparing to enter the University of Heidelberg, falls in love with a barmaid. The love affair comes to a halt, however, when his father, the king, dies, and the Prince must return to assume his kingly duties—one of which will be to marry another person to be his queen. Coolidge and her writers have reworked this story, itself perhaps a reworking of an ancient fairy tale in which a young girl becomes the beloved of a crown prince and lives happily ever after, into a fresh reading which focuses on the girl's point of view. Whereas Eddie's life is already detailed for him as the hereditary monarch of his country, Paige has carefully planned her life around going to a prestigious medical school and becoming a doctor—working part time as a barmaid to accomplish her dreams. Not only is she a workaholic, but she is single-minded about her own future.

In her introductory comments on the DVD of *The Prince and Me*, Coolidge says:

> The first image of Paige is looking through a microscope, and it's, I think, a real definition of her character, that sees very small things in a very detailed way, but she doesn't have a wide vision about her life. The point of the movie being, that she is going to learn, through loving the prince, to open herself up to other possibilities.

The differences between these two characters, established early in the film, are accomplished through alternate shots and episodes of Paige, a serious farm girl from a loving family who has set the arduous parameters of her life, and Prince Edvard Dangaard, dallying with girls and racing against Eddie Irvine, Formula One Racing Great, to avoid the responsibilities inherent in his birth. Coolidge notes the way the conflicts in the conflicting cultures were demonstrated: colors used for the Wisconsin shots are much warmer colors than those used for the cold, blue colors of Denmark. We see her driving home to the farm to change clothes for a friend's wedding, which is paralleled with the race between the Prince and Irvine through the city streets and into the country. Prince Edvard is shown with his groupie girls after the race, whereas Paige is seen with her friends celebrating the wedding. But, despite the fact that these episodes certainly suggest an impending crash of opposites, the chemistry that exists between these two characters is quite strong. The chemistry lab is significant regarding Eddie (the Prince's name in Wisconsin) and his growing attachment to Paige. He had never been on his own with a woman who did not know who he was and he was not automatically in control. He falls in love with her in the bar scene where she is cleaning up; she falls in love with him in the laundry room when he explains Shakespeare to her. This scene is significant: it shows that she is the scientist, and he the poet. She has no metaphorical bones in her body, being a scientist who is concerned with facts and not the likes of Shakespeare. In the Shakespeare/laundry room scene, he proves there is more to him than playboy, and his sensitivity toward the sonnet in question captures Paige's heart. The two are opposites, yet each provides the lack in the other.

Following the erotic scene in the library, where the pair are interrupted by Danish Photographers hounding the Prince, and Paige discovers the true identity of Eddie, Eddie is informed by his mother of his father's illness and abdication of the throne to the Prince. Paige follows him, undergoing an initial conflict with the Queen Mother (Miranda Richardson), who introduces Paige to the life of responsibility and public appearances—her future life if she becomes Queen. Paige understandably has doubts, and despite the Prince's victory over the Queen regarding his choice of mate, she cannot escape wanting to be herself and follow her plans to become a doctor. Paige says goodbye to Eddie and goes home. While the audience expects this to be the final scene, it is not. At her graduation from college, when Eddie appears with his plea, it is as if two people are coming out of themselves through the evolving dialogue to compromise and resolve the conflict. Coolidge, indeed, offers a "contemporary interpretation" of the fairy tale.

KATHRYN BIGELOW

Of all the mainstream women film directors, none is more unique than Kathryn Bigelow, who rejected the idea that women should make tame films and has

created a niche for herself as a director of action genres. She flaunts a stylized violence and visual intensity usually reserved for male directors, though blended so
masterfully with continuous revisions of major genres, echoes of earlier male directors and her own gender-related issues, the results are complex, layered artifacts.
Although aimed for a wide audience, Bigelow's films have faltered financially,
but have impressed critics with their originality, and more than one of them has
become a cult favorite.

Bigelow was born November 27, 1953, in San Carlos, California, to a paint
factory manager and a librarian. After high school, she studied at the San Francisco
Art Institute, graduating in 1972. She received a scholarship to the Whitney
Museum in New York, eventually moving from abstract art to film studies, and
graduated from Columbia Graduate Film School in 1979.

In 1978, Bigelow directed a short student film, *The Set-Up*; coscripted and
codirected with Monty Montgomery, a fellow student, her first feature film *Loveless*
in 1982; directed and coscripted (with Eric Red) her first mainstream film, *After
Dark*, in 1987; and, in 1990, directed *Blue Steel*, a film about a female cop who
tracked down her stalker. In 1989, she and director James Cameron were married;
they divorced in 1991, the same year of the release of *Point Break*. In 1995, her
best-known film, *Strange Days*, shocked audiences with its apocalyptic vision of a
society on the eve of destruction, followed by *K-19: The Widowmaker*, in 2000.
In 2002, she released a change-of-pace film, *The Weight of Water*, which centers
on a contemporary photographer's investigation of a gruesome murder in 1873.
Bigelow codirected a television mini-series, *Wild Palms* (1993), as well as various
episodes of television dramas, including *Homicide: Life on the Street* (1998–99)
and *Karen Sisco* (2003).

Bigelow once explained that her career shift from art to film occurred because
"she recognized film as this extraordinary social tool that could reach tremendous
numbers of people" (Webb 3). To endeavor to reach a wide audience, Bigelow
chose to work with the action genre, one most associated with male directors and
audiences, and also within the noir tradition—a prominent vehicle for male fantasy. Her own themes of violence, especially among society's outsiders, nihilism,
and a preoccupation with strong characters, both male and female, are developed
through unexpected genre twists and mutations, and extraordinary visuals that
essentially turn the genre on its head.

Bigelow's first film, *The Set-Up* (1978), announces her concern with violence
and its depiction on film. The twenty-four-minute experimental film recounts
an episode of two men fighting in an alley, while two theorists on voiceover
speculate about the causes for violence. This film led to Loveless, a story of an
outsider biker gang in the 1950s on their way to Florida, who pass through a
small town and generate a series of violent encounters with various citizens in
the town. Fresh from the art world, Bigelow was largely experimenting in this
film by attempting to "create this visual tapestry ... to give the illusion of a story
percolating ..." (Smith 30). Bigelow continues, "I hadn't embraced narrative at
that point; I was still completely conceptual, and narrative was antithetical to

anything in the art world" (Smith 30). Bigelow's interest in *Loveless* amounted to the "images of power" (Smith 31). This film seems to be a riff on several other biker films—*The Wild One* (Laslo Benedek, 1954); *Two-Lane Blacktop* (Monte Hellman, 1971); and most significantly, Kenneth Anger's *Scorpio Rising* (1963), which links "motorcycle culture to homoeroticism, the death wish, and desires aroused by mass media drawn from comic strips, movies and mystical traditions" (Thompson, Bordwell 591).

Willem Dafoe's film debut, *Loveless*, depicts Dafoe as Vance, who plans to meet up with other bikers on the way to Florida. In a small Georgia town, where they wait for bike repairs, Vance has a sexual encounter with a girl whose promiscuity derives from being a victim of incest. The slow-moving film, headed toward a showdown at the end between the bikers and the townspeople and punctuated by the girl's murder of her father and her own suicide, ends with the bikers going on their way to Florida. The film, containing long stretches of no dialogue and little action, functions as a meditation on violence and power in the sexually repressed 1950s.

Bigelow's first feature film, coscripted with Eric Red but directed by her, *Near Dark*, introduces a bizarre blend of western, noir, and vampire genres and inverted gender roles. The film's opening shots of a western landscape at sundown leading into the night world of vampires set up a clash of opposites that result from the mingling of genres. The expanse of sun-scorched flat earth and its historic association with civilization and cowboys in the classic western genre is replaced with the dark lawless realm of savage, ageless vampires whose only fears are of exploding in the sunlight. Bright material heroics of the western tradition contrast oddly with the nightmare world of the supernatural.

Caleb (Adrian Pasdar), an Oklahoma farm boy, on his way into town at twilight to spend an evening with his friends, sees Mae (Jenny Wright), a delicate, otherworldly girl who speaks to him of the beauty of the night. Caleb takes her to his father's farm to see his horse, which seems unsettled in Mae's presence. Mae lassos Caleb, who stops his truck later on determined to kiss her. Mae, again in an assertive role, draws Caleb's blood in a vampire kiss, which ushers him into the night world of blood craving, forever lost to the comforts of his home and family. He is, however, kidnapped by her family who demands that he adopts their lifestyle of sleeping in their aging, darkened Winnebago all day and killing at night. The vampire family descends on a bar, specifically a barmaid whose throat they cut, catching her blood in a beer mug and passing it among the family members. Caleb is urged to kill his first victim (thus, winning his spurs), but he lets the young man escape, as a violent brawl erupts in the bar, with the vampires killing the bartender among others, and burning the building as they escape. The film's end hinges on a final battle between Caleb's family and Mae's.

The film ironically depicts the total freedom of the west with the subversive vampire attraction of endless adventure and invincibility. Soon after he was "turned," Caleb asks Mae, "What do we do next?" Mae replies, "Whatever we want until the end of time." The film offers eroticism; Caleb's bite comes at the end of a kiss in an extended caress, and Caleb feeds from Mae's wrist like a helpless infant, as Mae becomes mother as well as seductress in an eerie episode under the stars. Bigelow omits traditional trappings of vampire lore, utilizing only the sun in her contemporary narrative. The film received, by and large, good reviews as most viewers were struck by Bigelow's playing with genre and gender.

It was with *Blue Steel* that Bigelow achieved the notoriety that comes with writing and directing a film whose main character is a female cop. Complexity of genre and gender representation elicited a great deal of feminist attention to the story of Megan Turner (Jamie Lee Curtis), who on her first day as a cop, kills a convenience store robber and is suspended because she forgot to get the killer's weapon. The weapon is surreptiously recovered by Eugene Hunt (Ron Silver), a customer in the store, who becomes unhinged by what he witnesses and begins to randomly shoot strangers with bullets that have Megan's name carved on them. He also "accidentally" meets Megan and they begin dating. Megan discovers the identity of Hunt and tracks him down.

Slick, violent, and bloody, the film is seen as an unrealistic action/thriller film. David Denby labeled the film as a "Dirty Harriet movie," referring to Clint Eastwood's *Dirty Harry* (1971), directed by Don Siegel, and continued, "I can't see that much has been gained now that a woman is free to make the same rotten movie as a man" (p. 77). The film is popular with feminist critics, who enjoy Curtis as a cop whose role of female victim and female hero is never really resolved.

Point Break, Bigelow's next mainstream film, was successful at the box office, earning around $100 million in its first year, but was perceived negatively by many critics, who saw it as a youth-oriented action film. Hannah Ransley believes it fared well because it fit the action genre so perfectly and its "examination of masculine relations and the lines between right and wrong is complimented by adrenaline-pumping action sequences" (47).

In order to apprehend bank robbers thought to be four surfers who call them-selves Ex-Presidents (Nixon, Carter, Reagan, Johnson), the FBI sends in Johnny Utah (Keanu Reaves) and his partner, Pappas (Gary Busey), to investigate. The plan is for Utah to infiltrate the surfer group, make friends with the leader, Bodhi (Patrick Swayze), short for Bodhisattva, Sanskrit for "being of wisdom," and gain information. Utah, taught to surf by Tyler (Lori Petty), makes the acquaintance of Bodhi, and a struggle between the beliefs and values of each ensues. Very slowly, Utah is seen coming under the influence of Bodhi, the exisitential, Zen-quoting Bodhi who surfs "out of time" in an endless ocean; time slows down and he is being set free. He is depicted as a free agent outside the system, and a part of a counterculture. The dominant culture, represented by Utah, a creature of schedules and deadlines who, because of its rigid concept of time, has not been able to apprehend the Ex-Presidents, because they view time as passing seasons. The surveillance agents and the surfers engage in a struggle between beliefs and values, which dominates the film. Bigelow views the surfers, who enjoy their own language, dress code, and conduct, as reflecting subversive, countercultural values that undermine the conservative law-and-order system. Bigelow first depicts this opposition in her opening shots of Bodhi surfing balletically in slow motion on the perfect wave intercut with Johnny Utah, the cop executing his training routine. A glittering ocean suggesting endless freedom where time and constraints are of no consequence appears to be Bigelow's alternative to the regulated, programmed, repressive lifestyle of Utah and the dominant system of values. Ultimately, Utah's attraction to the surfers' freedom prompts him to toss his badge in the water and allow Bodhi to go free.

Despite being a box office failure, *Strange Days* is a provocative look at the approaching new millennium, focusing on events during December 30 and 31, 1999, in Los Angeles. The story centers on Lenny Nero (Ralph Fiennes), a former vice-squad cop, who is now a prominent purveyor of a superconductor device (SQUID) that allows the wearer to relive the experiences, usually erotic or violent, of other people. Seedy and glib, Lenny proclaims himself the "Santa Claus of the unconscious" as he plies his trade among the zonked and jaded denizens of Los Angeles eager to perceive the ultimate virtual reality. But, Lenny has his ethics: he refuses to deal with "snuff" films, or any SQUID that results in the death of the individual wired to record his or her experience.

Lenny receives a "playback" of the horrifically brutal rape and murder of Iris, a prostitute friend of his lost love (significantly named Faith), and sets out to find the perpetrator. His search takes him through a society reeling from technological surfeit, violence, racism, and paranoia, as Bigelow invokes a formidable critique of an out-of-control civilization on the brink of self-destruction. Ironically, her depiction of a society of voyeurs bent on living through the experiences of others mirrors a nation of filmgoers whose need for the spectacular is alarming. At one point in *Strange Days*, Max says to Lenny: "Every kind of music's been tried. Every government's been tried. I mean ... hairstyle ... bubble gum. You know, breakfast cereal. Every ... peanut.... How we gonna make it another thousand years, for Christ's sake?" The film's postmodern vision of the world is one where everything has already been done, and the consumerist throwaway culture prods a constant search for new things, including, in this case, SQUID devices. Lenny, unable to establish a new relationship, dotes on his taped memories of happier days with Faith, because newer acquisitions fail to satisfy. The narrative, according to feminist evaluation, echoes a fragmentation characteristic of postmodernism through the interruption of the white male narrative with the various SQUID tapes involving women and minorities who represent the "Other." Although the film's voyeurism calls to mind Alfred Hitchcock's films that indict voyeurism, *Rear Window* (1954) and *Psycho* (1960), Bigelow also hints of Michael Powell's *Peeping Tom* (1960), a controversial film about a photographer who murders prostitutes with a tripod's hidden rapier as he photographs them viewing their own deaths.

But, as *Peeping Tom*'s photographer appears to be unbalanced from having been filmed, or looked at, every minute of his life by his father, who conducted scientific experiments, so does Bigelow assume a connection between the need for and the dangers of addiction to looking at and participating in the experiences of others. Bigelow comments:

> The movie explores the idea of watching and the need to watch, and Lenny is a kind of director-to-producer of heightened reality documentaries that put the viewer into the head of the person having a particular experience. . . . As our society progresses and genuine experience becomes a riskier and riskier enterprise, so the desire for it will increase. Lenny says, 'I am performing a humanitarian service. I probably save lives'. . . . I think cinema as we know it today satisfies that need; it's fundamental to the human condition. (Webb 1)

But it is through her genre inversion and gender reversals that Bigelow stamps her trademark and generates deeper meanings. Within the traditional noir pattern, the main character, usually an ex-cop, seeks and ferrets out truth from unsavory characters who are judged, while he remains an upright person of integrity. In other noirs, the main character, morally ambivalent and therefore susceptible to temptation, is undone by greed or lust and defeated by his enemies. In *Strange Days*, Lenny, who has lost his way in the morass he inhabits, turns to Mace (Angela Bassett) for help. Mace, an African American single parent who drives an armored limousine for the wealthy, emerges as the strongest person in the film. A person of integrity, she is fond of Lenny because he cared for her son when her husband was arrested, and, like many African Americans, Mace is economically incapable of participating in the technological explosion that specifically affects white individuals in the film. Moreover, when the cops assassinate Jeriko-One, a black leader and spokesman for the "Armageddon" to come, Los Angeles (reminiscent of the aftermath of the Rodney King beating) is on the verge of a racially charged riot. Lenny sees his discovery of the tape depicting the murder of Jeriko-One the ticket to possibly reclaiming Faith, but it actually becomes the crux of a critical situation between Lenny and Mace. Lenny wants only Faith and to return to his voyeuristic existence, immune to any responsibilities. Mace is the conscience of the film; as a mother who wants a better world for her son and is acutely aware of the racial oppression, she demands that the tape be used to bring the two murderous cops to justice. Lenny concedes, and his redemptive actions show him capable of more than mere self-indulgence.

Words are poor substitutes for the technical virtuosity of *Strange Days*. Bigelow is a master of action scenes; the fast-paced opening episode bristling with kinetic energy is a breathtaking example. Instances of her remarkable action skills include the episode when the maverick cops are chasing Lenny and Mace with intent to kill; Mace driving a flaming car off a cliff into water to extinguish the flames; Lenny and Mace breaking the windshield and surfacing; balletic scenes of mugging and violence choreographed in time to music on Lenny's car radio; the terrible struggle between Mace and the two cops who are attempting to kill her; the near-final scene where Mace is beaten (again referencing the Rodney King beating) and the unspeakable violence of the two murders caught on SQUID.

Bigelow followed up this film with *The Weight of Water*, completed in 2000, but because of a collapsed distribution agreement, it was shelved for two years. A departure from her usual "action films," this exploration of the connections between two women of different eras befuddled many critics who apparently felt that she had wandered out of her métier and was therefore lost. Despite the fact that she had always been involved in the scriptwriting process, Bigelow chose a 1997 novel of the same name written by Anita Shreve that presumably offered her opportunities to concentrate on feminine points of view. Shreve's historical drama is based on a true story that centers on the murders of two Norwegian immigrant women in 1873 on Smuttynose Island, ten miles off the New Hampshire coast. One woman survived and identified the murderer, who was later hanged. More recent evidence has raised suspicion about the hanged man's guilt.

The mysterious murder of the two women has lured Jean (Catherine McCormack), a photographer, her husband, Thomas (Sean Penn), a Pulitzer Prize–winning poet, his brother, Rich (Josh Lucas), and his sexy new girlfriend, Adaline (Elizabeth Hurley), to the island. But, as Jean reads the trial account, she becomes more vexed by the attempts of Adaline (Elizabeth Hurley) to seduce Thomas, her drunken husband. Little is known about the brother, who is attracted to Jean, or Adaline, who is provocative and scantily clad. We learn that Thomas has drifted into alcoholism after he caused the death of a woman in a car wreck, that his marriage to Jean is in trouble, and that they have a daughter at home. On the boat during a storm, Jean sees Adaline fall overboard, and says nothing. Thomas rescues her, but is drowned.

The nineteenth-century story shows Maren (Sarah Polley), the woman who survived in a loveless marriage, working endlessly to ease her loneliness. She is passionately in love with her brother, having created a family scandal by carrying on a sexual relationship with him in Norway. When her sister, Karen, and later her beloved brother and Anethe, his naïve new wife, immigrate to Smuttynose, the family situation soon disintegrates. During the absence of Maren's husband and brother, Anethe, pregnant and lonely, asks to sleep with Maren; soon, Karen bursts in shrieking about Maren's evil nature and her incestuous affair with her brother. In a blind rage, Maren murders Karen and Anethe. Perhaps, as Jean becomes preoccupied with Maren and her story, she shares a feminine sensibility across time and place that incites her own jealousy and rage. Strangely, Jean has an abrupt confrontation with and recognition of Maren in the turbulent water, as she tries unsuccessfully to rescue Thomas. The more deeply Jean investigates the double-ax murder and the newly recovered evidence of a letter Maren wrote after the man's execution that clearly makes Maren suspect, the more her marriage to Thomas seems to unravel. Sexual tension and repression in 1873 parallels the tension on the boat as Adaline flaunts herself. But to what end? The muddled film was a miserable failure at the box office.

Bigelow's most recent film, *K-19: The Widowmaker*, is a grim story of an actual incident of 1961 that was kept secret for years by the USSR. In the frenzy of the Cold War crisis, a Russian atomic submarine, hastily put together and ill equipped for its mission, was sent to fire a test missile in the Arctic Circle and then assume a conspicuous station in the Atlantic Ocean as a warning to the United States. In the ocean's depths, the reactor malfunctioned, and men were ordered to repair it. Wearing only plastic raincoats, the men were contaminated and consequently doomed, and the rising radiation level threatened everyone aboard. Moreover, the reactor's temperature had climbed to a point that a nuclear explosion was feared, which, in view of the ship's proximity to the United States, might set off World War III.

Another crisis rampant through the ship pertained to the command of the vessel. Captain Polenin (Liam Neeson), the ship's well-liked captain, who had complained to officials about the ship's unseaworthiness, was forced to step down to Captain Vostrikov (Harrison Ford), whom the crew resented. Vostrikov forced the ship and crew into an alarming series of tests, designed to whip them into fighting shape, and managed to gain the men's allegiance when the test missile was successfully fired. When Vostrikov refused help from the United States, waiting instead for aid from the USSR fleet, which was delayed by the Commander's suspicion, hard-line supporters of Polenin seized the ship's control from Vostrikov. Polenin was offered the command, but refused it and ordered the traitors arrested. When the crew was finally rescued, the two captains went home in disgrace, and were never given a command again. News of this tragedy was not known to the world until the 1990s when a documentary of the event, produced by National Geographic, was aired on PBS.

MIMI LEDER

Mimi Leder was born January 26, 1952, in New York to Paul and Etyl Leder. Paul Leder met Etyl, a survivor of Auschwitz concentration camp, when he served as an Army medic in General Patton's troops in World War II. Mimi, her brother, Reuben, and sister, Geraldine, were heavily influenced by their father, whose career as an independent filmmaker spanned three decades, and whose filmmaking involved every member of the family. "He threw us on the set," Leder recalls. "My mother cooked for everyone, and my brother, sister and I would do every job there was to do. Once you do that, it's not such a mystery, making films" (*She Made It*).

Leder applied to the American Film Institute's cinematography program, and in 1975 became the first woman to graduate from AFI with a degree in cinematography. After graduation, Leder became a script supervisor on the television program, *Hill Street Blues*. She made a short film, *Short Order Dreams*, which induced Steven Bochco and Greg Hoblit to invite her to direct an episode of *L.A. Law*. From there, she worked for two seasons as director/producer of *China Beach*, before leaving episodic television to direct several television movies and pilots. Lured back to full-time work by her former colleagues from *China Beach*, she joined them as a director of *ER*, whose production was overseen by

Steven Spielberg's company, Amblin. Leder was awarded two Emmys for her work on ER.

On the strength of her directing on ER, Spielberg asked Leder to direct *The Peacemaker*, a $50 million action-adventure film featuring George Clooney and Nicole Kidman in a search for stolen warheads. The first movie from the Steven Spielberg, Jeffrey Katzenberg, David Geller company, Dreamworks SKG, *The Peacemaker* opened in September 1997 to reviews that are divided somewhat along gender lines. Janet Maslin proclaims the film a "forceful, feature-directing debut" (NYT 9/26/97). James Berardinelli laments that the "task was just too much for first-time director, Mimi Leder," and adds that "Dreamworks is not off to a flying start" (1997). Charles Taylor claims Leder is a "hack," in a punishingly dull movie, and views Leder's breakout direction of an action-adventure film as a "leap forward for women directors to prove that they can be as brutal and stupid as men" (Salon.com).

Written by Michael Schiffer, the script is based on an article written by Andrew and Leslie Cockburn that was carefully researched for detailed accuracy concerning nuclear smuggling out of the former Soviet nations. The film follows the efforts of Colonel Thomas Devoe (Clooney) and nuclear scientist Dr. Julia Kelly (Kidman), who are on the trail of Russian terrorists who have stolen nine nuclear warheads and are thought to be preparing to sell them to the highest bidder, specifically a Serb/Croat who has a score to settle with the United States. Although Dr. Kelly, acting head of the White House Nuclear Smuggling Group, is actually Devoe's superior—he is an intelligence officer in the U.S. Army Special Forces—much of her time is devoted to tiresome instruction by Devoe about the "real world." The one-upmanship justified by his brawn against her brain seems, at first, to be Hollywood's appeal to adolescent viewers, but is actually Leder's rejection of the time-honored practice of males and females being thrown together in the typical Hollywood film and overcoming their initial dislike of each other by becoming involved romantically. Devoe and Kelly, who have little in common except their job, are sent to France, Germany, Macedonia, Vienna, the Russian–Iranian border, where they work through their mutual dislike to its conclusion.

The film begins with a manipulated train wreck, designed to cover the theft of the warheads, and is followed later by a nuclear explosion in the heart of the Urals that allegedly kills 150,000 people. And, despite the car chase in Vienna that Leder labored to get just so, plus explosions, fights, and assassinations that provide the masterful action sequences she was hired to deliver, Leder insists she sees the film primarily as a "drama." Both Leder and her producer, Walter Parkes, had planned early on to add a dimension to the film, a dimension not usually present in a typical action film. The terrorist (Marcel Iures) who eventually smuggles a nuclear bomb in the United States with plans that hinge upon the United Nations Building in New York is no soulless cypher. He was a concert pianist whose personal tragedy—his family and friends slaughtered, his homeland (Bosnia) ravaged—drives him to payback the so-called "peacemakers" responsible for it. In fact, the distinction between wrong and right blurs as the film's heroes, whose determination never waver, become sympathetic toward the film's villain. To the special effects, Leder adds a clear emotional aspect with regard to the man in pain, who is tortured by the memories of his dead friends and family members.

Before The Peacemaker was playing at theaters, Leder was working hard on the second film steered her way by Spielberg and Dreamworks and in a coproduction effort with Paramount. *Deep Impact*, intended to be a summer blockbuster for 1998, followed *Titanic* (James Cameron, 1997), which had succeeded in balancing its gender appeal. Leder's mission in *Deep Impact* was to combine the high-adrenaline drama with the most impressive special effects to date. Containing at least three interconnecting stories, the film was a logistical nightmare that made the direction of *Deep Impact* an extremely challenging task. While critics almost unanimously lamented the ineffective script written by Michael Tolkin and Bruce Joel Rubin, Leder's action sequences and special effects impressed viewers sufficiently for the film to set record earnings of $41.2 million in its opening weekend and to go on to gross $350 million worldwide.

Leder begins the film with a depiction of the initial discovery of the Wolf–Biederman comet by high school student Leo Biederman and the finding of the existence of the ELE (Extinction Level Event) one year later by intrepid television reporter Jenny Lerner (Tea Leoni). ELE was first thought by Lerner to be the name of a woman and, intrigued by the possibility of a sexual scandal, Lerner keeps digging and soon hears from the President (Morgan Freeman) himself the real story. Announcing to the country that a comet the size of Manhattan is on a collision with the United States, he says the government is not without a plan. Retired astronaut Spurgeon Tanner (Robert Duvall) is heading a mission into space to destroy the comet or alter its course. The mission fails, whereupon a national lottery is set up to choose 800,000 ordinary individuals under the age of 50, along with 200,000 scientists, soldiers, and government officials—a total of 1,000,000 people—to be relegated to underground caves for preservation against total extinction.

Most of the remainder of the film is occupied with the great mass of the population facing its own death and either trying to escape it or preparing for it. And, while Charles Taylor sees the film as the "epitome of Hollywood's crassness to introduce the extinction of human life as an excuse for a series of Hallmark moments" (Salon.com) Leder, daring to display a woman's touch, spends time with the characters and the unfinished business of their lives, and not just on special effects. Leo Biederman (Elijah Wood), the young discoverer of the comet, has fallen in love with Sarah Hotchner (Leelee Sobieski), and being one of those chosen by the lottery to escape annihilation by his removal to the cave, quite naturally exerts every effort to take her with him. Lerner herself is emotionally trapped between her mother (Vanessa Redgrave) and her divorced and alienated father (Maximilian Schell), who again in the end proves undependable. The scenes of desperate humanity fleeing the doomed East Coast for safety farther inland, of women choosing a quiet place with their children to wait for the end and, significantly, the episode near the end of the father holding his infant child above his head hoping for someone to save him all have an emotional impact not always seen in summer event films. The mammoth tidal wave that destroys the Statue of Liberty and the Manhattan skyline and the comet's passing are certainly impressive, but trying to catch what makes characters tick seems to be Leder's trademark. She noted that in preparation for the making of *Deep Impact*, she had watched *On The Beach* (1959), Stanley Kramer's drama of the world's few remaining survivors of a nuclear holocaust, who have taken refuge in Australia as they wait for the radioactive cloud to reach them. Indicating that the aspect of the characters in *Deep Impact* facing their own deaths is the thing that drew her to the film, she expresses hope that moviegoers, upon leaving the theater, would pause to ask of themselves what might be the final acts of their lives in a similar situation, and to consider their decisions. That the film lingers over the dramatic events to the end (much to the dismay of critics) and that the catastrophic event occurs quickly say volumes about Leder's priorities in *Deep Impact*.

Anxious to distance herself from action-adventure films, Leder accepted the direction of *Pay it Forward*, based upon a 2000 book by Catherine Ryan Hyde, about an eleven-year-old student who takes to heart his social studies teacher's extra-credit assignment to think of an idea that could change the world and put it into action. Released in 2000, *Pay It Forward*, much like *Deep Impact*, features an all-star cast, in this case Kevin Spacey, Helen Hunt, and Haley Joel Osment. Set in Las Vegas, the story follows several months in the life of seventh-grader Trevor (Osment), the son of Arlene (Hunt), an alcoholic who works two jobs to pay the bills, and the student of Mr. Simonet (Spacey), who has both physical and emotional scars from childhood abuse.

Trevor conceives the idea of *Paying it Forward*, in which he elects to help three people who are unable to help themselves, each of whom in turn would help three more individuals, and so on. The plan functions much like a pyramid scheme, and ironically a homeless person (James Caviesel) who is trying to become a successful ex-drug addict is given shelter by Trevor but relapses. Trevor believes his mother and Mr. Simonet would make an ideal couple, but mutual attraction between the two is not enough for a real relationship. Meanwhile, in Los Angeles, the *Pay it Forward* idea is catching on, as we see a man giving the keys to his Jaguar to a stranger (Jay Mohr), whose car was demolished in a police standoff gone bad, that he as a reporter was attempting to cover. The stunned reporter begins his search for the originator of the idea, going from an arrogant criminal to elderly alcoholic Grace (Angie Dickinson), who lives in her car and turns out to be Arlene's estranged mother.

Toward the film's end, the two narratives connect as the reporter finally traces the idea to its originator, Trevor, who had inadvertently begun a movement. By that time, Arlene has refused to be a victim to her abusive ex-husband, Ricky (Jon Bon Jovi), has stopped drinking, and has a relationship with Eugene Simonet. She has located her own mother, Grace, and has invited her to visit the family (when sober) and assume her grandmotherly duties to Trevor. And, yet, Arlene has only recently forgiven her mother for her childhood traumas, she finds out that Eugene Simonet is a wounded, defensive person whose own father poured gasoline on him and set fire to him, and Trevor, in coming to the aid of his small, helpless friend is knifed in the side by a bellicose gang member. The film raises questions about humanity and if it might be redeemable.

⟶⟫ 3 ⟪⟶

Independents, Experiments, Documentaries

For every Nora Ephron or Amy Heckerling who has managed to find a formula that would accommodate a number of films appealing to both genders and to more than one age group—therefore approaching the main stream designation—countless other women could not or would not attempt to follow that path. In a male-dominated industry where biases against women in positions of power limit their capacity to express themselves creatively, many women have chosen to participate outside the mainstream in alternative cinema. Women whose voices have been stifled opt to tell stories about what they know, or their own emotional experiences, and to reject formulaic or action-oriented film. Emanuel Levy notes the "greater talent and tough-mindedness" required to make "personal films about relationships—to put a personal sensibility on the screen" (349), yet he suggests the difficulty personal films encounter in an audience largely addicted to escapist films.

The women directors discussed in this chapter have all begun in independent film. A few—Borden, Anders, and Spheeris—have at some point crossed into studio films: Borden's last film, *Love Crimes* (1992), made with a $6 million budget, was not well received and she has not made another film; Anders' *Grace of My Heart* (1996), although executively produced by Martin Scorsese, floundered with critics and at the box office; and Spheeris ventured into mainstream films only to amass enough money to continue making independent films. Each woman has sought, through independent film, to explore themes dearest to her heart: Borden's engagement with radically feminist themes; Harron's pursuit of social criticism; Dash's incredible perseverance to tell the story of the Gullah; Savoca's interpretation of Italian American rituals; the compulsion of Anders and Spheeris to reflect psychologically upon the distress of their early lives; and Barbara Kopple, who began in documentary to tell stories of those who had no means of self-expression. With the exception of Maya Deren, whose interest was experimental, avant-garde film, all these women have worked extensively in television.

Aside from various film festivals and regional organizations that promote women's films, the most important showcase for American independent films is the Sundance Film Festival, known to be especially kind to first-time women directors. Established by actor Robert Redford in 1980 with the primary mission of displaying fresh talent, the Sundance Institute provides professional help for aspiring filmmakers with its Screenwriters and Filmmakers Labs and offers unknown filmmakers opportunities for film distribution.

MAYA DEREN

Eleanora Solomonovna Derenkowsky was born in Kiev, Ukraine, on April 29, 1917, into a troubled marriage; her mother, Marie Fiedler, and father, Solomon, a psychiatrist, both members of Kiev's intelligentsia, were incompatible and later divorced. The Derenkowsky family was split up when during one of the many government transitions following the Russian revolution, Dr. Derenkowsky and all the other physicians in Kiev were taken away by the Bolsheviks to an unknown locality. He was able to return, whereupon he bribed the guards at the frontline and escaped into Poland. Later, he sent for Marie and little Eleanora, who in a harrowing night ordeal, fled to Poland, and from there to France, eventually emigrating to Syracuse, New York, to join Dr. Derenkowsky's brother. While Dr. Derenkowsky studied at Syracuse University for an American degree in medicine, Marie and Eleanora stayed with relatives in Columbus, Ohio, where Marie worked in a factory. Once he received his diploma and passed the State Board examinations, the family was reunited in Syracuse, where he accepted a position at the State School for the Mentally Defective, a position he held the next eighteen years until his death in 1943. Dr. and Mrs. Derenkowsky became naturalized citizens and changed their names to Deren.

After she finished elementary school in Syracuse, Deren, accompanied by her mother, traveled to Switzerland to enter the Ecole de Internationale de Geneva in 1930. Deren was in Switzerland for three years, studying French and German, returning to Syracuse in 1933. During 1932–33, Marie lived in Paris and took courses at the Sorbonne.

Back in Syracuse, Deren entered the University of Syracuse at the age of 16. Under the guidance of her father, Deren experienced a dramatic shift from the female world of her mother, roommate, and friends and found it difficult to adjust. While studying journalism, she and other Russian immigrants read and discussed Russian literary figures and the Russian classics. She became involved with the Young People's Socialist League, later moving to New York City with Gregory Bardacke, a Russian immigrant, whom she married in 1935. She transferred to New York University, from which she graduated the following year, and separated from Bardacke. She enrolled in the graduate program at Smith College and was awarded an MA in English literature in 1939. In 1940, Deren moved to Los Angeles and was hired as secretary and editorial assistant to choreographer

Katherine Dunham, on the cross-country road tour of the musical, *Cabin in the Sky* (1941).

In Los Angeles, Deren, divorced from Bardacke, met Alexander Hammid, a Czechoslovakian refugee, and a professional filmmaker of documentaries. Deren and Hammid married in 1942, at a time when she was writing poetry. In 1943, Deren's father died unexpectedly of a heart attack, an event that prompted a new start for Deren. Although grief-stricken, Deren believed that her father, who had opposed her journalistic and artistic career, would never have respected her desire to pursue filmmaking; his death apparently released her to follow filmmaking. Ironically, with the small amount of money left her by her father, she bought a second-hand Bolex 16 mm camera she used for all her films, and she and Hammid made *Meshes of the Afternoon*, her first film. After the film was completed, she elected to create a new identity, and chose the name Maya, Hindi for illusion, to go with her new film and her new freedom to become her own person. She created an exotic free spirit image, wearing her dark hair long and curly, and dressing herself in a dirndl and peasant blouse, complete with large hoop earrings.

After *Meshes* was made, Deren and Hammid moved back to New York, where she began screening the film regularly and lecturing on independent filmmaking. She began a second film, *Witches Cradle* (1943), which was never finished, and followed it with *At Land*, a fifteen-minute film featuring Deren herself on various landscapes and including Hammid, composer John Cage and critic Parker Tyler. In 1945, Deren and Hammid made the thirty-minute *The Private Life of a Cat*, and in the same year, Deren finished a two-and-a-half-minute film, *A Study of the Choreography of the Camera*. The following year, Deren booked the Village's Provincetown Playhouse for a public exhibition titled *Three Abandoned Films* that included *Meshes of the Afternoon*, *At Land*, and *A Study for the Choreography of the Camera*. She also published a book of theory, *An Anagram of Art, Form and Film*, completed *Ritual in Transfigured Time*, and was awarded a Guggenheim Fellowship of $3000 for creative work in the field of motion pictures, the first Guggenheim ever awarded to a filmmaker. Deren presented *Meshes of the Afternoon* at the Cannes Film Festival in 1947, where it won the Grand Prix International in the category of 16mm Film, Experimental Class—the first award to a U.S. film and the first to a female director. Divorced from Hammid, Deren began to transfer her interest in film to Haiti and Voudoun culture, a subject that captivated her for the next eight years. She used the money from the Guggenheim Fellowship to travel to Haiti for a period of nine months, where she observed Voudoun rituals for a planned film on rituals and dances in different cultures. After three trips to Haiti, Deren was to forsake the plans for a film, publishing instead the results of her studies in a book, *Divine Horsemen: The Voodoo Gods of Haiti* (1953), with the assistance of anthropologist Gregory Bateson and Joseph Campbell, in which, according to Lauren Rabinovitz, Deren "compares the priests in Haiti to western artists because she identifies with their social status as individuals whose special talents are exploited or mocked" (78). Following an outline of the parts of the book and their discussions of the evolution of Haitian religion, Deren concludes with a subjective account of her possession by a Haitian god, a loa, its ecstasy and spiritual fulfillment, which formed the basis of her high status as "high priestess" in the artist community in New York City (Rabinovitz 79). Stressing the importance of ritual symbolic structures in the community, Deren reenacted some of the Haitian rituals at artists' meetings, which Rabinovitz claims "imposed a 'ritual' on her friends that contributed more to her status and popularity than to the group's unity" (Rabinovitz 78–79).

Nevertheless, Deren's call for ritualistic structures in group activities stemmed from her perceived need for the deemphasis of the individual and the assertion of the importance of a larger group consciousness. Her tireless efforts to gain recognition for independent film and artists through a "shared framework of distribution, exhibition, and critical discourse" (Nichols 7) and the indefatigable efforts of Jonas Mekas, Amos Vogel, and others "formulated the terms and conditions of an independent cinema that remain with us today" (Nichols 8). In November 1953, forty filmmakers met as the newly formed Film Artists Society, and continued meeting until 1955 when the group expanded, renaming itself the Independent Film Makers Association, Inc. (IFA), whose regular meetings included participation in local film festivals as guest speakers and screenings of members' films and discussions. In 1955, Deren also founded and operated by herself the Creative Film Foundation (CFF), a nonprofit organization that awarded filmmaking grants to independent filmmakers—the grants being funded by small contributions from her filmmaking friends. The CFF was the first organization in this country to present money grants and citations to independent filmmakers regularly (Rabinowitz 80–82).

At the Cinema 16 symposium, "Poetry and the Film," in 1953, when Deren argued that film operates on two axes, "a horizontal, narrative axis of character and action and a vertical, poetic axis of mood, tone, and rhythm" (Nichols 8), participants, Welsh poet Dylan Thomas and playwright Arthur Miller, reacted in a dismissive, exasperated manner. Aside from the fact that more recent film scholars recognize the validity of this film theory, Deren utilized this concept in her own films, particularly in her footage of the Haitian rituals, emphasizing the vertical line in the ritual of the descent into the abyss, or "plunging into the depths." But the idea was a part of the distinction she had made early in her career between recording and creating reality: as the horizontal line, for her, represented film's domination by narrative with characters as motivating agents, the vertical line corresponded with imagery reflecting creativity, specifically creating the invisible for the visible. Deren's interest in dance, games, and ritual "stemmed from her belief in the vital necessity to decenter our notions of self, ego, and personality" (Nichols 10). By the time she made her third film, she had begun combining the horizontal–vertical axes of her films with the ritualistic structure, in order to emphasize the individual's departure from what is known as he moves into a ritual journey more collective than personal. Deren's intense involvement in the Haitian Voudoun ritual dance led her to shoot 20,000 feet of film and produce 1,000 still photographs. She had received permission from a priest outside Port-au-Prince and proceeded to shoot ceremonies or benedictions to the specific god, or loa, which included sacrifices and possessions, in which the individual is dressed either as a deity or an ordinary person. Also, drumming, singing, and various forms of prayer were filmed. But, in her attempts at editing the material she encountered difficulties in structuring it; and the fact that the footage remained mostly unedited, Deren saw as evidence of the ritual's essential formlessness. Her pursuit of myth and ritual in dance and film, which captured the fluid, spontaneous movements of Haitian ritual that charted the process of connaissance, or possession, created a groundbreaking method of representation in her use of art in ethnography.

While many critics saw Deren as changing artistic directions, others saw something else altogether. Of those who insisted her filmmaking was never the same after her experience with the Voodoun rituals, fellow filmmaker and friend Stan Brakhage was one of the most vocal: "Something happened to Maya in Haiti which has happened to a lot of artists in every century. She became deeply and personally involved in a religion, and, essentially, that religion destroyed her as an artist" (Brakhage 111). In addition to her Haitian activities and her organization building, Deren found time to complete *Meditation on Violence* in 1958 and *The Very Eye of Night* in 1959, both of which bore evidence of her immersion in ritual. In 1960, she married Japanese musician Teijo Ito, her third husband, who composed soundtrack music for her films. She suffered a massive cerebral hemorrhage and died on October 13, 1961, in New York.

When Deren made *Meshes of the Afternoon*, she introduced avant-garde, a kind of filmmaking associated in Europe with art and which, though outside the mainstream of film production, attempted to incorporate the principles of modernist art into film. The European avant-garde film of the 1920s and that beginning in America with Deren and other artists in the 1940s who emigrated to the United States during World War II, sought freedom from traditional patterns of filmmaking, specifically narration, photographic realism, and logical progression, to emphasize the subjectivity of film, the manipulation (and creation) of images through editing, and the privateness of the filmmaker's experience. Also, the fact that avant-garde cinema is as dependent upon the medium as it is upon the artist is evident in Deren's observation: "If cinema is to take its place beside the others as a full-fledged art, it must cease to merely record realities that owe nothing of their actual existence to the film instrument. Instead, it must create an experience out of the very nature of the instrument that shows it to be inseparable from its means" (Deren *Cinematography*).

One of the major impulses behind Deren's *Meshes of the Afternoon* seems to be a preoccupation with self-definition, as the film deals simultaneously with the exterior world and the interior realm of dream, fantasy, memory, and imagination. The film's central action begins when an arm drops a large flower on a sidewalk and disappears. A woman catches a glimpse of a hooded figure vanishing around the curve in the road. The woman then knocks at the door of the house, finds it locked, locates a key in her purse, but it slips through her fingers. Recovering the key, she opens the door: a newspaper is scattered on the floor; a knife in a loaf of bread removes itself and falls on the table. As she climbs the stairs to the bedroom, she moves past a telephone receiver off its hook, and discovers an unmade bed and a record spinning on the turntable. The woman turns off the record player, descends the stairs and sits in a chair facing the front of the house. She holds the flower on her lap, strokes herself sensuously, and falls asleep. The film repeats these events three more times with variations, each one ending with the woman looking out the window and observing herself walking down the path and entering the house. In the plot structure of *Meshes*, it becomes obvious that the first sequence of the film contains the incident, and the dream consists of the manipulation of the elements of time. Everything that happens in the dream has its suggestion in the first sequence—the knife, the key, the repetition of the stairs, the figure disappearing around the curve in the road.

Obviously, the emphasis in the film is on the complexity of the dream within a dream, reflecting a concern with both the interior and exterior action within the film. When the woman falls asleep in the chair, the camera focuses on her eye and appears to move from the outside world into her mind, and through a kind of fabricated editing, shows the woman, her lover, and the hooded figure wearing a mirror for a face, and passing repeatedly in and out of the house. Numerous Deren figures appear, presumably representing the woman's multiple selves, and, at one point, one of them menacingly approaches another with the knife, followed abruptly by episodes of feet walking outdoors on various surfaces, and, quickly, the character enters the room again. Abruptly, a man appears, who wakes her; and, quickly, they go upstairs, where he lays the flower on the bed and she lies beside him. He caresses her, whereupon the flower becomes a knife with which she stabs him in the face, which then becomes a mirror, its pieces falling on a beach. Almost immediately, we see the same man walking on the road, picking up the flower and entering the house to discover the woman lying in an easy chair with her throat slit among broken glass. Although Deren contends this film "externalizes an inner world to the point where it is confounded with the external one" (S31), the violence of the dream and its transfer from male to female and waking to sleeping seem to affirm the dream over the reality (Sitney 14). But, as the objects shift and fragment, their transformation producing unresolved questions of whose dream it is and who perpetrated the violence and when, the reworking of the elements in succeeding sequences seem to assure that no one interpretation of the film should prevail.

In *Meshes*, indoor and outdoor space seem to represent the interior and exterior worlds, a doubleness that reflects Deren's idea of the dual functions of filmmaking: photography, by which actuality is recorded and revealed, in its own terms; and editing, by which those elements of actuality proper may be re-related on an imaginative level to create a new reality (Deren *Cinematography*). As the creative property in film, according to Deren, resides in the editing, the world of keys and knives, of bread knives suddenly appearing in the bed, of two Deren figures, through superimposition, sitting side by side, and of individuals merging into one another, need not follow the laws of physical reality, as Deren's intention was to "put on film the feeling which a human being experiences about an incident rather than to record the incident" itself (Deren *Cinematography*). Discussing the American avant-garde film, Parker Tyler avows: "The chief imaginative trend among experimental or avant-garde filmmakers is action as a dream and the actor as a somnambulist ... the world in view becomes that of poetic action pure and simple: action without the restraints of single level consciousness, everyday reason, and so-called realism" (Tyler 96). Despite the fact that Deren maintained her films should not attract surrealistic or psychoanalytic evaluations, *Meshes*'s dream state and the filmmaker's use of herself as the protagonist suggests, even beyond an autobiographical component, the fact that it "becomes a process of self-realization" (Sitney 18). And as many filmmakers of avant-garde films found it impossible to project the highly personal drama into another character's mind, realizing their themes only through making the films and acting in them, these films became true psycho-dramas (S 18).

The inward exploration of *Meshes*, enhanced by the interlocking of sequences of scenes and frames bespeaks the contribution of Hammid, Deren's husband and photographer, whose creative presence is missing in her other films. In *At Land*, Hella Heyman films Deren rising from the ocean, crawling over logs, and, unnoticed, to the middle of a banquet table, stealing a chess figure from a board and then losing it. Deren's protagonist is an unseen intruder, who, disinterested in the various social activities she invades, is intent upon the chess boards.

Unlike the editing in *Meshes*, which was used to join the outer world with the inner one, it functions here as a connector of the unlikely areas that Deren traverses and serves to relate her pattern of movement with a chess game. Nichols compares her "search for autonomy" through her interaction with the males and females she encounters in her journey, to the power each chess piece accrues through its mobility and pattern of movement. Males respond to her intrusion with hostility and threats, hoping to limit her mobility, whereas females tend to ignore her unless she caresses their hair, distracting them from the match—whereupon, she steals their chess pieces. The two chess pieces stolen from male and female players by Deren, who absconds with them back into the sea, suggests her defiance of the rules of the game. Noting that the film has nothing to do with the internal world, Deren says "it externalizes the hidden dynamic of the external world" (Deren,"Letter to James Card").

A Study in Choreography for Camera, three minutes long, marks a change from the previous two Deren films in that it abandons the narrative form, focusing instead primarily upon a single gesture as a complete film form. The film provides a very brief glimpse of black dancer Tally Beatty in his prime, whose movements explore spaces shown in the film, accomplished through Deren's belief in the function of photography and editing (partially quoted above) as they combine in the imaginative creation of reality.

Ritual in Transfigured Time was intended to be the first of several filmic examinations of ritual. Already a guiding force in her creative work, ritual had been used in *Meshes* and in *A Study* to some extent, but all her films that follow *Ritual* use ritualized dance as a primary tool of communication. In *Ritual*, the individual becomes somewhat depersonalized and is part of a larger collective consciousness. The opening sequences follow the actions of three women in the slow movement of the trance film, which changes to normal action. A party scene follows, in which a crowd of people begins to dance through several repetitive patterns that are stopped and suspended in air. Deren accomplishes this effect of dance movement through printing several copies of a few of the most intricate steps, repeating these identical shots at exact intervals and then interrupted with freeze frames. Through her transformation of trance movement into dance and her fusion of traditional and mythological elements (goddesses in Greek mythology) with her private psycho-drama, Deren searches for perfect fusion. In 1985, using the original footage Deren shot in Haiti, Cherel Ito completed and narrated *Divine Horsemen: The Living Gods of Haiti*.

LIZZIE BORDEN

Linda Elizabeth Borden, born February 3, 1958, in Detroit, Michigan, studied art at Wayne State University and later transferred to Wellesley College, where she majored in art. Never intending to be a filmmaker, Borden continued her art studies at New York City's Queens College, earning an MFA, then working as a painter and as critic for Artforum. She began drifting farther away from art, and while attending a Jean-Luc Godard Retrospective, she was captivated by his experimental features and film's possibilities for fostering political discussions.

Determined to direct films, Borden rented equipment and taught herself how to use it; her first film, *Re-grouping* (1976), about a women's consciousness-group, was Borden's exploration of the idea of women's groups and what might be gained from their solidarity. But Borden's group scenes are intercut with the voyeurism that was designed to confront the issue of cinematic voyeurism head-on, and the film was almost universally damned. B. Ruby Rich notes that "Women retaliated by vehemently attacking Borden's abdication of feminist principles of process, complete with a statement read at screening" (Rich 113). Her first low budget feature, *Born in Flames* (1983), concerning the mobilization of a Women's Army was very controversial. Her second film, *Working Girls* (1987), uses its boring, repetitive aspect to target middle-class prostitution and serve as its agent of demystification. Since her first studio film, *Love Crimes* (1992), which centers on a woman who must investigate her own victimization, Borden has directed one segment of *Erotique* (1994) and an episode of *Red Shoe Diaries* (1995) for television.

Lizzie Borden's independent films blend documentary and pseudo-documentary styles to provide a powerful effect on a tight budget. *Born in Flames* started as an exploration of marginal, black, gay and underworld women, and Borden's effort to find a common language of communication. The film perceives the differences of women not as a hindrance but as an advantage in Borden's fantasy of the unification of women. *Born in Flames* dwells on media fragments— headlines, sound bites, news bits, talk shows—all designed to indicate the distortion and confusion of the media with regard to the political stances of women. But, when Adelaide, one of the women characters, is killed by the government, a lengthy debate ensues among women reporters concerning the best utilization of photographs of the dead woman, thereby accomplishing the mobilization of women against the government. Consequently, some women unite to write a newspaper article, while others begin the construction of a women's underground radio station. Slowly, the mobilized women overcome obstacles of race, class, sexual preference, and political affiliation to bomb a network television station and gain control of the dissemination of information and images of them by the media. The film received some criticism for its violence and for its use of fantasy as a means of surmounting serious disparities among women who seek answers to complex, concrete problems. Of the responsibility of being a feminist filmmaker, Borden has noted: "The only thing I feel about a feminist approach to filmmaking is just that we as women have to make our own images about whatever we see" (Dale and Cole 40).

Borden's second film, *Working Girls*, a pseudo-documentary about middleclass prostitution in a brownstone New York dwelling, grew partially from *Born in Flames*. The cast of *Born in Flames* included some prostitutes who worked in up-scale brothels; through them and others of her acquaintance who were "working girls," Borden learned of the existence of far more women who supported themselves by prostitution than she ever had guessed, and determined to make a movie about them. The laborious search for financing, the process of writing, rewriting, and directing finally culminated in the production of this film with a budget of $110,000 (Lane 133).

Working Girls features Molly (Louise Smith), a two-degreed graduate of Yale University, whose career options are so limited as to make prostitution preferable to a demeaning job that devours the best part of her life and leaves her exhausted. Molly lives with her African American girlfriend and the girlfriend's daughter, who know nothing of Molly's line of work. We see Molly bicycling to work at the dwelling and beginning her day's work. As the film aims at the demystification of prostitution, its narrative covers one work day in Molly's life. Her first encounters with her clients are treated as economic agreements only, as the camera then records the ritual of preparation. When Molly's "john" arrives, and the service to be performed is agreed upon, they proceed upstairs where money is transferred and other perfunctory activities are performed before the sexual encounter takes place. Borden has commented: "I wanted to make a very simple film about work and allow the viewer to see it up close. To see the condoms and the rituals, and the towel room, and the hygiene, and the downtime, the boredom and the humor. . . . By focusing on exactly what happens, how they deal with their sessions, the bedroom scenes, and even the comedic aspects or the horrible aspects of it . . .

I could somehow objectify the work and have references to other kinds of work outside of the realm of prostitution" (Dale and Cole 38).

Like all the girls, Molly is exploited by Lucy, the Madam, who extends work shifts autocratically while bombarding everyone relentlessly with tales of her married boyfriend and her ploys for extracting more money from him. The "girls" who work in this brothel are there for the money, and the film implies that prostitution has nothing to do with a woman's sexuality. Borden is mindful of the traditional Hollywood depiction of women's motivations for becoming prostitutes—nymphomania, childhood abuse, drug habits that demand to be supported; she seems to have in mind Jane Fonda's Oscar-winning performance in *Klute* (Alan J. Pakula, 1971), where, as a prostitute, Bree is in therapy to understand why she feels compelled toward that lifestyle, and is "saved" by a detective (Donald Sutherland), who proposes marriage (which she accepts) and a "normal" life together in America's heartland. In *Working Girls*, Borden depicts a fantasy of prostitution for economic reasons, asking might it not be preferable to rent out one's body for two or three "shifts" a week than to work at a debasing, mindless job that leaves one debilitated at the end of the day? Borden shows Molly, who quits her job at the end of a double shift, depositing $900 in the ATM. But unlike the screwball comedies of the 1930s, where chaotic, subversive action only appears to undermine the status quo, which actually reasserts itself at the end, Borden suggests that under certain conditions, prostitution could be considered. In the middle-class residence in New York, the "girls" are protected from street life, drugs, cops, pimps, and undesirable clients, therefore placing them in control of the situation. And as long as they are in control, Borden contends, prostitution is no longer degrading. "Making a film about prostitutes [that] shows them controlling prostitution ... therefore shows me as a female director controlling the images that I want to be seen about prostitution. I think that's the most we can do as women. By putting out our own images, and choosing how we want to show these images, we are in fact changing the world" (Dale and Cole 40).

Love Crimes, Borden's first commercial feature, is similar to Kathryn Bigelow's *Blue Steel* in that both films depict women investigating their own exploitation within an environment of political backlash against women. In the course of their investigations, both women are fired from their jobs. These films and others, namely *Silence of the Lambs* (Jonathan Demme, 1991) and *Sleeping With the Enemy* (Joseph Ruben, 1991), are usually categorized as psycho-thrillers in which women investigators attempt to overcome their own powerlessness or deep-seated trauma to expose and bring a halt to a specific male victimization of a woman. But Borden never intended *Love Crimes* to become a psycho-thriller; it fell into that category because of pressures exerted by Miramax to make the film marketable. Although Borden saw the film as a small one focusing on women over 30 (Lucia 7), Miramax perceived it as a mainstream thriller, targeting males between 18 and 34, and designating it for wide distribution. Also, the film seemed pigeon-holed with the casting of Patrick Bergin in the male lead, in view of his portrayal of the abusive husband in *Sleeping With the Enemy*.

Because *Love Crimes* was financed by two companies, one American and one European, two versions of the film exist on video. The Miramax video emphasizes the story of Hanover, the voyeuristic photographer, whereas Borden's director's cut features Dana's experiences. Dana (Sean Young), District Attorney in Atlanta, becomes obsessed with her investigation of the exploitation of women by Hanover, a photographer who seeks out women who "need" him to help make their secret fantasies come true. He gains their confidence, photographs them, learns their secrets, and has sex with them. Many of his victims prefer not to sign a complaint, even though they were exploited, because they feel confused by the experience.

Borden insisted upon revising the original screenplay for *Love Crimes* to include an African American woman detective, Maria, whose function in the plot is to balance Dana's perspective. Both women are seen as interlopers in a man's world, where the authority of each is undermined; but most important, Maria, who has spent much time studying the photographs of women deceived by Hanover, has detected a look of "mutual fascination" on their faces—a foreshadowing of the ambivalence Dana comes to feel for him. Dana's own desires, which stem from childhood trauma of watching her father having sex with various women and being locked in the closet as punishment, have seemingly become perverse—and, ostensibly her curiosity about them motivates her to follow Hanover to his remote cabin. He, of course, discovers her and locks her in the closet. The next morning, he leads her out of the closet, handcuffs her to the sofa, and proceeds to cut her clothes off. Two scenes excised by Miramax demonstrate the perversity that Borden was concerned with: at a campfire, Dana screams hysterically about her dislike of sex and, later, when she attempts to stab Hanover with a knife, he lays her across his lap and spanks her. Hanover bathes and photographs Dana, who fantasizes about him. On the porch, when Hanover stops massaging Dana because she won't resist him, she retrieves her gun, fires it in the air, and takes him to the police station.

The ending of *Love Crimes* occurs in Dana's apartment when Hanover enters and photographs her in the dark, an "assault" that takes her through flashbacks to her childhood when her father murders her mother, who had attempted to kill him for his infidelity. Lane insists that "Dana's reactions suggest that she perceives his photography as rape" (143). Dana smashes a vase into Hanover's head, seemingly substituting him for her father, and thus confronting the "damage of male voyeuristic desire" (Lane 143), and through confronting the victimization of other women and thus resolving her own traumatic childhood experience. In the final scene, the audience witnesses Dana burning the photograph Hanover took of her in the bathtub, thus destroying all evidence of her own desires, but, nevertheless leaving any real answers about them shrouded in ambiguity.

One of the more interesting aspects of *Love Crimes* is Dana's sexual metamorphosis in the film. At the beginning, Dana is dressed in a dark, mannish, professional suit, with her hair slicked back for masculine effect. When she begins to feminize herself as bait for Hanover, she first applies mascara heavily, all the while experiencing flashbacks to some of the women whom she had watched in sexual escapades with her father, an episode that Borden seems to overlay with Oedipal overtones. Dana, however, settles for releasing her hair into soft curls and donning a blouse and skirt. This sequence clearly associates her "perverse" desires with her father and Hanover, whom she both desires and wants to arrest. It also serves to emphasize the ambivalent fantasies that motivate this film and, presumably, make up a significant part of the lives of women, as Borden sees it. The fantasies elaborated upon in these three films—a fantasy of feminine mobilization, of prostitution for pure economic motives, and "perverse" Oedipal desires engendered by childhood witnessing of traumatic "primal" scenes—provide a means of understanding and perhaps challenging the social and economic circumstances that contribute to the oppression of women.

MARY HARRON

Born in Toronto, Canada, in 1952, Harron, daughter of actor Don Harron, was raised in London and educated at Oxford University, receiving a BA in English Literature in 1975. In 1976, she moved to New York and became one of the founders of *Punk* magazine, the first magazine devoted totally to punk rock. The first American to interview Sex Pistols for an American publication, she contributed a lengthy article to *Village Voice* in 1977 on the punk scene in London, which was viewed as an underground phenomenon by mainstream America. For London's *Melody Maker*, Harron wrote an historical account of Andy Warhol and the Factory; and, for the *New Musical Express*, she authored a history of the Velvet Underground. Harron's cinematic career began while researching for a prominent U.K. arts documentary program, *The South Bank Show*, and later hosting a sophisticated talk show, *UK Late*, in 1990. For BBC and Channel 4, Harron directed several documentaries and six short films, including *How to Make an Oliver Stone Movie*. Back home in 1991 to produce segments of *Edge*, a PBS documentary series, she proposed the idea of a documentary on Valerie Solanas to producers Christine Vachon and Tom Kalin, who encouraged her to pursue a dramatic feature instead. Harron, who coauthored the script with Daniel Minahan, finally secured financing for the film from American Playhouse International and entered it at the Sundance Film Festival in 1996. A controversial indie, *I Shot Andy Warhol* (1996) received the Independent Spirit Award nomination for best film director and a Special Jury Award for Lili Taylor.

Harron's plans for a film about Valerie Solanas, the delusional lesbian and militant man-hater who shot Andy Warhol, the king of pop art, had begun years before 1996 with her acquisition of Solanas' *SCUM Manifesto* (referring to the Society for Cutting Up Men, of which Solanas was the founder and only member) while she was in London, as well as her early and continuing fascination with the pop-culture landscape. Harron's extensive research on Solanas and her obsession with Warhol and the Factory—his studio used for painting, silk screening, filmmaking, writing, manufacturing, gatherings of groupies, and the creating and promoting of Warhol "superstars"—is evident throughout the film.

In scenes of Solanas' early life, episodes of abuse and displacement are shown, seemingly mixed with Super 8 movies, and later Harron depicts her struggle to attend and graduate from the University of Maryland—a venture financed by prostitution. Her radical hatred of men leads to her writing of the SCUM Manifesto, a fifty-page diatribe that holds men responsible for all that has gone wrong in the world and insists that women, the superior gender, do not require men to reproduce. One day, outside the Factory, she gives her play, entitled Up Your Ass, to Warhol with the hope that he will be influential in getting it published. Initially intrigued by its title, Warhol soon loses interest in the play and misplaces it. Solanas gains access to the Factory, and although she remains on the fringe of Warhol's glittering circle, she fastens her expectations on his capacity to help her. She meets Maurice Girodias, of Olympia Press, who wines, dines, and convinces her to sign a worthless contract for her Manifesto, which he steals from her. Growing more deranged by this turn of events, she redoubles her efforts to reclaim her play from Warhol, who finally admits that it has been lost. On June 3, 1968, she enters the Factory, shooting Warhol, an assistant, and missing a second assistant because the gun misfires; on the street, she hands the gun to a policeman, saying, "I shot Andy Warhol . . . he had entirely too much control over my life."

Harron's first feature effort portrays Solanas sympathetically, but makes no attempt to hide her disturbing, abrasive behavior in the process. Punctuating Solanas's desperate endeavors to write down her beliefs, where she is usually ensconced on a rooftop scattered with books with written pages and papers blowing in the wind, she is seen in paid sexual encounters with men, begging small change from passersby, proposing to "say a dirty word" for fifteen cents, or peddling her manifesto. Periodically, Solanas is seen, in black and white, reading to the audience from her Manifesto—a document that seems to be less on the lunatic fringe the more she reads. Obviously, with her background and lack of resources other than prostitution, she finds men repugnant. Harron's documentary-like presentation of life at the Factory—the enlightened goings-on of the artsy, drugged-out group—and its general rejection of Solanas emphasizes her growing desperation for recognition and acceptance. The silver-hued studio, headquarters for a community of artists, seems an unlikely refuge for a radical, ragged individualist such as Solanas. The theft of her Manifesto and Warhol's indifference to her desperation induced further paranoia and violence in someone who had always been on the fringe and who appeared to be just waiting to explode.

American Psycho, Harron's second feature film, also focuses on the life of a deranged main character. Based on the controversial novel of the same name by Brett Easton Ellis, Harron's film turns a violence-detailed book into a satirical black comedy that targets main character, Patrick Bateman (Christian Bale), high-powered mergers and acquisitions expert, as a mad serial killer, crazed by the materialistic excesses of the 1980s. Harron, who almost lost her bid to direct the film to Oliver Stone, avoided an NC-17 rating by editing an early sequence of Bateman and two prostitutes; typically, the Review Board was offended by sex, but not violence, whose quotient, though restrained compared to that in the book, soars. Despite indications within the film that the murders occur only within Bateman's mind, filmgoers witness him killing a homeless man and his dog, an ex-girlfriend, prostitutes, functionaries, and policemen. He has urges to kill his secretary, who is smitten, but holds off on them; he kills his friend and associate, Paul Allen, because Paul's business cards are classier than Bateman's and his more costly apartment affords a superb view of Central Park.

Harron replaces much of the book's endless lists of consumer products and minute descriptions of Bateman's murders with dark-humored social satire. The connection between 1980s Yuppie consumerism and serial murder is vividly established during the film's titles when what appears to be blood dripping is actually drops of red berry sauce drizzled onto elegant cuisine on a dinner plate. The exclusive restaurant where Bateman and his Wall Street friends dine serves, as do designer suits, elegant apartments, and limousines, as an emblem of 1980s greed. Hanging out at trendy bars, they all look similar and interchangeable; in fact, identities are frequently mistaken. Filled with disgust and rage, Bateman loathes his friends, treats his vacuous fiancée (Reese Witherspoon) cruelly, and mutters murderous threats to anyone he does not like. By day, Bateman is a Wall Street broker, who is never seen doing any work; by night, he picks up prostitutes and tortures them, sometimes killing them.

The acquisitiveness that drives Bateman's life cannot fill the void he feels; nor can he, through it, escape the emptiness it brings. As viewers witness him preparing himself for the day with gels, scrubs, and peels, he confesses that his emotions are only greed and disgust. As a killer, Bateman, whose name suggests Norman Bates, appears to have become monstrous, much like Alfred Hitchcock's famed film murderer, through the deterioration of some faculties, and eerily calling to mind some more famous serial killers, specifically Ted Bundy (who is mentioned at one point by Bateman). In Bateman's case, empathy or concern for other humans has been eroded by succumbing to his own fierce desires. Harron also adds, politically, the resonance of the "me" generation from the 1980s. Early on in the film when Bateman encounters the homeless man and his dog, he interrogates the bewildered, destitute African American person about looking for a job. Suddenly, screaming, "We have nothing in common," Bateman stabs the man and kicks the dog to death.

Harron's third film, *The Notorious Bettie Page* (2006), continues her interest in pop culture with the story of the famous pin-up girl of the 1950s, Bettie Page (Gretchen Mol). Born in Nashville, Tennessee, Page came from a Christian fundamentalist background. As a teenager, she married a man who hit her, and was later gang-raped. Page's history as well as her inner life is given short shrift in this film that focuses on Page's great willingness to pose for cameras. Harron's film follows no argument about pornography or morality, emphasizing Page's sweetness and innocence in displaying the body God gave her.

Shot mostly in black and white, Harron shows Page posing for camera clubs and becoming associated with the brother-and-sister team, the Klaws, who push her into bondage photos, from which most of her fame derives. We see Page being investigated by Senator Estes Kefauver, Democrat from Tennessee, in his anti-smut campaign; we see her dressed primly outside the proceedings in the Senate Chamber, waiting to testify. We see Page in nature pictures, crawling on a carpet, spanking another female, or trussed up in boots and corsets and smiling directly into the camera, and all reflect Page's love of life and what Manohla Dargis refers to as a "genius of the body" (*New York Times*, April 14, 2006). When asked how she reconciled nudity with Christianity, she would remind the person of Adam and Eve in the Garden of Eden. In 1957, she gave up posing and returned to full-time Christian work.

Harron has directed many episodes from television series, including *Homicide* (1998), *Animal Farm* (1998), *Pasadena* (2001), *Liberally* (2004), *The Rainbow of Her Reasons* (2005), and *Roberta's Funeral* (2006).

JULIE DASH

Born October 22, 1952, in a Queens, New York, housing project, Julie Dash first became interested in filmmaking while attending an after-school program at the Studio Museum of Harlem in 1969. After studying psychology at the City College of New York for a brief time, she enrolled at the Leonard David Center of the Arts in the David Picker Film Institute to study film. While she was there, she wrote and produced *Working Models of Success*, a promotional documentary for the New York Urban Coalition. She received her BA in film production from City College of New York in 1974 and headed for California. Dash's discovery of 1970s black women novelists, specifically Alice Walker, Toni Morrison, Toni Cade Bambara, marked a directional turning point. As in the case of most women directors, Dash realized she wanted to direct not documentaries, but narrative films, and later recalled thinking, "How do I learn to make films like this?" At the Center for Advanced Film Studies at the American Film Institute, courtesy of a two-year fellowship, she studied under several eminent filmmakers, including William Friedkin and Jan Kadar, and developed a solid filmmaking style. Interested in kinesthetic movement, Dash produced *Four Women*, an experimental dance film, for which she was awarded the Gold Medal for Women in Film at the 1978 Miami International Film Festival. At the University of California at Los Angeles, Dash continued to perfect her filmmaking style, directing *Diary of an African Nun* (1977), her first narrative film based on an Alice Walker short story. For the next two years, she was a member of the Classifications and Ratings Administration for the Motion Picture Association of America, whose duty was to screen films and assign audience ratings. On an assignment at the Cannes International Film

Festival, Dash cosponsored a screening of short films at the Marche du Cinema, which resulted in the historic retrospective of Afro-American films held at Paris' Forum Les Halle in October of 1980. In 1983, Dash directed *Illusions*, a short film depicting an African American woman "passing" for white; the film received the Black Cinema Society Award in 1985 and the Black Filmmaker Foundation's Jury Prize for best film of the decade. *Daughters of the Dust*, a project long researched and studied, and aided by a Guggenheim Fellowship and the support of the Corporation for Public Broadcasting, finally moved into production with a budget of $800,000. Widely acclaimed at its release, it was given the best cinematography award at the Sundance Film Festival, 1991, and garnered several prestigious awards.

In order to support herself and her daughter during the years of struggle to make *Daughters of the Dust*, Dash continued to make documentaries for various organizations, including the National Black Women's Health Project, Morehouse College in Atlanta, Southern Christian Leadership Conference, the American Civil Liberties Union, and the National Association for the Advancement of Colored People.

Funding films for women directors is a perplexing issue at best, but for a black woman director who wants to alter the stereotypical roles of black men and women on screen, the odds against her are enormous and the accomplishment of her goals uncertain. Dash seeks to redefine the traditional images of black women on screen from the "Mammy" roles played by Hattie McDaniel in *Gone With the Wind* and Ethel Waters in *The Member of the Wedding*, by portraying on screen black women who are central to the plots of films that focus on African American women and speak to African American women. In *Illusions*, Dash confronts Hollywood's images of black women in the cases of Mignon Dupree, a black woman studio executive who passes for white, and Esther Jeeter, a black singer who dubs for an important white Hollywood star. This complex film examines Hollywood's "illusions" about black women that are manifested by Dupree's light skin, a phenomenon that protects her from discrimination, but forces her to witness the treatment of the other black women who understand she is black although the white people do not. Jeeter, however, is too black to be seen on screen, but her voice perpetuates the career of a white actress. Made on a tiny budget that Dash skillfully maneuvered to allow lyrical images, this film refutes the Hollywood stereotypes and establishes Dash's black woman as a complex human being.

In 1992, *Daughters of the Dust*, in the works for more than ten years, was released to critical acclaim and an audience already prepared for it by intensive direct communications from a small group of publicists to black churches, social organizations, black radio, television stations, and black newspapers. *Daughters* was a successful independent film that provided a voice for black women habitually denied in mainstream cinema. The film is set in the Sea Islands off the coast of South Carolina and Georgia in August 1902 on the occasion of a Gullah family's "last supper" just before most of the family members migrate north to the mainland for a new life. Functioning as Ellis Island for the Africans, the Sea Islands were the primary drop-off point for Africans brought to North America and were home to generations of Africans (the Gullah) since the first slaves were brought from Africa to the new world.

Daughters concentrates on the women in the Peazant family who are faced with the prospects of abandoning their ancestral traditions as they become assimilated into American culture. Nana, the matriarch, refuses to leave the island and desperately urges all those leaving to continue the old traditions. Yellow Mary, Nana's granddaughter, who has worked in Cuba as a wet nurse and a prostitute, has returned with her girlfriend, Trula, to the island seeking her identity. Eula, who has married Nana's grandson, Eli, is pregnant; but she has been raped by a white plantation overseer, and Eli is tortured by the likelihood that the child she carries is not his. Hagaar, also a member of the family by marriage, is eager to leave the past and begin a new life; outspoken and critical, she denies Nana's traditions and magic. Viola, who returns from the mainland a Christian missionary, having "violated" her own past, traditions, and myths by hiding herself in Christianity, proceeds to give the Peazant children Bible lessons. Iona, Hagaar's daughter, has been asked by St. Julian Last Child, the last child born of the Cherokee Nation in the Sea Islands, to stay on the island with him.

Challenging prevailing Hollywood perceptions and traditional film-making practices, Dash tells the story in the oral manner of an African griot, a storyteller hired at celebrations to recount a family's history in a circular, nonlinear fashion. Dash's goal is "to touch something inside of each black person that sees [the film], some part of them that's never been touched before" (Dash 32). As a result, and despite the accuracy of her research, she moves away from "real" and "accurate" into the realm of the imaginative and the poetic, as the story just unravels through an evocative, dreamlike series of tableaux, underscoring the fact that the film is "about memory and reflection" (Dale and Cole 62). Dash was not interested in using the meticulous research she had amassed to make a documentary of the Gullah; she wanted to depict historical moments in a more meaningful way whereby she could create new icons of the scars of black people, and therefore transmit myth, memories, and feelings to the audience. One of the ways Dash accomplishes this is by using the indigo stains—which, in reality, are very poisonous and would not have remained on the hands of old folks who had worked in the indigo processing plant. Nevertheless, she uses them as a new, lasting symbol of slavery, as opposed to whip marks or chains. Another scene that Dash wrote into the script (but was ultimately excised for lack of time) flashes back to a period of slavery when Nana Peazant's mother encloses a lock of her hair in a baby-quilt for her baby, Nana, who has been sold to another plantation, to find later and treasure as the only thing she has of her mother. And, instead of traditional tears flowing from the mother's eyes, milk tears flow from her engorged breasts and droplets seep through her dress and onto the ground as a graphic indication of the pain she feels when her child was taken from her.

Daughters is portrayed from the point of view of a black woman, a fact Dash believes has much to do with her difficulty of finding money to make the film.

Dash observes, "I think a lot of people are severely disturbed by the film because they're not used to spending two hours as a black person, as a black woman" (Dash 36). The film is about women as a group with men in the background and on the periphery; placing the camera inside a group situates viewers within the group of women, and not as outsiders. And, as women have become the griots of their culture, the film's two narrators, Nana Peazant, the aging matriarch, and the voice of the Unborn Child become, in Nana's words, "the last of the old and the first of the new." Nana is the repository of tradition and memory, who perpetuates the myths of Ibo Landing, a source of strength to the slaves and a powerful retentive aid for those still living in the region. She recalls the myths of the Ibo captives, who were brought to the new world wearing "collars, like dogs"; and upon realizing what lay in store for them, many of them refused to live in slavery and walked on the water back to Africa. Another myth insists that some even flew back to Africa. Others, men women and children, all marched out into the ocean in their chains and drowned rather than become slaves" (Dash 29–30).

Dash utilizes the narration of the Unborn Child of Eli and Eula, whose visual presence is indicated by slow motion, indistinct background and a brown-yellow color, to provide continuity between the past and the future, to keep the family together and to "convince my daddy that I was his child." The child, who has not yet been born, is speaking from the future back to the viewers about events related to her by her great-great-great-grandmother, Nana, but spoken in the film in the present tense. The Unborn Child begins her recollection: "My story begins on the eve of my family's migration north. My story begins before I was born. My great-great-grandmother, Nana Peazant, saw her family coming apart, her flowers to bloom in a distant frontier. . . . And then, there was my ma and daddy's problem. Nana prayed and the old souls guided me into the New World." The Unborn Child, as heard and seen in the film, reinforces the spirit world of the Gullah, as emphasized by Nana in the tradition, memories and the "protection" she seeks in the bottle trees, magic rituals, and the continued spiritual contact with the ancestors. The Child appears to Eli, soon after he, in despair, renounces all of Nana's magic and protective religion because it failed to protect him or Eula from the white rapist. Eli, of course, does not recognize her as his child, but through Nana's prayers, he undergoes a transformation from contact with the spirits of his ancestors and comes to believe Eula's child is his. Also, the Child is visible to those family members who are capable of believing in her presence—only very young or very old members. At one point, she appears in the viewfinder of the photographer hired to take the final photographs of the family; but, to suggest the limitations of his own perception, he can see her only through his lens. The superb, expressive cinematography of Arthur Jafa provides a sharp perspective on the "documents" that Mr. Snead, the photographer, is preparing. Mr. Snead is portrayed by Dash as someone who, once back on the mainland, would display the photographs of very primitive people publicly; in fact, Dash equates him with the viewers" (Dash 38). On the other hand, Jafa's evocative photography includes exquisite shots of girls in white dresses playing on the beach, with lingering, appealing angles and close-ups of the faces of black women, and sweeping shots of the island's beauty. Through Nana, we see flashbacks of the first slaves arriving on the island, flashbacks into slave quarters, scenes of her as a young woman with her husband, Shad, planting seeds in the dusty earth, the Unborn Child observing her ancestors working in the indigo processing plant with eternally stained hands, and Nana sifting the dust of the past through her fingers. We see Yellow Mary, Trula, and Eula, "ruined" women, lying under a ruined parasol on the beach; a turtle (used in the family blessing before the meal) whose back bears a symbol of ancient African cosmology—continuing evidence of the family's life before slavery; and the surviving figurehead of an African warrior taken from the prow of a slave ship, seen to be doubly ironic as it floats by Eli, who is struggling with his misfortune.

The predicament in which Eli and Eula and, to some extent, Yellow Mary find themselves reflects the historical facts of sexual abuse and rape during slavery, but Dash emphasizes the victims' attempting to cope with the effects of such acts. Yellow Mary, favored by Nana, but treated contemptuously by Hagaar and Viola, the two daughters who seek to forget the old ways and forge ahead full of ambition and Christianity, also represents one of the many new kinds of women depicted on the island—in her case, independent and undomesticated. Eula's impassioned speech to the women in defense of Yellow Mary and the unspoken legacy of sexual abuse is a plea to all to consider the impending radical change in their lives. She goes on to say, "As far as this place is concerned, we never enjoyed our womanhood. . . . Deep inside, we believed that they ruined our mothers, and their mothers before them. And we live our lives always expecting the worst because we feel we don't deserve any better. . . . Deep inside we believe that even God can't heal the wounds of our past or protect us from the world that put shackles on our feet." In her final entreaty, Eula proclaims, "If you love yourselves, then love Yellow Mary, because she's a part of you. Just like we're a part of our mothers . . . because we're all good women. Do you understand who we are, and what we have become? We're the daughters of those old dusty things Nana carries in her tin can. . . . We carry too many scars from the past. Our past owns us. . . . Let's live our lives without living in the fold of old wounds."

Just before the family embarks on the journey north, Nana conducts a religious ceremony of communion with the ancient souls and future generations intended to provide rootedness in the dissolution into the mainland. She holds a "hand" she has created with her ancient magic, wrapped with Yellow Mary's St. Christopher's Medal and placed upon each family member as a source of strength in the New World. The film ends with the voice of the Unborn Child, whose parents and Nana and Yellow Mary remain on the island. As Nana, Eula, and Yellow Mary walk across the horizon, the Unborn Child runs behind in slow motion; each woman disappears into dust shifting in the sunlight, as the Unborn Child intones, "We remained behind, growing older, wiser, stronger."

Of Dash's enormous television output, one of the most interesting is *The Rosa Parks Story* (2002), which provides background information for Parks (Angela

Bassett) concerning her work with the NAACP and the family tensions exacerbated by her civil rights activities. The film details Parks's defiance of Jim Crow legislation for public transportation, by refusing to give up her seat on the bus seat to a white man.

NANCY SAVOCA

Nancy Laura Savoca was born July 23, 1959, in the Bronx, New York City, the daughter of Sicilian and Argentine immigrants. She graduated from New York University's Film School, having been awarded the Haig P. Manooghian Award for overall excellence in her short films *Renata* and *Bad Timing*. Her first professional work was as production assistant to John Sayles on his *Brother From Another Planet* (1984) and as assistant auditor on two films directed by Jonathan Demme (*Something Wild*, 1986, and *Married to the Mob*, 1988).

Savoca's first film, *True Love* (1989), coscripted with her husband, Richard Guay, and financed by John Sayles, depicts an Italian American couple about to be wed. The film begins with preparations for the wedding of Donna (Annabella Sciorra) and Michael (Ron Eldard), who have been engaged for a long time, and seem to be buoyed along toward the wedding day by the excitement of their friends and families. Donna sees marriage as her fulfillment as a woman (and because she has no other real alternatives), but Michael views it as a crimp in his own masculinity. His concept of the ideal romantic evening is going out with his buddies and watching re-runs of *The Honeymooners*. On the way to the church, Donna's father asks if she is sure she wants to go through with the wedding, and while she seems not so sure, she indicates she does. At the wedding banquet, Michael objects to eating blue mashed potatoes (dyed to match the bridesmaid's dresses) because potatoes are not blue "in real life." But the supreme moment of frustration occurs when, at the banquet, Michael declares to Donna that he is going out with his buddies on their wedding night, for "one last night" with them, rather than stay with her.

While Michael is not only immature, but dense, and gives no indication of growing up anytime soon, the wedding—a traditional culmination of "true love"—is complicated by a clash of notions and influences concerning the idea of "true love." Besides the great gap that exists between Michael's and Donna's idea of true love, each is influenced by images of love in television, music, and movies. In Michael's lovemaking to Donna, he attempts to recreate memorable scenes from films. Pictures of beautiful brides adorn the refrigerator in Donna's house and images of sexy women on Michael's walls perpetuate a fiction of "true love," But, most important, are the expectations generated by the Italian American community. Within these conventions, Donna seems largely powerless to halt the wedding, despite her doubts about Michael as a suitable husband, and powerless to go beyond the bounds of marriage and the domestic sphere that is assigned to her at marriage. The wedding and festivities, filmed by Donna's father, signifying the approval and supervision of the family patriarch, capture the adherence to the rituals that are ethnically appropriate, yet fail to assist her in self-realization. The color used in the beginning of the film that becomes the black and white of the video images of the celebration parallel the fading of the dream of "true love" for Donna throughout the film.

Savoca's second film, *Dogfight*, cost $8 million (eight times the cost of the first one) and expanded Savoca's range beyond the Italian American neighborhood. Written by Savoca and her husband, this film depicts the antics of Cp. Eddie Birdlace and his three friends (the four Bees—whose names all begin with the letter B) in 1963, who are on a stopover in San Francisco shipping out in two days to Okinawa and on to Vietnam. To have some fun, they plan a "dogfight," a male chauvinistic ploy, in which each searches for the ugliest female he can find (a dog) to take to a dance the following night. The winner would grab the pot into which each has contributed $50, for a total of $200. They rent a dance hall and each goes in search of his "dog."

Birdlace (River Phoenix) finds Rose (Lili Taylor), a shy girl who listens to Joan Baez songs and wants to become a folk singer, who agrees to accompany him to the nightclub. The proceedings there are heartless, as the guys parade the women—one elderly—on the dance floor for the judges to decide the ugliest and therefore determine the prizewinner. Rose, who figures out the game, is surprisingly rough on Birdlace, and makes her exit. He follows her home, apologizes, and they go out to a late dinner and get acquainted. With his buddies again, he tears up Rose's address, but at the film's end, in 1966, he comes back to town, looks up Rose, and they silently embrace.

In *Household Saints* (1993) scripted by Savoca and her husband from a novel by Francine Prose (1993), Savoca returns to her own ethnicity and crafts a strange film of miracles. The story begins retrospectively in 1949 in New York City's Little Italy during an unbearable heat wave. During a pinochle game in his back room, butcher Joseph Santangelo (Vincent D'Onofrio) bets Lino Falconetti (Victor Argo) unlimited blasts of cold air from his meat locker. He wins Catherine (Tracey Ullman), Falconetti's sullen seventeen-year-old daughter, whom Santangelo sets about convincing to marry him. After the wedding, Santangelo and Catherine live with his insufferably unkind mother, Carmela (Judith Malina), who insults Catherine's cooking, talks to her dead husband, and forces Catherine to pray she does not give birth to a chicken. During Catherine's first pregnancy, the superstitious old woman regales her with stories of witches, monstrous births, and expertly discusses the religion in the "old" country.

When Carmela dies, Catherine paints the dark rooms with pastel colors. She and her husband are prospering in the butcher shop—especially with the "magical" sausages—and Catherine gives birth to a daughter, Teresa, named for St. Therese of Lisieux, the Little Flower of Jesus. In adolescence, Teresa (now played by Lili Taylor) begins to follow her namesake by finding miracles in small, everyday things such as scrubbing the floor or other domestic chores. Intent on becoming a bride of Christ, Teresa wants to become a Carmelite nun, but her father refuses. She gives up her plan, enters college, and moves in with Leonard, her boyfriend. One day, while ironing his shirt, Jesus appears to her and thanks her "for grooming one of my lambs." Teresa's frustrated parents place her in a Catholic institution.

Savoca utilizes magical realism, a term that relates to the incorporation of the fantastic along with the ordinary. It is popularly related, although not confined, to Latin American authors, including Chilean Isabel Allende, author of *The House of Spirits*, and Mexican Laura Esquivel, author of *Like Water for Chocolate* (1992), both of whom wrote novels in the magical realism tradition that were made into popular films. In the latter film, a memorable instance of magical realism is the scene where Tita transmits her sorrow into the food she cooks and the guests become afflicted with sadness. The inclusion of magical realism in literature or film usually occurs without explanation and is presented matter-of-factly. Despite Savoca's specific examples—the wedding night bliss of Santangelo and Catherine whose bed soars above the sleeping Carmela; the "magical" sausages; flowers that bloom where they previously had not; Teresa's various religious experiences, culminating with Jesus appearing at the ironing board—the entire film seems suffused with a fated aura, stemming from the night Santangelo wins Teresa. Moreover, the film's journey from Carmela's superstitions and miracles to Teresa's obsession with miracles and sainthood seem somehow connected. Carmela would certainly have understood Teresa's longing for sainthood, whereas her parents, obviously more worldly, do not. "Man deals, but God stacks the deck," one character says, which echoes the action of the film.

In 1996, Savoca turns to television with *If These Walls Could Talk*, three stories about three different white women with unwanted pregnancies in 1952, 1974, and 1996. Savoca directs "1952" and "1974," featuring Demi Moore and Sissy Spacek as women who are confronted with unplanned pregnancies that turn their lives upside down, sometimes with disastrous consequences.

The Twenty-Four Hour Woman (1999) features Rosie Perez as Grace Santos, a woman with a high-pressure job who discovers she is pregnant. Her husband is the good-looking host of the funny women's daytime television show that Grace directs, and her boss is a no-nonsense go-getter. Grace's conflict between career and motherhood begins soon into her pregnancy and escalates through it, and there is no help to be seen. After the baby is born, Grace, stricken with guilt, no energy, resentment of her husband who, for the most part is totally self-absorbed, seems headed for a breakdown. The film proposes no saccharine Hollywood solution for the problem, which seems, despite being funny, to have been written by someone who has experienced the same wrenching issues.

Following her filmed performance of Latina comic Reno (*Reno: Without a Pause*, opening in New York in October 2001) in which Reno did her take on the events of September 11, 2001, Savoca began work on *Dirt* (2003), the story of an undocumented Salvadoran woman immigrant who cleans luxurious uptown apartments in New York by day, and returns to her small quarters in a multi-Latin neighborhood in Queens, where she lives with her unemployed husband,

Rodolfo, and their son, Rudy. The film confronts the numerous difficulties of Dolores (Julieta Ortiz) and Rodolfo (Ignacio Guadelupe), and by extension, the problems facing illegal aliens in the United States. Dolores is soon fired by one employer because she doesn't smile enough, and by another because she has political aspirations and cannot keep an illegal in her employ any longer. She looks for more work as she and Rodolfo came to the United States to make money to build their dream house back in El Salvador. Her husband gets work with a construction company, but soon after he is killed in an accident. Dolores and Rudy take Rodolfo's body back to El Salvador for burial, and are shocked that, having been in the United States, they now no longer belong in El Salvador. Dolores and Rudy decide to return to the United States, but are refused admission. She finds a man who will help them, whose fee is such that Dolores sells the unfinished home she and Rodolfo were sending money back for, and she and her son return to New York, where she continues her work as maid in the luxury apartments. She thinks about her situation, and considers herself fortunate to have her son and her job.

ALLISON ANDERS

Born November 16, 1954, in Ashland, Kentucky, Anders survived a difficult childhood and young adult life. Her mother was a secretary, and her father, who was a bartender, abandoned the family when Anders was five. Anders endured the abuse of various other men, including her stepfather, who once held a gun to her head, and at the age of twelve was raped by a group of teenagers. Anders had run away from home several times; but at age fifteen, when it was rumored that Beatle Paul McCartney had died, she retreated into an imaginary world with "dead Paul," which later became the basis of her autobiographical script, *Paul Is Dead*.

Anders suffered a breakdown and was placed in a mental institution for two years. At age seventeen, she was released into foster care, and after several suicide attempts, she dropped out of high school in Los Angeles, where her mother then lived, and resolved to return to Kentucky. On the bus, she met a British student whom she followed to London; she worked as a barmaid until she became pregnant, whereupon she returned to Los Angeles and gave birth to a daughter, Tiffany. She survived by working as a waitress and receiving welfare benefits. She entered Los Angeles Valley Junior College, gave birth to another daughter, Devon, and later, attended the UCLA Film School.

Having wangled an internship on Wim Wenders' film *Paris, Texas* (1983), Anders released *Border Radio* (1987), originally a student film from UCLA, for which she, Dean Lent, and Kurt Voss had shared the Best First Film Award in 1982. In 1992, her film *Gas Food Lodging* based on *Don't Look and It Won't Hurt*, a young adult novel by Richard Peck, debuted at the Sundance Film Festival. She received a fan letter from Martin Scorsese, and the film was awarded the Best

New Director Award by The New York Film Critics' Circle. Anders followed this internationally acclaimed film with *Mi Vida Loca* (1993), a feature that focuses on girl gangs from Echo Park in north-central Los Angeles; "The Missing Ingredient," an episode in *Four Rooms* (1995); *Grace of My Heart* (1996), the story of a young ambitious singer; *Sugar Town* (1999); and *Things Behind the Sun* (2001). In 1995, Anders received the MacArthur Foundation Fellowship (cash award of $20,000) "Genius" award.

Allison Anders excels at the portrayal of strong women struggling to raise children without husbands or support of any kind—in other words, narratives that reflect her mother's life as well as her own. In her bleak view, women drop out of school, work as waitresses to support children the transient men in their lives have left them with, establish only marginal communication with their children, who, if they are female, grow up to perpetuate the cycle and, in the end, are alone. Anders seems to always have a woman alone at the end of her films.

Anders' first feature, *Gas Food Lodging*, a critically acclaimed film set in a small, bleak town in New Mexico, is concerned with the changes that occur over a period of about a year in the lives of Nora Evans (Brooke Adams), a truck-stop waitress and her daughters, Trudi (Ione Skye), sullen and rebellious, and Shade (Fairuza Balk), an adolescent who is obsessed with romantic Latino movies. Trudi, who has been missing school, drops out entirely following a fierce confrontation with her mother and starts work as a waitress. Desperate to avoid following her mother's path, she throws herself at most of the boys in town in pathetic attempts to make a real connection with one of them and escape the mobile home and oppressive lifestyle she loathes. She meets a British rockhound, Dank (Rob Knepper), with whom she spends a night in the desert and becomes pregnant; he disappears, and she goes to a home for unwed pregnant girls who agree to offer up their newborn babies for adoption. After her daughter is born and placed with a new mother, Trudi arranges to stay in Dallas and get work, ironically treading the same course her mother is on. Shade and the audience, but not Trudi, discover that the baby's father did not leave Trudi but died in a cave accident while searching for exotic, glowing rocks.

The film opens inside the Sunn Cinema, where Shade regularly catches the Latino matinee featuring Elvia Romero in Anders's clever manipulation of 1950s movies. Adolescent Shade looks to romantic movies for the solution to her family's problems. The film's main character, portrayed by the famous Latina movie star, is assailed with difficulties involving romance, marriage, childbirth, and desertion—all of which seem to be directly relevant to Shade's wretchedness about the absence of her father. Shade sneaks her mom's home movies into the theater, where her friend Javier works and, when everyone is gone, they run the movies and watch Shade, as an infant, being bounced and kissed by her father. Shade determines to look for her father, who left them years before, and in the meantime to search for a man for her mother. Shade surprises her mother with a dinner guest, who is the same married man with whom Nora recently broke off relations in order to be a good role model for her girls. Shade eventually locates her father, who lives nearby, but whose ability to help her is limited by his current relationship.

Anders's striking photography of the desert actually expresses the awakening of both girls to love. As perceived from the opening scenes, the desert is lifeless and dead, a vivid metaphor for the barren, arid lives of the three women. Shade is seen in Javier's arms in a field of grass outside of town. On the magical night with Dank that Trudi experiences in the desert, she discovers it is alive with colors and lights that seem to resonate throughout her being. The morning's flowers are vibrant with life and beauty.

But, in Anders's films, happiness and perfect unions are not meant to be. People leave, communications break down, as in the case of Shade and her mother, who talk very little. Interestingly, Javier and his mother, who is deaf and loves to dance, have a close relationship, possibly because they are not both females or because they are not American. Nora begins a new relationship with a television cable salesman, and the film ends on a note of profound despair regarding the inability of women to find what they need, and the absolute necessity of carrying on anyway.

The prevailing melodrama in Anders's films is an indication of her regard for her female characters. During an interview, Anders said, "Melodrama is a genre of film which tells the story from the inside out. It charts the interior journey of a character, and their actions happen as a result of what's going on inside of them. In most films you have the action going the opposite way. The action happens and affects the character. In melodrama, the action happens from the inside out. . . . I think it's all heightened by people's need to address their spiritual yearning" (Mercurio 26). Peter Brooks views melodrama as a "central fact of the modern sensibility" that exists in a void, expressing meanings which have no certain justification because "they are backed by no theology and no universally accepted social code" (21).

Anders's melodramatic mode involves placing her characters and their conflicts at the heart of her films and utilizing expressive techniques to illustrate their emotional situations. *Gas Food Lodging* uses strategic shot composition that takes advantage of the desert surrounding the characters to reinforce the loneliness, isolation, and aridity of the women's lives. Repeated use of close-ups highlights the women's disappointments and evokes the lack of any emotional fulfillment, specifically in the disappearance of Trudi's lover, in Shade's blighted hope of a reunion with her father, and in Trudi's brief gesture of reaching for her baby as it was lifted from her body. The excess of Elvia's appeals tracing her route through marriage, childbirth, and desertion speaks to the adolescent Shade, while the female vocalists on the soundtrack intone issues that the characters cannot bring themselves to address.

Melodrama, traditionally associated with femininity, is a strong point in Anders's follow-up film, *Mi Vida Loca*, which depicts a group of Latino gangster girls in Los Angeles, who raise their children and carry on with their lives after their men have been killed. In a world of poverty, illiteracy, and violence, most of these girls have few illusions about their future. Although Anders cast some actresses in this film, many of the girls were real gang girls, whose confidence she gained and who agreed to be in her film. The film is actually three stories, all concerning Mousie, whose child was fathered by Ernesto, and Sad Girl, whose child was also fathered by Ernesto. Mousie and Sad Girl have been friends all their lives and belong to the same gang, The Homegirls, now hate each other because of Ernesto. The girls meet one night and, armed with weapons, confront one another. At that same moment, Ernesto is killed in a drive-by shooting, resulting in the renewal of the girls' friendship. Mousie and Sad Girl discover a fancy truck Ernesto had kept hidden from them, and they resolve to seize it, sell it, and use the proceeds to raise their children.

Mi Vida Loca received mixed reviews, but Anders's status in the independent film circle was such that she was the only female contributor in *Four Rooms*, a film of four segments—the others directed by Quentin Tarantino, Robert Rodriguez, and Alexandre Rockwell. Soon after the disaster of *Four Rooms*, Anders began *Grace of My Heart*, with Martin Scorsese as executive producer. The story of Edna Buxton (Illeana Douglas), Philadelphia heiress, who wants to be a singer, includes career setbacks typical of those experienced by Anders herself. The winner of a singing contest, Buxton is awarded a contract in New York, which does not materialize. She meets Joel (John Turturro) who renames her Denise Waverly and becomes her manager. Learning that the days of Tin Pan Alley are over, she is installed by Joel in Broadway's Brill Building in 1958, and in an oddly shaped room, begins to write successfully for girl group singers. Broadly following the career of Carole King, the film shows Denise being swept away by Howard (Eric Stoltz), who wants to ride her coattails to success. Together, they write teen songs that explore unwed motherhood and other topics that reflect Anders's experimental use of music as a central place in the narrative.

After their child is born, Denise is confronted with his infidelity and leaves him. She becomes infatuated with a married DJ (Bruce Davison) and reinvents herself again in Malibu with Jay (Matt Dillon) of the Riptides—reminiscent of Brian Wilson of the Beach Boys—who goes off the rails on drugs and commits suicide. Finally, after twelve years of following the wrong men and writing for other people, she records her own song.

The film is another Anders saga of a woman undone by men, taking painful detours from her original path, yet finding at the end her own authentic voice. Songs throughout the film, supposedly written by Denise, repeatedly reflect her own emotions or the pain of the person singing them. Denise's trip through the music industry also allows Anders to include original music written by some veteran 1960s composers such as Burt Bacharach and Joni Mitchell, and some written by 1990s groups, including Los Lobos.

Anders takes us on another jaunt into the music industry in her next film, *Sugar Town* (1999), a story of a group of has beens in the music world who want to make a comeback. Coscripted by Anders and Kurt Voss, who partnered on her first film, *Border Radio*, in 1988, Anders poses a satiric look at a number of musicians, including John Taylor of Duran Duran, Martin Kemp of Spandau Ballet, and Michael des Barres of Power Train, part of a would-be supergroup whose demo, containing song titles like "Gravy Stain Girl," has been rejected. As holdovers from the 1980s, they have few groupies, and some of them request autographs for their parents. Into this Robert Altman–like tapestry of people coming and going are several opportunists and a back-stabbing ambitious climber. Despite emphasis on several female characters, Anders's usual struggling lone female is not present.

However, Anders returns to her own personal experiences in her next film. *Things Behind the Sun* (2001), a fictionalized story of an aspiring musician, includes a brutal gang rape scene filmed in the same house where Anders was raped. The years since she had been raped at the age of twelve had included therapy, mental institutions, working on getting over it, but in 1996 she reached a crisis and concluded she had to do something. The following month, she went back to the house where the attack occurred and realized she could not have escaped from the dead end outside the bedroom. In 2000, when she returned to the house to shoot the rape scene (also shooting others in Cocoa Beach, Florida, where she had lived and attended school), she felt more at peace with herself. Part of her recovery could be attributed to the revelation that the three siblings who raped her were themselves the victims of horrific child abuse by their father. Making the film, for Anders, was "complete alchemy. I changed that experience forever" (Jacobson).

Anders's film describes Sherry (Kim Dickens), an alcoholic singer-songwriter who has written a song about a gang rape. In California, a music editor is sent to Florida to interview Sherry because he knows the boys who raped her. He interviews her, and being one of the boys himself, talks with her about the attack. The film is an incisive look at the long-term effects of rape.

PENELOPE SPHEERIS

The grim, hard-edged reality of the films of Penelope Spheeris is not just the outgrowth of her wild imagination, but reflects a preoccupation with incidents in her own life. Born December 2, 1945, in New Orleans, Louisiana, to parents who worked in a traveling sideshow called the Magic Empire Carnival, Spheeris and her three siblings were forever moving around. When she was seven, her father was murdered while trying to defend a black man in Alabama (the killer served no jail time); afterward, her mother became an alcoholic and married nine times. Later in life, her brother was killed by a drunken driver, and her long-time boyfriend, the father of her daughter, Anna, overdosed on heroin in 1974.

Supporting herself by working as a waitress for twelve years, Spheeris entered the University of California at Los Angeles eager to study behavioral psychology but, lured into filmmaking by its sheer self-expression, she changed her major. In film school, Spheeris made two edgy student films, *Hats Off to Hollywood* and *I Don't Know*, an account of a love affair between a drag queen and a lesbian.

She graduated with an MFA in filmmaking. After college, Spheeris worked as a film editor and director of music videos, founding her own music video company, Rock 'n Reel, which produced short promotional films for groups, including the Doobie Brothers. Reaching beyond music videos, she was given an opportunity by Lorne Michaels of television's *Saturday Night Live* to produce short segments for Albert Brooks, a contributor to the show. In 1979, she produced with Brooks her first film, *Real Life*, and resolved to do no more producing.

Realizing she would like to direct, she was fortuitously steered by a friend to two businessmen from San Fernando Valley who had some money to invest in a film, and she convinced them to finance her punk rock documentary, *The Decline of Western Civilization*. The title was a joke, aimed at narrow-minded people who believed that punk and heavy metal in regular doses "rotted brains and endangered society" (Athitakis). The film itself explored the punk rock movement in Los Angeles through concert performances, profiles of band members and fan interviews. Groups including X, Black Flag, Fear, and The Germs forged a vital shift away from conventional music, and also, says Spheeris, produced the "most psychologically disconcerting music" she had ever heard (Savlov). Eager to preserve the movement for musical history, Spheeris approaches her subject with a sociological perspective and a sympathetic attitude toward musicians and fans whose alienation from the mainstream shocks through their dress, behavior, and attitudes. As the primary emotion fueling punk rock is anger, the music, as Berardinelli observes, "is a kind of primal scream against society's ills" (DWC:PT III). Spheeris insists she relates to alienation philosophically because of her "rough upbringing" and declares, "Punk rock is true to my soul and my soul is true to punk rock" (Bobrow). But despite Spheeris's empathy with the punk rockers, or perhaps because of it, she recognized in them a hope that they might be able to provide some help for those like themselves. And while film critic Janet Maslin, among others, saw the film as a comment on "teenage disaffection in its most extreme forms" (NYT), Spheeris saw the phenomenon as a positive movement capable of effecting change.

In 1988, Spheeris produced *The Decline of Western Civilization: The Metal Years*, and Maslin observes that both films "say a great deal about how self-destructive adolescent behavior reflects the society that shapes it" (NYT). In *Decline II*, Spheeris turns her attention to the Los Angeles heavy metal scene, shifting to bands including Aerosmith, Alice Cooper, and Kiss, in a more comic heavy metal–oriented installment about the excesses of the late 1980s—hair, drugs, alcohol, loud music. Spheeris had been offered the job of directing the rockumentary, *This Is Spinal Tap* (1984, Rob Reiner), but loved heavy metal so much she could not bear to make fun of it. However, her interviews with heavy metal idols and groupies allowed most of them to "hang themselves" with their attitudes and behavior.

In 1998, Spheeris decided to return to the punk rockers and make a follow-up documentary of their progression over the last twenty years. She went to shows in the counties surrounding Los Angeles to acquaint herself with the "new wave" punk music and discovered a shocking reality: the title chosen twenty years previously as a joke had become a "profound prophecy" (Hejnar). The idealistic beliefs professed by the 1970s rockers about changing the world no longer existed: the 90s crowd is "trying to escape it" (Berardinelli). The kids that Spheeris interviews in *Decline III*, aware that most of them were not even born when *Decline I* appeared, wear tattered shirts bearing the names of the original punks, and blazing no musical trails themselves, continue to echo those of their prototypes. In answer to Spheeris's off-camera voice asking them where they plan to be in five years, the homeless gutterpunks respond with "I don't know" or "Dead, probably." Life for them, as depicted by Spheeris, is a dreadful pattern of panhandling for change, consuming alcohol, attending punk shows, returning to the streets or their "squats" to consume even more alcohol, and waiting to die (Athitakis).

In this third documentary, Spheeris shifts her focus from the music to the people themselves. Despite her original intent to immerse herself in the music she loves and make some money doing so, she found it unconscionable to make money off the unfortunate kids; she, therefore, financed the film with her own money from her foray into mainstream cinema or, as she says, "the million dollar movies with nothing to say" (*Filmmaker*). Spheeris saw no better use for the money for the kids "with absolutely no future" (*Filmmaker*). To these kids she interviewed—those far more desperate in terms of survival than the earlier punk ones, and those for whom daily survival is the only goal—she paid each $50. She also designated the money from the film to be used for a shelter for children and teenagers. But Spheeris herself had survived a horrible childhood and as a single parent had raised her daughter. And after filming countless horror stories reported by teens about the neglect and abuse of their parents, she has become very outspoken about parents mistreating their children or failing to guide their children. *Decline III* won the Jury Award for Best Documentary at the Chicago Underground Film Festival, the Freedom of Expressions Award, and a nomination for the Grand Jury Prize Sundance Festival in 1998.

Spheeris's first feature film, *Suburbia* (1983), was an answer to those critics who complained about documentaries: she transformed the same subject matter into a feature film. *Suburbia* is a sympathetic story of angry, desperate teenage runaways who live at the edge of Los Angeles in an abandoned house boarded up by the city in preparation for the construction of a freeway through the area. The opening episode sets the brutal tone of the film, in which a toddler is ripped apart by wild dogs. This event and other shocking ones throughout the film were based on true events. Witnesses to the horrible event were the child's mother and Sheila, a runaway from her sexual predator father, being given a ride by the mother of the child. Other newcomers to the house of runaways are Ethan, abused by his mother, and Josh, whose father and another man carry on a homosexual relationship in the home. All the young people there have been essentially discarded by their parents, who are too distracted or self-absorbed to function as caretakers for their children. Jack, who left a painful family situation, and whose stepfather is a cop, has a beat-up car—the only transportation for the group. The kids, who survive by looting and panhandling, are actually happy living together. The title ironically refers to the family of runaways living "happily" in the suburbs.

The antagonism between the kids and their neighbors begins to escalate when the honcho males shoot the wild dogs roaming the neighborhood and decide the kids represent a filthy menace and should be forced to leave. Before the situation reaches a boiling point, we see scenes of the punks attending punk rock concerts, punkettes approaching middle-aged, middle-class ladies for money, Jack and his friends liberating pantries and freezers of food in houses with open garage doors, and taunting the "respectable" neighborhood. We also see runaways dealing with "family" runaways with great tenderness and hear wrenching stories of parental abuse. Sheila still has marks on her back from her predator father, who took turns molesting her and beating her. When it becomes clear that the homeless kids will be forced out, Sheila commits suicide, leaving a note saying she does not want to go on. Not knowing what else to do, her friends deliver her body back to her parents, who ban the broken-hearted kids from her funeral, thereby provoking a fight that dooms the kids' existence in their house.

Spheeris reflects her own upbringing in *Suburbia*, specifically in following the struggle between the angst-ridden punkers and their infuriated self-righteous neighbors who blame them with crimes they did not commit and ultimately oust them from the community. In a sharp comment on their hypocrisy, Spheeris films the two leaders of the community group in a bar ogling a stripper, when they finalize their plans to run the kids out. She places the blame squarely on society for the cast-off children and the mayhem they engender.

Suburbia was followed by *The Boys Next Door* (1985), wherein Spheeris revisits similar territory in depicting two high school seniors who, three days before their graduation, go to Los Angeles on a killing spree. Vincent Canby, of *The New York Times*, describes it as a "well-made movie about inarticulated despair and utter hopelessness" (VCNYT). The dark film begins with the approaching graduation of Bo (Charlie Sheen) and Roy (Maxwell Caulfield), who are alienated from their optimistic, anxious-to-move-up-in-the-world classmates, because the end of school for them means going to work in a factory. After the boys crash a party and steal a dog, they head to Los Angeles for some fun before their life "ends." On the way, Bo comes to understand that Roy is troubled. Once there, a misunderstanding at a service station results in the pair (mainly Roy) beating the attendant, and going on their way in search of girls. With the police on their trail, the pair proceeds to kill people randomly, for their implied sexual orientation or because they "look happy"; Roy is shown enjoying it all thoroughly and wanting to do more. The film was shocking in 1984.

Later in that decade, Spheeris directed *Hollywood Vice Squad* (1986), a comedy–action mix film about a mother who goes to Los Angeles searching for her daughter who has gone missing and discovers she is a heroin-addicted prostitute in the pornography business. The film, sporting one storyline about pornography and the other about bookies on the East Coast, features Carrie Fisher as the young, ambitious detective who breaks the pornography case. In 1987, Spheeris directed *Dudes*, a film that details the adventures of New York punks who tire of waiting for the end of the world and decide to migrate out West. They camp beside the road, whereupon they are attacked by a vicious gang who kills one of them and flees. The narrative then follows the two survivors, who search for the killers. In 1988, Spheeris directed *Thunder and Mud*, a tale of women mud-wrestlers involving Jessica Hahn; in 1989–1990, she advanced into television as the story editor for *Roseanne*.

Spheeris's move to mainstream came with *Wayne's World*, a *Saturday Night Live* skit with Mike Myers and Dana Carvey, self-appointed "party dudes" who cohost their own cable TV show. Made for $14 million, *Wayne's World* follows the long-haired pair, Mike and Garth, whose popular show in Aurora, Illinois, is exploited by Ben (Rob Lowe), who signs them to a stringent contract with the odious operator (Brian Doyle-Murray) of the largest chain of video stores in Chicago. Myers's original skimpy sketch is fattened up with the addition of guest actors and musicians, but most of the humor is fed by jokes, the dude phrases used by Mike and Garth ("Party On, Dude!" and use of the word "NOT!") and humorous scenes that were not in the script but added as Spheeris and the actors went along. One of these, a scene parodying the television show *Laverne and Shirley* was shot on the original set from the program. The film was a box-office success, and Spheeris was asked to direct other mainstream films. She declined *Wayne's World II*, accepting instead *The Beverly Hillbillies*, the remake of the 1960s television program of the same name that was almost universally panned for its crude adolescent humor. The film included intertextual references to television programs including *Jeopardy* and *People's Court* that a great many viewers enjoyed. Spheeris profited from the film and continued to amass money in the hope of returning to her documentary career.

In 1994, Spheeris's next film, *The Little Rascals*, a '90s version of Hal Roach's famous 1950s television series *Our Gang* was released. Alfalfa (played by nine-year-old Bug Hall) and Darla (five-year-old Brittany Ashton Holmes) have fallen in love, to the dismay of the other characters, Spanky, Stymie, Buckwheat, Porky, Froggy, and Woim (all played by child actors), who belong to the He-Man Woman Haters Club. As the annual derby race is usually won by the Club, males fraternizing with females is forbidden and used to justify spoiling Alfalfa's romantic picnic with Darla. But the prank goes awry, accidentally burning down the clubhouse, and then the derby vehicle is stolen. But, all ends well, and the winning money is used to build a new club house that allows girls as members. Despite criticism for putting adult jokes in children's mouths and perpetuating stereotypes of girls and boys, the film, updated with contemporary references and cameo appearances by Donald Trump, Reba McIntyre, Whoopi Goldberg, Mel Brooks, and Darryl Hannah, seemed to entertain movie audiences.

Spheeris then made *Black Sheep* (1996), featuring David Spade as someone assigned to look after Chris Farley, the doofus younger brother of the gubernatorial candidate in Washington. Spheeris followed with *Senseless* (1998), a comedy that pits Darryl (Marlon Wayans), a poor student working his way through college and supporting his family at home, against Scott (David Spade), who seeks grades that would guarantee a job on Wall Street. After this, Spheeris swore off making any more studio films; with the money from those already made, she could go back to her real interest—independent, documentary films.

Following making several short productions for television, Spheeris turned to Ozzie and Sharon Osborne for their permission to film a documentary of *Ozzfest*, an annual summer road tour of heavy metal bands. The 2001 documentary, *We Sold Our Souls to Rock and Roll*, features bands touring in 1999, including Fear Factor, Slipknot, Deftones, Rob Zombie, Primus, and Black Sabbath. The Ozbornes granted Spheeris access to themselves on tour and provided help with filming of the various bands. Spheeris focuses on the bands, the fans, and their drunken, drug-prompted antics, as well as the manic, religious protestors along the way. Spheeris's film was named best documentary at the Australian Film Festival, Boston Underground Film Festival, and San Francisco Indiefest.

In 2005, Spheeris directed *The Kid and I*, written and coproduced by Tom Arnold, a film about his neighbor Eric Gores, son of Alec Gores, Los Angeles billionaire technology magnate. In a combination of fact and fiction, the father, whose character, Aaron Roman (Joe Mantegna), hires Arnold, an out-of-work comedian, to write a script for his son, who has always dreamed of starring in an action movie. Arnold is commissioned to write a script and costar in an action film for the eighteenth birthday of Davis Roman, played by Eric Gores, to be directed by Penelope Spheeris "on the cheap" and produced by Linda Hamilton. Also appearing in the film is Arnold Schwarzenegger, Governor of California, basketball star Shaquille O'Neal, actress Jamie Lee Curtis, and many of Arnold's friends. The independent film financed by father Alec Gores, features Tom Arnold as the washed-up comedian bent on suicide, but who finds renewal in his relationship with Gores. Essentially a sweet film about an endearing character, *The Kid and I* was a labor of love by Spheeris, Arnold, and most of the other participants.

BARBARA KOPPLE

One of America's preeminent documentary filmmakers was born on July 30, 1946, in New York City. She grew up in Scarsdale, New York, with loving, supportive parents who instilled in her the belief that she could accomplish anything she wanted to. After graduating from Northeastern University in Boston, Massachusetts, with a degree in psychology, she signed on with documentary filmmakers Albert and David Maysles, advocates of Direct Cinema, and worked with them in various capacities to learn filmmaking.

Although veterans David and Albert Maysles created a landmark Direct Cinema film, *Salesman* (1969), in their account of an unsuccessful Bible salesman who hounds and intimidates his prospective customers, the most widespread use of Direct Cinema was in the developing genre of "rockumentary." The invention of lightweight, hand-held cameras and direct sound recording made it possible to shoot film quickly and cheaply and propelled directors to film musical tours—notably D.A. Pennebaker's Bob Dylan film, Don't Look Back (1966)—or to focus upon a single event, such as Michael Wadleigh's Woodstock (1970). The most provocative film to emerge during this period, the Maysles' Gimme Shelter (1970), intercuts the Rolling Stones' 1969 United States tour with a single "free" concert at Altamont, California, in which a fan's murder by Hell's Angels "security" is inadvertently caught on camera (Thompson, Bordwell 667–668).

During the making of Gimme Shelter, Kopple, as an uncredited apprentice, learned editing and sound recording and soon became an assistant for the Maysles as well as for other producers. She too became an advocate of Direct Cinema and of the general practice of allowing form to follow content. Kopple also took with her the Maysles' "style of letting life unfold" (Cunha) and adapted that to her own determination to allow a voice to those denied a voice. When she had gained experience and confidence, she began to make her own films and imbue them with social conscience.

During three days in January and February 1971, Kopple and fifteen other filmmakers who were part of a collective converged upon a Howard Johnson hotel in Detroit to film the testimonies of 125 devastated Vietnam Veterans Against the War concerning their observations or involvement in the torture of Vietnamese civilians. The film, now a historical document titled Winter Soldier (taken from a quotation of Thomas Paine) was edited into ninety-five minutes of testimony that includes an interview conducted by decorated war veteran John Kerry of Massachusetts. Receiving the Film Festival Award at Cannes in 1972, the film, shown at some colleges, film circuits, and then mainly forgotten, was re-released in 2005.

In 1972, Kopple formed her own film production company, Cabin Creek Productions. She went down to the coal fields of Harlan County, Kentucky, and spent nearly four years researching and recording the struggles of the union miners that eventually became Harlan County U.S.A., a documentary that received, among many other awards, an Oscar for Best Feature-Length Documentary in 1977. Kopple had originally intended to film the Miners for Democracy movement. But after the murders of United Mine Workers Union's presidential candidate for reform, Joseph Jablonski, his wife and daughter in 1970, the miners wanted new leadership to represent them and to be rid of the present dictatorship. "And that was how the film began," recalls Kopple. "We wanted to record that moment, that turmoil" (Rosenthal 304). Kopple was given a loan of $9,000 at the beginning with the promise that the benefactor would finance the entire film. But, when she had finished the first shoot, "this fine gentleman decided that a twenty-six-year-old woman couldn't possibly make a major political film and decided not to fund it" (Rosenthal 304). Kopple applied to hundreds of foundations for grants and sought bank investments and was rejected by most. When the film was finished, she was $60,000 in debt.

Influenced by the Direct Cinema method, Kopple and her cameraman, Hart Perry, lived in the community for eighteen months, becoming acquainted with the

108 families, and making a direct record of the miners'struggle to join the United Mine Workers Union. At no time does Kopple make any pretense about where her own sympathies lie. Beginning the film with coughing coal-dust-covered workers emerging from the mine, Kopple shows them going to their thrown-together shacks where their families exist without indoor plumbing and other substandard conditions. The people in Harlan County community are depicted as courageous human beings, who are fighting the mine authorities for the barest essentials—decent wages, health benefits, and retirement. To indicate how this situation fits into the long struggle with the coal companies, Kopple intercuts background material and related events that provide historical perspective on the Harlan County War. Using stills and interviews, Kopple traces a brutal history of miners' bitter battles with the company. An old-timer recalls being cautioned about the treatment of mules, because they were much harder to replace than humans; women retell stories of hardship and black-lung disease endured by their fathers, which is apparently the self-same legacy being passed on to their own children. Florence Reece sings "Which Side Are You On?"—a song she wrote during the bloody 1931 mining dispute that is still relevant in 1973. To emphasize the gravity of the miners' cause, Kopple includes information on the Mannington Mine Disaster in 1969, in which seventy-eight lives were lost in a mine that had failed inspection repeatedly, and on the murders of Jablonski, his wife and daughter. Kopple's film tells a story of intermittent, temporary successes in an unending battle. Three months after the ratification of the unionized Brookside miner's contract, the National UMW contract expired and a nationwide strike began. Documented updates continue to appear on the screen as the credits roll at the film's end.

Kopple gained the confidence of the women in the community by joining them on the picket line at 5 AM (Winokur), thereby establishing a rapport with them and maintaining an intimate knowledge of the transpiring events. Perry's hand-held camera and Kopple's sound recorder went into the homes, meeting places, and were privy to conversations and actions that traditional filming would not have allowed. Women were the focus of much of Kopple's interest, as they supported their husbands, squabbled among themselves, staffed the picket lines (many of them with their children), goaded the company-paid law-enforcement officer into arresting a gun-carrying thug, and stood up to the threats from the strike-breakers. Brutal confrontations erupted between the strike-breaking workers called "scabs," who were convicts on furlough from prison brought in to mine coal (Winokur) and the striking miners, their wives and children on the picket line. In a clear demonstration of the immediacy of Direct Cinema, Kopple and Perry were beaten, and their camera battered in a scene that, according to Perry, was "one of the most dramatic . . . in the film, but is underexposed because it all happened at 4:30 in the morning" (R 307). Kopple adds, "The scabs and gun thugs told us that if we were ever caught alone we would be killed" (Hall).

Amid the constant threats and escalation to the miners, who were hit by cars, hit with baseball bats, shot at—including a young miner who was shot and killed by a company foreman—the community, bolstered by the tireless efforts of the women, maintained its solidarity. Kopple also features noted Applalachian protest singer and songwriter Hazel Dickens both in the film and on the soundtrack. And in a region where music conveys cultural memories and reinforces identity, the voice of Dickens singing "They'll Never Keep Us Down" and the rousing "Whose Side Are You On?" expresses the Harlan Community's struggle for dignity and its determination to stand up for its rights. Kopple's experiences in the documentation of the people of Harlan County have profoundly affected her; she says, "They've made me understand what the human spirit is all about and have made me an optimist in my own life" (Winokur).

Kopple followed this documentary with the No Nukes (1979) concert footage of Musicians United for Safe Energy, codirected with Haskell Wexler, and a television movie Keeping On (1983), aired on CBS's American Playhouse, which deals with the unionization of textile mills in the South. In 1986, she became interested in the labor dispute at the Hormel Meat Packing Company in Austin, Minnesota, and began working on American Dream, a documentary that took almost five years to finish. Kopple's previous success with Harlan County, U.S.A. was of no help at all in the funding of the new documentary; and with no money for editing, Kopple bought used refrigerators, whose freezers were used for the storage of exposed stock until the time when money could be raised.

In 1984, Hormel, coming off a year of posting $29 million in profits, cuts employees' hourly wages from $10.69 to $8.25 and slashes benefits by 30%. While the workers had been promised that they would never make less than their present rate of pay, Hormel claims the measures reflect a need to remain competitive. Rejecting that explanation, the union local P-9 of the International Food and Commercial hires a consultant from Corporate Campaigns Inc. of New York, an organization that specializes in unionizing through public support and publicity. Despite the lack of backing by the parent union, P-9 is convinced it can force Hormel to reconsider its position, but Hormel's offer is so far off the mark that the union has no choice but to strike.

The euphoria enveloping the local P-9, whose zeal anticipates certain victory, blinds it to the harsh realities that lie ahead. Advised by a member of the Meat-packing International Union, whose wisdom comes from an understanding of the change in American attitudes toward workers, to make concessions to Hormel, P-9 opts, naively, to go it alone. Before too long, it becomes obvious that Hormel has but to hang on and wait for the beleaguered town to admit defeat. After six-teen weeks, dissension at the local P-9 erupts into screaming arguments and fist fights; and by the end of week 21, 75 of the plant's 1,400 workers have returned to work along with 400 from outside, and the mood has shifted to despair and gloom.

Unlike Harlan County, U.S.A., which boasts a clear division of sympathies that are generally indicative of right and wrong sides, American Dream is a more complex and disillusioned rendering of the labor problem in Minnesota. The film, as Kopple observes, is "gray" (Hall) and, as such, portrays the painful test of allegiances, of decisions called for that provide for one's family yet defy the traditional beliefs of that family (specifically, the wrenching matter of whether or not to cross the picket line), the looming uncertainties, and the conflicting points of view within the movement. Families pack up their belongings and move away, brother turns against brother, and the consultant, unaccustomed to defeat, leaves town.

The intricacies of the labor problem are also denoted by the various techniques employed by Kopple. Rather than the Direct Cinema method used in *Harlan County, U.S.A.*, which includes interviews, Kopple's own background information, and material shot on the fly, Kopple utilizes various sit-down interviews, several narrations of principal participants including her own voiceover narration to clarify situations, as well as the direct filming of events and activities. And, unlike *Harlan County, U.S.A.*, where there was no uncertainty about Kopple's sympathies, she now considers management's viewpoint, and actually films workers crossing the picket line, although she could not bring herself to allow the camera to cross it (Winokur). As one might expect from such involved circumstances, the ending of the film brings no satisfactory conclusions for the striking meat-packing workers, and events are being updated as the credits roll at the end. Similar to her narrative development of *Harlan County, U.S.A.*, Kopple places the events in *American Dream* within the history of labor and management disputes—but the entanglements of the latter film indicate fewer clear-cut divisions between the two historically opposed sides, and depict an environment where the status of workers has undergone a decline. Despite being labeled an "activist" director, Kopple insists her main interest is in people who, caught up in crisis and change, are pushed to the brink. Of the many prestigious awards she has received for *American Dream* were her second Oscar for a feature-length documentary in 1991 and the Director's Trophy at Sundance Institute the same year.

The next year, 1992, Kopple codirected with Danny Schechter a documentary, *Beyond "JFK": The Question of Conspiracy*, at the request of Oliver Stone to serve as a companion piece to his film *JFK*. The documentary provides information not included in Stone's film, footage of the arrest of Clay Shaw and Lee Harvey Oswald, and interviews with Shaw, Jim Garrison, Marina Oswald, and other individuals who furnish reflections on Garrison's trial. Kopple follows this work with a 1993 television biography, *Fallen Champ: The Untold Story of Mike Tyson*, for which she received the Director's Guild Award in 1994 for Directorial Achievement in Documentary/Actuality, the Television Critics Association Award in 1993 for Outstanding Achievement in Movies, Miniseries and Specials, and an Emmy nomination. The two-hour documentary, aired on NBC on February 12, 1993, during prime time, approaches Tyson with curiosity rather than exploitation, with Kopple wondering why Tyson's life unraveled at the height of his boxing career. Using conversations with Tyson's old friends, footage of old training films, interviews, and home movies, she follows him from his troubled childhood in Brooklyn, through his rise in boxing, his association with boxing promoter Don King, his difficult eight-month marriage to Robin Givens, and to his conviction for rape of beauty contestant Desiree Williams in 1991. Most interesting is Tyson's relationship with Cus D'Amato, his first manager, who, as a father figure, groomed and nurtured Tyson, but died in 1985, presumably leaving a void that Tyson could not fill. Kopple's lifelong interest in individual response to crisis and change led her to focus, understandably, upon Tyson's plummet from the top and his increasingly scornful attitude toward women. Also, Kopple confesses, "The huge interest for me is men, so I . . . want to keep making films about men and male issues . . . to have some sort of understanding who these beings are" (Kopple).

In 1994, Kopple codirected a two-part television miniseries, A Century of Women. The first part, A Century of Women: Work and Family, narrated by Jane Fonda, examines the contributions of women, both real and fictional, who have faced the challenges of balancing their homes and careers. Meryl Streep, Gloria Steinem, Twyla Tharp, and Maya Angelou are featured in a documentary that offers through photographs, interviews, and diaries historical women who struggled to maintain a satisfactory relationship between work and family. In the second part, A Century of Women: Sexuality and Social Justice, the ninety-five-minute documentary follows feminists fighting to control their own body's reproductive rights, the Roe v. Wade decision and the efforts to overturn it.

In 1997, Kopple seems to make a complete about-face in her choice of material by accompanying and documenting Woody Allen, his sister, Letty Aronson, his soon-to-be wife, Soon-Yi Previn, and Eddie Davis and the band on their 1996 Spring Tour of Western European cities. In Wild Man Blues, using her fly-on-the-wall camera technique, Kopple shows the sixty-two-year-old camera-shy icon, whose films are enormously popular in Europe, visiting eighteen cities in as many one-night stands, playing the clarinet and enjoying it immensely. Allen takes his musicianship very seriously.

Allen's anxieties about the public's perception of him as a musician, about his audience's interest in New Orleans Jazz, and its ability to keep them interested are all lovingly addressed by Soon-Yi, who also dispenses advice to him. Carefully reflecting the importance of Allen's musical career, Kopple was granted complete access to the couple on the trip, and films them enjoying one another's company. He appears to be much the same neurotic nebbish that he is in his films, and she seems the calming person whose opinion is always important. The funniest part of the film details forty minutes of a visit to Allen's parents in New York, who express reservations that Soon-Yi is not a Jewish girl and opine that Allen might have done well as a pharmacist. Allen's ninety-six-year-old father has seen none of Allen's films, and his mother, with three of Allen's Oscars prominently displayed behind her, says that Allen "tried a lot of good things when he was young, but never pursued any of them." Kopple's technique in this film—and one honed to perfection—is to make herself as anonymous as possible, allowing the audience to experience as closely as possible "what's happening through the character's point of view" (Cunha). The scene in Madrid of the couple having breakfast is characteristically one of Kopple's efforts to help viewers feel as if they are having breakfast with Allen and Soon-Yi, with no one else present, and lose themselves in the scene" (Cunha).

Following her direction of three episodes (1997, 1998, 1999) of television's *Homicide: Life on the Street*, Kopple turned to the making of *A Conversation With Gregory Peck* in 1999. As Woody Allen and Mike Tyson were made accessible to the public and were also presented from perspectives other than their public images, Kopple's look at Peck is one that goes beyond his fame as an actor. At the film's beginning, the credits, designed to imitate those introducing *To Kill a Mockingbird*, suggest that Peck's most famous role as Atticus Finch is also his favorite. As the film progresses, viewers become aware that Peck's role as Finch is very similar to Peck himself. The film begins with Peck preparing for one of his touring one-man shows, and continues with segments of six of his town-hall-type discussions with questions and answers, while stills of him in various famous roles appear on the screen. Peck's wit and charm are apparent as he speaks candidly to the audience in the meeting hall as observed by documentary viewers. The film shows that despite Peck's great status as an actor and friend of the powerful, he is a devoted husband and father who is happiest amid family gatherings. Originated by Peck's daughter, Cecilia, who also functioned as one of the producers, the film reaches a grand celebratory finale at the end with Cecilia giving birth to a baby boy, who was named for Harper Lee, author of *To Kill a Mockingbird*.

Back in 1994, Kopple had been asked to film *Woodstock '94*, planned as a twenty-fifth anniversary tribute to the original 1969 event. The concert and the film were to be generously financed by PolyGram, a giant music corporation that soon began to have second thoughts about its huge investment. Fearing possible repercussions concerning audience safety issues or unforeseen hitches in the concert itself, PolyGram withdrew its support from Kopple's film. Her position on that development was, "I wasn't going to let money stop me from doing it, so I just kept going" (J. Wood). In fact, she finished the shooting and, with no money for editing, she worked on it piecemeal—editing bits when she had money. As she completed editing a mix of the '69 Woodstock with the '94 Woodstock, another unforeseen development occurred: she was asked to film *Woodstock '99*. Kopple recalls: "I took a deep breath and went and did '99 with a really small crew. . . . I then had to reopen the film again and begin the editing process all over. But I was glad that happened because, in a way, it just came around full circle" (J. Wood).

My Generation (2000) emphasizes the '94 Woodstock over the '69 or '99 Woodstocks, seeing it as a kind of bridge connecting what went before and after, but it is actually concerned with the interaction between the three concerts, or more specifically, the three generations. Whereas the '69 Woodstock was perceived as an outpouring of peace and love, the '94 Woodstock was viewed as a disgraceful exhibition of merchandizing and commercialism (Slurpees sold for $7 each), and the Woodstock of '99 generated shameful television clips of violence, Kopple believes that all three events were pretty much the same: "My feeling is that all of us—no matter who we are—want to get together and be part of a community and have a sense of ritual and be with people we like and then listen to music we love, no matter what the music is" (J. Wood).

While each generation seemed preoccupied with overwhelming social issues— women's rights and Vietnam in '69; AIDS, environmental concerns, and "corporate takeovers" of music in '94 and '99—Kopple points out that certain misconceptions have arisen. She notes that Woodstock '69 was not entirely peaceful; in fact, hamburger stands were burned down and women were raped then and in '99. She concludes, "I think we're all the same, no matter what generation we come from. I think it's all of us trying to find ourselves in our own skin, no matter who we are or no matter how old we are" (J. Wood).

Kopple's return to television, *The Hamptons* (2002), a four-hour reality miniseries aired on ABC in June, 2002, looks at the summer playground of the wealthy and well-known at the notorious beach resort on Long Island. The residents were understandably wary of Kopple, the famous chronicler of striking workers and champion of the downtrodden, fearing she might target their glitzy lifestyle with her unsympathetic camera. But Kopple, welcoming an opportunity to once again be featured on prime-time television, approached *The Hamptons* by putting her preconceptions behind her and letting "people's lives unfold" before her camera (Patterson).

Kopple begins the somewhat ambling film with Alec Baldwin explaining that the place seems to have a hold on him and moves on filming the local Hamptonites in their habitat. She talks with a fisherman in his trawler, who notes that people come there in such great Numbers that they destroy what they came for. Kopple cuts to a group of young men and women signing up for a stay in a large rental house holding thirty-five people on weekends. Her camera lights on Jacqueline Lipson, a young matrimonial lawyer who has designated that summer as the time to find a husband: according to her life plan, she must be married before age thirty in order to open up her own office by age thirty-two. She plunges enthusiastically, if not desperately, into the mating game. Kopple continues to divide her time between the locals and the affluent. Of those who work and live there year-round, we meet a woman who writes a regular column in the local paper, a singer-waitress who is preparing to quit her job and make a CD, a few farmers, and the town's police lieutenant of thirty-five years, whose retirement party Kopple attends and films. We see California native Tracy Hotchner, an emergency services technician who cowrote the screenplay for *Mommie Dearest*. Kopple spends time at Christie Brinkley's birthday party for her daughter.

We meet entrepreneurial types like Jason Binn, publisher of *Hamptons* magagine; Josh Sagman, an oxygen-bar salesman; and Steven Gaines, author of, among other works, *Philistines at the Hedgerow*, a social history of the Hamptons and occasional tour guide for Kopple. When Gaines's little dog, ill with "doggie Alzheimer's," dies, Gaines mourns his loss by purchasing for himself a black BMW as a "grief gift." Kopple films sport fishermen singing out "Yeah, Baby!" when they make exciting catches and presently cuts to an elderly black woman stuffing her catch into a plastic bucket. Kopple also notes the antics of publicist and socialite Lizzie Grubman, who backs her large SUV into a nightclub crowd, injuring sixteen people. At night in clubs, Kopple's camera picks up James Lipton of Bravo's *The Actor's Studio*, Jerry Seinfeld, Chevy Chase, the Hilton parents, sisters Paris and Nicky, Craig Kilborn, Russell Simmons, the Hip-Hop mogul, and the ever-present Billy Joel.

Kopple's film begins with the 2001 Memorial Day exodus from New York to the resort itself and ends on September 12, when the summer residents pack up and leave. The summer ritual for the moneyed few and those who aspire to that status is, quite naturally, defended by Steven Gaines as "the American Dream" (Kopple must have winced) and he goes on to assert that all who come there have "made it." "This will be remembered as the golden age," prophesies Gaines. Indeed, as summers go at the Hamptons, it was certainly one of the more memorable. With the bizarre incident involving Grubman, the untimely death of popular restaurateur Jeff Salaway, and the September 11 attack on the World Trade Center that marked the summer's end and cast a pall on all its splendor, Kopple's film certainly seems if not to have captured the end of an era, then to have signaled the return of summer residents to a world forever changed. At the end of the film, we see scattered on tables at the resort newspapers filled with accounts and pictures of the burning Twin Towers.

In 2005, Kopple codirected *Bearing Witness*, a documentary of five women journalists who have harrowing stories to tell about their experiences as foreign reporters from around the world. Funded by A&E Network, the film refers to the survivors who understand and bear witness to the cost of the struggle and to the personal cost to the professionals who report it. Significantly, the women who report the events seem to grasp the significance, as they also comprehend the personal sacrifice they have made to become top professionals in their field.

Using stock footage, personal photographs, and home movies, Kopple and her codirectors Bob Eisenhardt and Marijana Wotton follow two *London Times* reporters, a CNN camerawoman, an American working for Al-Jazeera, and a still photographer, as they are seen performing their high-pressure duties and reflecting on the difficulty, for women, of balancing the home–work responsibilities. Janine DiAntonio, *London Times* reporter, covered assignments in Iraq until twenty-one days before her son was born. She is married to French journalist Bruno Girodon and they live in Paris with their young son, Luca. Having reached a different perspective about covering dangerous assignments, Janine has written a memoir of war and has visited refugee camps in Israel. But few find the personal fulfillment of Janine and the elusive equilibrium of career and home life. Mary Rogers, a CNN camerawoman, recalls that when she was twenty, she met a young man whom she liked and could have married, but she wanted to continue her work. Now, she has no one to come home to. Marie Colvin, a Yale graduate from Oyster Bay, New York, who is also a *London Times* reporter, lost an eye in a grenade attack in Sri Lanka and was present at the unearthing of mass graves in Iraq. She has lost two husbands in divorces. Freelance photographer Molly Bingham, of a newspaper family in Lexington, Kentucky, was captured by Saddam Hussein's Secret Police in the early days of the Iraq War and thrown in Abu Ghraib, miraculously escaping torture. She returns to photograph the women held prisoners there. And finally, May Ying Welsh, a videographer and documentarian from San Francisco, reports for Al-Jazeera and is held in contempt by both Americans and Iraqis.

4

International

The women directors in this section have risen to prominence amid circumstances favorable to their personal and artistic inclinations, with the exception of Riefenstahl, whose talent became subservient to the Nazi regime, which ultimately destroyed her. Gillian Armstrong was one of the first to participate in Australia's creative explosion of the late 1960s and early 1970s, when Australia established the Australian Film Commission and subsidized a national cinema, opening the Australian Film and Television School and training filmmakers to make films emphasizing Australia's cultural history. Armstrong was a role model for Jane Campion, from New Zealand, who also attended AFTS.

Agnes Varda, from France, hails from a culture that has long encouraged creative independence and accepted women's sensibility in mainstream culture (Levy, *French Cinema*). The French openness to women directors is evident in the career of Varda, which began with the New Wave in the 1950s and still continues.

Lina Wertmuller began as an assistant to Federico Fellini, who, along with Michelangelo Antonioni, created the Second Italian Film Renaissance in the late 1950s and 1960s. Wertmuller was mentored by a master film director, who aided her in beginning her own career.

GILLIAN ARMSTRONG

Gillian Armstrong, the daughter of a real estate businessman, who was also an amateur photographer and a teacher, was born December 18, 1950, in Melbourne, Australia. At Swinburne Film and Television School, she studied stage and costume design and presented her graduation film, *The Roof Needs Mowing*, in 1971. After working for a time as an assistant editor of short films, and as tea lady, she was awarded in 1973 a film scholarship for the elite Interim Program at the newly established and prestigious Australian Film, Television and Radio School in Sydney. Created by the government in a period of arts support that started in the early 1970s and became known as the Australian New Wave, the school offered Armstrong a unique opportunity to direct short films with professional casts and crews and gain entrance to the film industry. The vital new Australian cinema featured a group of young filmmakers—Bruce Beresford, Peter Weir, Fred Schepisi, Philip Noyce, and Armstrong—whose films were required to utilize indigenous casts and crews and to focus on national themes.

Armstrong's first three films won critical acclaim and illustrate the thematic and stylistic preoccupation that has become characteristic of her work. *One Hundred a Day* (1973) and *The Singer and the Dancer* (1976), adapted from stories by Alan Marshall, portray defeated hopes and illusions against a working-class background. *Smokes and Lollies* (1976), a short documentary, which was the first in a series of four short films, brought together three young working-class women, who were featured in three succeeding documentaries at later points in their lives: *14's Good, 18's Better* (1980), *Bingo, Bridesmaids and Braces* (1988), and *Not 14 Again* (1996). The end of this period in her life marked the end of her apprenticeship and began the pattern for her future accomplishments with notable producers, screenwriters, and actors.

With *My Brilliant Career* (1979), Armstrong achieved critical acclaim, box office success, and national prominence as the first woman to direct a feature film in Australia in forty years. And, unlike her peer group of male directors who left Australia for Hollywood, Armstrong, though traveling to Hollywood occasionally to direct a film there, has remained loyal to the Australian industry and continues to provide inspiration for aspiring film directors. Armstrong followed up *My Brilliant Career* with a musical, *Starstruck* (1982), another period drama, *Mrs. Soffel* (1984), the award-winning *High Tide* (1987), and the disastrous *Fires Within* (1991), from which Armstrong has publicly disassociated herself. She rebounded with *The Last Days of Chez Nous* (1992), a dramatic representation of a family falling apart. In 1994, the release of *Little Women*, the fourth remake of Louisa May Alcott's classic story, brought Armstrong commendations and monetary rewards; in 1997, the provocative *Oscar and Lucinda*, based on the Booker prize–winning novel by Peter Carey, was released; and in 2001, Armstrong ninth feature film, *Charlotte Gray*, opened to mixed reviews.

While Armstrong's films beginning with *My Brilliant Career* are often perceived to center on strong, independent women, her first film appears to focus on the transformation of a spirited, ambitious young woman from life in the bush to a budding author. Along the way, Sybylla Melvyn (Judy Davis), the poor headstrong girl from Possum Gully, is faced with being placed in service by her family because they can no longer afford to keep her. Despite the fact that she has resisted her parents' efforts to transform her unattractiveness into something appropriate for polite society, she is being pursued by Harry Beecham (Sam Neill), the area's most eligible bachelor. The film is based on the novel of the same name by Miles Franklin (1901), who herself secured her future by writing, feminism, and

Australian cultural nationalism, rather than through marriage. At the beginning of the film, we see Sybylla finishing a letter in which she unabashedly describes herself as egotistical, and is beginning the book that is finished at the end. She is oblivious to the dust storm drawing near and threatening the clothes that should be removed from the line. In the second scene, she plays "Schumann's Scenes from a Childhood" on the piano badly and loudly in an effort to assert herself within the family. And, when her mother tells her she must become a servant to another family, Sybylla is angry, and remarks to her sister that she might as well be dead. Sybylla goes to live with her grandmother at Caddagat and becomes caught in a serious effort by the grandmother and Aunt Helen to tame her. The poles of wild and tame throughout the film are seen primarily through Aunt Helen's lessons in cultivating feminine values; each point, however, is undermined by Sybylla, culminating in a formal dinner where Sybylla drinks port and entertains with naughty pub songs and suggestive dancing. When Harry takes her out on the river in a boat, Sybylla initially recites poetry, then gleefully upsets the boat, as she and Harry fall into the water.

But the transformation of Sybylla is not wrought by the feminizing efforts of her relatives, all, of course, aimed at helping her make a good "match," but the realization of the poverty and adversity suffered by many of her countrymen who are much less privileged than herself. She is deeply affected when a letter from her mother arrives regarding a debt and she cannot help her pay; however, she survives the experience and benefits from it. She manages to teach the children to read—not books but the newspapers that line the walls of their cabin. Realizing the parallel between the hardships of her parents and the family she lives with, she acquires a measure of compassion and humility. When the debt is paid, and she returns home, she recognizes the fact that her mother had married beneath her—an event that had led to a life of adversity—and became even more determined never to marry. She rejects Harry's proposal and, because of her newfound compassion for other humans, comes to believe she has acquired enough wisdom to write stories.

Mrs. Soffel, Armstrong's first American film, is based on the true story of Kate Soffel (Diane Keaton), a repressed warden's wife who falls in love with convicted murderer Ed Biddle (Mel Gibson) and aids in his escape from prison. Cinematographer Russell Boyd's murky photographs of the prison interior and the exterior shots of snowy Pittsburgh in 1901 foreshadow a dark, doomed love story. In the film, Kate is a frail, deeply religious woman who hands out Bibles to inmates when she is well enough, and occasionally reads Bible passages to them. This exercise is carried out at the discretion of her warden husband (Edward Herrmann), as are all her activities as she is under the watchful eye of him whom she married at a young age. The couple's three younger children are mostly cared for by their sixteen-year-old daughter, who is being pursued for marriage by a devoutly religious young man—a prospect that delights the warden but saddens Kate. This film follows the transformation of Kate from the pious, angelic woman praying for the souls of those awaiting execution, through a circular narrative of passion, rebellion, betrayal of husband, and abandonment of family to her return to the institution as a prisoner, refusing the prayers of the pious. Her attraction to Ed, who elicits her sympathy and then uses her to help him and his brother (Matthew Modine), leads her to make a public denouncement of capital punishment which embarrasses her husband and jeopardizes his position as warden. She provides Ed and his brother with saws and a weapon to accomplish their escape and accompanies them on a frantic trek into Canada in an attempt to elude the law enforcement officers. She and Ed manage to spend one night together, which allows those in pursuit to catch up with them. Not wanting to live without him, she persuades Ed to shoot her shortly before he and his brother are killed. She, of course, does not die and is transported back to prison.

Meanwhile, her husband, disgraced by her actions, and her motherless children have left the prison. Her oldest daughter visits her in hospital to tell her mother that she has married the zealous young man. Kate sees her own unfulfilled life continuing on into her daughter's readiness to assume the role of repressed wife and mother, at the same time that she, in one swift action, having betrayed and abandoned her husband and family for a few hours of passion and rebellion is now faced with years of solitude. She has exchanged her life of protection by God, her husband, and family for the supervision of the prison authorities in a secular world. Kate forsakes Christianity for love and passion, succumbing to Ed's absence of piety and sentence of death (in the scene where he shoots her, she murmurs, "Yes, yes," as an intense acceptance of death for her actions), but the motivations for her transformation are as ill-defined as the dimly lit interior of the prison. This uncertainty bids the viewers to ponder the implications of the chiaroscuro for what cannot be said, but only shown in images.

High Tide, Armstrong's follow-up film, is another meditation on women's abandonment of children. The story follows Lilli (Judy Davis), a back-up singer for an Elvis impersonator who, fired from her job and needing expensive car repair, is stranded in Eden, a small beach town. She agrees to strip twice in the local bar for money for the car repairs. In Eden, a name that carries Biblical overtones of a fallen world, Lilli discovers her daughter, Ally, whom she had given up in infancy, and Bet, her former mother-in-law, to whom she had given her baby daughter. Because the transaction that occurred shortly after Lilli's young husband, Bet's son, died was never legalized, Bet fears Lilli is there to take Ally away from her. Since her husband died and she abandoned Ally, who had been told her mother had died, Lilli has led a transient life, joining a traveling entertainment group and rejecting any hint of commitment to anything or anyone. A new relationship with Mick, who has a small daughter his mother helps him raise, falls by the wayside when she meets Ally. Lilli's crisis in the film centers around her conflicted desire to run away from Ally and continue on her uncommitted life, or become a mother to her child.

Abdication of motherhood is depicted in *High Tide*, as in *Mrs. Soffel*, by an empty space beside the child where the mother was accustomed to being. Kate Soffel's family is seen having to leave the prison while she is on the road with

Ed Biddle, and Kate's daughter is seen at the piano and the space beside her, usually occupied by her mother, vacant. Also, an empty space exists across the table from Ally at the service station where she waits for her mother, who is in the car fighting her desire to run away again and reject any obligation to Ally.

The Last Days of Chez Nous did not receive sparkling reviews from male reviewers, who apparently found the story of a woman's emotional journey through the ending of one relationship to the beginning of another somewhat lacking in interest. The film returns again to the figure of the woman writer, but one who is a wife and mother in a contemporary setting in Sydney. Beth (Lisa Harrow), a writer of novels and mother of teenaged Annie, is married to J.P., and has alienated him through her inattention to him. A new boarder, Tim, very focused on Annie, is teaching her to play piano duets with him and they soon become engrossed in each other. Into this tension comes Vickie, Beth's baby sister, who is several weeks pregnant, back from Europe. Vickie agonizes over her predicament and is encouraged by Beth to have an abortion, but before she leaves the clinic, she begins to question the wisdom of her painful decision.

Although there are three women in this film, the focus is upon Beth, middle-aged and sensuous, a successful author who is a maternal person, eternally cleaning, shopping, and cooking, looking after her daughter and keeping the family going. She asks her husband, J.P., a transplanted Frenchman soon to be granted Australian citizenship, "Will we ever make love again?" J.P., an egotistical person, who tells her that her books reflect life as she would like for it to be, replies tartly that she has asked the wrong question. He longs for a child of his own and someone to "notice" him. He prepares elegant French cuisine, derogates Australian culture, and insists upon "real news," as opposed to mere sensationalism. He chastises Beth severely for eating a piece of his brie before it has ripened—an evidence of the little things that irritate in a relationship that is floundering. Beth's sister, fresh from her failed relationship, becomes the catalyst for the end. Her initial gesture of greedily devouring a large piece of her heart-shaped welcome cake (and throwing it up) metaphorically indicates her lifetime behavior pattern. She looks upon Beth as her mother, because her own parents are "too old" for her. Pampered and immature, Vickie never helps with food preparation, cleaning up, or any chores, preferring instead to daydream about the future, sing, and dance. Envious of Beth's life and career, Vickie makes it known that she wants to write but has no discipline or drive.

Beth, who organizes everything and tries to take care of everything and everyone, attempts to make peace with her aging, ailing, cantankerous, taciturn father, with whom she has never gotten along or been able to communicate. He and Beth travel to the desert, where after repeated criticism of her driving and general sniping, they reach the primal red earth of Australian outback. Here, they speak haltingly of death, God, and peace, managing to talk briefly, if circuitously, of their troubled relationship. One of Armstrong's more insightful scenes, occurring during a night when Beth and her father, in separate motel rooms, and Vickie, back in Sydney, are all simultaneously watching the same television program involving the birth of a baby. Beth's father changes the channel to sports. Beth watches the tiny baby as tears stream down her cheeks, while Vickie, hysterical, is comforted by J.P., who inquires why she had not decided to give birth to her aborted baby and give it to him. In comforting Vickie, J.P. initiates a closeness with her; despite her indolence, he had responded to her energetic dancing and the way she hungrily seized experience. Soon, they are sharing soup, conversation, sympathy, and the same bed. J.P. has convinced Vickie that Beth does not love him and would not mind about their affair, and she responds immediately, refusing to acknowledge any allegiance that might be owed to her sister. To the lovers' surprise, when Beth discovers the shift in loyalties, she destroys the bathroom in a rage. Heartbroken, she rallies to go on with life; she even manages to salvage a friendship with J.P. but cannot forgive Vickie for her betrayal. Vickie and J.P. move into a new place, and the film ends with Vickie, dismayed by the work required to make a home for her and J.P., stares glumly at the mop bucket.

For Beth, the film ends on a more upbeat note. She, Annie, with whom she is very affectionate, and Tim remain in the terraced house in downtown Sydney. After much thought, Beth walks down the street from her house, and turns the corner into an area she had not been seen in previously, suggesting that she intends to widen her sphere from the maternal one to expand her writing and perhaps embark on a spiritual quest.

Little Women, a film very similar to *My Brilliant Career*, also concerns a spirited girl who doesn't fit in, and wants to become a writer. Much like Sybylla, Jo March, independent and tomboyish, serves her apprenticeship through the transitions of time and change upon her family before she finds her real subject. Only after Sybylla's realization of the poverty and deprivation of others less fortunate than she could she gain the compassion and vision to write a book, and only with the death of Beth, Jo's beloved sister, could Jo write from her heart and abandon romantic stories of derring-do.

Based on Louisa May Alcott's book about her own family in Concord, Massachusetts, in the nineteenth century, Gillian Armstrong's film captures the timeless story of the March family and the journey of its girls to adulthood. Armstrong had refused the directorship of the film several times because she thought of it as a little girls' film, until her producer convinced her to look at the book as a story of family. In addition to family, other recurring Armstrong themes and subjects are present in this film, notably sisterhood, a young woman who wants to become a writer, and the strength of family bonds. The film specifically ties in Jo's marketable success as a writer with her own personal transformation, which is seen in her journey to New York to "become a writer" and in Beth's death. As Bronson Alcott, father of Louisa Alcott, was a believer in Transcendentalism—a movement that insisted, among other things, upon self-fulfillment and development—Marmee, who represents Mrs. Alcott, urges Jo to go in the world and transform her gifts into accomplishments. Also, by the way, the film notes the Alcott family's strong social-mindedness and compassion for the poor and for the wounded, dispirited Civil War soldiers returning home. But despite the family's support and her hard work, Jo has been hurt to the core with Beth's death and the breaking up of her family—both proving to be life-altering events. But new family members are arriving through marriage, including Jo's own, and by birth, and an even larger family now exists; but the necessity of impermanence countered by strong family ties has left its mark on Jo, and through her book and Armstrong's film, on us, the viewers.

In *Oscar and Lucinda*, Armstrong considers a relationship between two ec-centrics set in Australia's nineteenth-century colonial period. Adapted from the 1988 Booker Prize–winning novel by Peter Carey, the story is presented through a lengthy flashback by Oscar's great-grandson, who guides us through a series of events preceding his birth. The voiceover narration, rendered by Geoffrey Rush, emphasizes the extremes in the respective childhoods of Oscar and Lucinda; Oscar was raised by a stern father, who was a preacher, while Lucinda was taught and influenced by an intelligent, forceful mother who was an early active feminist. Oscar, a product of the colonial era of patriarchal religion emphasizing God, Death, and Judgment is juxtaposed with Lucinda, who represents the more mod-ern, secular, industrial, technological world. Forced out into the world in 1848, following a game of chance whose result Oscar interprets as God's Will that he train for an Anglican minister at Oxford, he appeals to an Anglican rival of his fa-ther, the Reverend Stratton, who sends him to college to benefit his own standing in the community. At Oxford, Oscar, lonely and nervous, does not "fit in." His friend, Fish, introduces him to horse betting and he catches "the gambling bug." He makes a large amount of money and gives it to the poor. Shocked to realize that he cannot stop gambling, and as he views the results as God's Will, Oscar lets the toss of a coin decide that he would go to New South Wales to become a missionary. On the boat trip to Sydney from London, Oscar meets Lucinda, who, having inherited a fortune from her mother, is returning to Sydney with the latest equipment she has acquired for her new glass factory. Lucinda approaches Oscar to hear her confession, and instead of absolution for her gambling compulsion, he exonerates her by citing Blaise Pascal's famous wager concerning the exis-tence of God. They play cards most of that night and others, continuing to see each other and to play cards. Lucinda, a wealthy, modern, independent woman who does as she pleases—visiting gambling parlors, dens, or gentlemen's quarters to gamble—is undaunted by society's injunction concerning a "woman's place." Oscar is soon excommunicated from the Anglican Church for his scandalous behavior and his association with Lucinda, with whom he makes a pact to gamble no more. But Oscar, who persists in searching for signs of God's Will, misreads Lucinda's relationship with the Reverend Dennis Hasset, who was sent down to a remote area of New South Wales to minister because of his association with Lucinda. Inasmuch as no church building exists in the village to which Hasset was banished, Oscar proposes a huge wager with Lucinda to the effect that if she would design and build a glass and iron church, he would be responsible for trans-porting it overland to Hasset and his congregation by Good Friday. Both stake all of their inheritances in support of the project; Lucinda seeks relief through deliverance from the burden of her inheritance, and Oscar hopes for redemption for his insults to God.

Before Oscar leaves on the trek through the "unmapped area," he learns that the Reverend Stratton has hanged himself after losing the family money while attempting to replicate Oscar's "system" of betting on horses. Oscar's guide through the outback, Jeffris, is a brutal, unprincipled man who forces laudanum into Oscar to quiet him, leads the massacre of a group of indigenous inhabitants of the area, and tortures Oscar mercilessly until Oscar plunges an ax into his head. The fact that Oscar arrives within the deadline is within itself miraculous, given his addled, traumatized state. Aiming for much more, Miriam Chadwick, a widowed member of Hasset's congregation, takes Oscar to her home to care for him. Predictably, she bathes him, seduces him, and becomes pregnant. He spends the night, his last, in the church moored in the village landing; during the night it sinks and Oscar drowns. Because Miriam never knew of the wager, she does not challenge the right to Lucinda's fortune. Lucinda befriends Oscar's son; the final scene of Lucinda is with Oscar's red-haired son in water, swimming together. At the film's close, we see Oscar's great-grandson and his daughter in a motor-propelled boat, presumably after he has completed his narration of the mystery of his existence, returning home.

Along with the water imagery throughout, the fluid narrative carries the audience through characters' memories, dreams, pasts, conscious and unconscious states, as well as Christianity's conflicts and dilemmas evident in nineteenth-century Australia. The struggle between the transplanted British patriarchal religion and the secular, technological "faith" of the approaching industrial revolution of the later eighteenth century is somewhat reflected in the glass-and-iron church. Floating by mystified naked indigenous children along the banks, with Oscar inside, the church begins to lose roofing pieces before it arrives at Bellington. Once there, Oscar, recovering from his ordeal with Jeffris, barely makes his presentation of the church to the Reverend Hasset, when he is taken ashore for medical attention. By the film's end, Oscar seems to have lost much of his insistence upon God's Will with regard to his behavior. His final prayer, heard echoing over the landscape, is a plea for forgiveness for causing the deaths of Stratton, and Jeffris, for his betrayal of Miriam, Lucinda, and his father, and for his pride and ignorance. At Oscar's funeral, Lucinda asks if the shattered church could be repaired with weatherboarding "and such" so as to be useful, suggesting that the technologically modern religion is inappropriate for an Australian bush town in mid–nineteenth century.

Armstrong's fondness for documentaries which kept her in Australia through much of her career is evident in her series. Unlike the distinctive spatial aspects of Armstrong's feature films that meld character and landscape to form the narrative, her four films in the series—*Smokes and Lollies* (1976), *14's Good, 18's Better* (1976), *Bingo, Bridesmaids and Braces* (1986), and *Not 14 Again* (1996)—emphasize the passing of time. The first one in 1976 was intended to document the attitudes and goals of three working-class fourteen-year-old girls, Diana, Josie, and

Kerry. This film came about through Armstrong's association with the Women's Film Fund and its sponsorship of film projects concerning girls and their positions toward school, work, sexuality, and family. On film, the girls discuss pregnancy, abortion, a proper age to marry, motherhood, and much more, all the while seeming optimistic about the future.

The succeeding films in this series, while showing the girls at ages eighteen, twenty-six, and thirty-four, who recount the events in their lives since their last meeting, also return to their comments in the previous films. Amongst the complaints of boredom were the stories of women getting married, getting divorced, raising children, working jobs, and still continuing to think of the future. The repetition of daily activities punctuated with infrequent dramatic events, such as the birth of a child, a wedding, a divorce, or substantial change of job, seem to characterize the existence of these women into the approach of middle age. And now that they have teenage daughters, whose options for careers may have expanded with time, Diana, Josie, and Kerry compare their recorded comments with those of their daughters.

In *Charlotte Gray* (2001), Armstrong directed a film from Sebastian Faulks's novel based on true stories of women who were agents for Britain's Special Operations organization. Kate Blanchett plays Charlotte Gray, a Scotswoman who goes to London to work as a medic and falls madly in love with RAF pilot Peter Gregory, who is shot down and rumored to be with the French Resistance. Gray allows herself to be recruited as a secret agent in support of the French Resistance. She assumes a false identity, that of Dominique Gilbert, whose husband has been taken prisoner. After her training, she parachutes into France and meets up with Julien (Billy Crudup) and his father, Levade (Michael Gambon), in rural France and delves into French Resistance activities. Her first mission, destruction of a train carrying German troops and weapons, leaves her devastated. Taylor insists that "no director has consistently brought a woman's viewpoint, a woman's experience and acute perception of female rites of passage to the movies" than Gillian Armstrong (1998).

JANE CAMPION

Jane Campion, born April 30, 1954, in Wellington, New Zealand, was the second child of Edith and Richard Campion, founder of the New Zealand National Theatre. Clearly the paramount influences in her life and work were her colorful, eccentric, theatrical parents, older sister, Anna, and younger brother, Michael, who may well be detected as shadowy figures lurking behind the unusual characters mired in sibling rivalry and dysfunctional households in her writings and films thirty years later.

Edith, a shoe-factory heiress, and Richard, whose own family belonged to a severe religious group that forbade radio, television, or films, believed they were celestial twins when they met; but over time the relationship deteriorated.

The parents poured Edith's inheritance into the establishment of the National Theatre of New Zealand, and threw themselves into the project. The management of it took them away from home for long periods of time, leaving the Campion sisters in the care of an insensitive nanny whose ferocious temperament forced them to repress their own individualities for fear of punishment. Competition for attention and achievement grew between the sisters, whose difficulties with each other fostered essentially solitary childhoods, and caused each to withdraw into a world of fantasy and imagination. When Campion was nine, the money ran out, marking the demise of the theater, and although the family had more time together, the antagonisms and resentments multiplied. At one point, the family took a trip to Europe—a huge influence on Campion's interest in painting—but, essentially, the family unit was eroding.

Campion's mother, Edith, who aspired to acting, was coerced by her husband to give it up and stay home with the children. Edith's frustration led to severe depression, and eventually electric shock therapy as treatment for her anxiety and despondency. Her mother's agony left its imprint on Campion's life and work; she feared that she too might suffer from depression, but she also gained new insight into the domination of women, and the afflictions some women endure while struggling for a means of expression.

Following her completion of a BA degree in anthropology in 1975 from the University of Wellington, she was still casting about for a direction and seemed no closer to finding one. Convinced that she needed to leave New Zealand, she enrolled in 1976 in London's Chelsea Art School. Living alone in a dreary flat and oppressed by miserable weather, Campion devoted many evenings to sampling London's art house cinema culture. After traveling about Europe for a time, she entered Sydney College of Arts, graduating in 1979 with a BA in painting.

While at the College of Art, Campion resolved to enter the prestigious Australian Film and Television School (AFTS), created by the government in a period of arts support that started in the early 1970s. Campion was keen to follow Gillian Armstrong, an AFTS graduate whose film My Brilliant Career (1979) had received national and international acclaim, and to take advantage of the flourishing film industry in Australia. Knowing that gaining admission would be difficult, especially for a woman, she learned to operate a Super 8 camera, and after graduation, put together a twenty-minute film that ensured her acceptance. Tissues (1980), written, directed, and edited by Campion, is a black comedy that concerns a father who has been charged with child molestation and his family's efforts to cope with their predicament.

In her first year at AFTS, Campion wrote, directed, and edited Peel (1982), a nine-minute film that depicts fantastic family behavior that could be seen as bordering on madness. From the back seat of a car driven by his father, a boy tosses an orange peel out the window, and the father, screeching to a halt, demands that the son retrieve the peel. When the son refuses, the situation becomes volatile and family members exhibit irrational and bizarre behavior. Despite the film's winning Best Experimental Film from the Australian Film Institute in 1984, and the Palme d'Or at Cannes Film Festival in 1986 for Best Short Film, AFTS showed little support for Campion's films beginning with her first year. At the generally conservative institution, many lecturers insisted that Campion's approach to filmmaking and startling subject matter would restrict audience appeal, while others contended that she was without talent. Never one to avoid controversy, Campion, in fact, seems to have sought it out and thrived on it. She continued at AFTS to make her own student films *Passionless Moments* (1983/84) with her boyfriend, Gerard Lee, as cowriter, director, and editor, and *A Girl's Own Story* (1983/1984), a twenty-nine-minute film about sisters who appear to hate each other, and whose parents have not spoken to each other in two years. Both films provide fragmentary looks at the lives of strange characters from oblique camera angles that cultivate a sense of uneasiness in the viewer.

After she left AFTS, Campion went to work for the Women's Film Unit of the Commonwealth Employment Scheme, making a twenty-seven-minute film titled *After Hours* (1984), whose avowed aim was to raise awareness of sexual abuse of women in the workplace. In 1986, she directed an episode of *Dancing Daze* and *Two Friends*, both for television, and received a citation for Best Director in a Television Feature. Two years later, she published a short story, "Big Shell," in *Rolling Stone* (Australia), followed by a role in *The Audition* (1989), directed by her sister, Anna.

In 1989, Campion's first theatrical feature, *Sweetie*, caused another storm of controversy when it premiered at Cannes, although it actually propelled her career into serious consideration. She followed this with *An Angel at My Table* (1990, originally for television), filmed in New Zealand and based on the autobiographies of Janet Frame, one of New Zealand's most famous authors. Also filmed in New Zealand was the Australian-produced film, *The Piano* (1993). In 1992, Campion married Colin Englert, second unit director on *The Piano*, and at the time of the film's premiere at Cannes, they were expecting their first child. The film garnered the Palme d'Or award and was proclaimed a masterpiece. However, the astounding success at the festival was completely overshadowed by the death of her twelve-day-old son, Jasper, who was delivered by emergency caesarean, but could not live outside the incubator. Her daughter, Alice, was born a year later. Campion, her husband, and two children make their home in Sydney.

In 1966, Campion released her next project, a film version of Henry James's *Portrait of a Lady*, and was criticized for taking liberties with the book. She followed this up with *Holy Smoke* (1999) and *In the Cut* (2001). Although four of Campion's short films were invited to Cannes in 1986—with *Peel* winning the Palme d'Or for short films—it was Sweetie, her first feature film, that gained international recognition. This idiosyncratic film about two sisters, one spontaneous and the other repressed, is a dark-humored, yet disastrous story of passions and tensions within a family. "I think . . . families . . . are incredibly funny at times, and yet there is a tragic underbelly," notes Campion in an interview (*Sydney Morning Herald*). Narrated by Kay, the film is Kay's story, despite the film's title and despite the fact that Sweetie does not appear until thirty minutes into the film. Kay and Louis, her boyfriend, live together; after a year has passed, her sister, Dawn (Sweetie), appears and proceeds to wreak havoc upon the entire family.

But, as a brief summary of the film tells little about the largely interior action of the film, so do Campion's films focus on feelings and states of mind, rather than narrative, and explore various levels of meaning through the use of expressive techniques. The chief symbol in the film— trees —and the attitudes of the family members toward trees illustrate much of the family's tensions and dysfunction. In her opening voiceover, which reveals her state of mind, Kay declares: "We had a tree in our yard with a palace in the branches. It was built for my sister and it had fairy lights that went on and off in a sequence. She was the princess; it was her tree; she wouldn't let me up it. At night the darkness frightens me. Someone could be watching from behind them—someone who wishes you harm. I used to imagine the roots of that tree crawling, crawling right under the house, right under my bed. Maybe that's why trees scare me. It's like they have hidden powers."

Kay's anxiety about trees that began in jealousy and resentment of her sister has progressed to feelings of dread and menace. When we first see her walking to her job as bank clerk, she avoids stepping on the cracks in the sidewalk, apparently having resorted to superstition in an effort to bring meaning into her life. She stops off to see a fortune teller; later, at work, she meets Louis, who has a curl like a question mark in the center of his forehead, and she decides that he is the one.

They move in together, and thirteen months later, Louis, over Kay's objections, plants an elder tree to celebrate their year together. During the night, she dreams of roots spreading uncontrollably and, fearing the tree's decay would kill their relationship, she slinks out into the dark yard, yanks up the tree and hides it. Almost immediately, she loses physical interest in Louis and moves into the spare bedroom. Campion reinforces Kay's anxiety with numerous shots of trees, shadows of leaves on walls and on curtains, and Kay's preoccupation with the patterns formed by branches. Curiously, Campion has said that of the characters in *Sweetie*, Kay is most like Campion when she was younger (Bourguignon and Ciment, 1993, 111).

When Sweetie appears, at about thirty minutes into the film, Kay's discomfort becomes more pronounced, as the symbolic trees reflect the psychopathology of the family unit. Sweetie, overweight and unstable, has left the mental institution, and along with Bob, a hopeless addict who purports to be her "producer," has broken into the home of Kay and Louis in their absence. Sweetie and Bob make love loudly and interminably, exacerbating Kay's alienation from Louis; Sweetie compulsively mutilates Kay's clothing, and upon being reprimanded, tries to eat Kay's collection of small, ceramic horses (at another time, Sweetie, in an agitated state, barks like a dog); and, Sweetie, as spontaneous as Kay is repressed, has offered to "lick [Louis] all over." In the midst of this, Gordon, the girls' father arrives at Kay's house, seeking comfort because his wife and their mother, Flo, has finally found his obsession with Sweetie intolerable, and has gone "out West" and cook for jackaroos. Sweetie, his childish, pampered, minimally talented favorite daughter, for whom the tree house was built, immediately begins to perform remnants of childhood routines in a desperate attempt to gain approval and communicate with her father.

Gordon's encouragement of Sweetie to become a performer has prompted her addiction to monstrous behavior in order to secure attention and love. It has also established, for Sweetie, a connection between belief in her talents and sexuality. A disturbing scene in which Sweetie bathes Gordon hints at an incestuous relationship between the two; also, Bob becomes her producer because he "believes" in her, and when Louis appears sympathetic, she offers him sexual favors.

Because of Sweetie's manipulation of Gordon, neither Flo nor Kay wants anything to do with her. Kay feels the family bonds, like tree roots, strangling her. She refuses to acknowledge any filial bonds with her sister; she says that Sweetie "has nothing to do with me . . . she was just born." At another time, Kay announces that Sweetie is "evil." Flo, also strangled by Gordon's "sickness" with Sweetie, improves as soon as she gets away. In her new location, she sings a tender love song—to the amazement of Kay, who never knew Flo could sing, and who, unlike her mother, has not yet found her own "voice" or means of expression. Flo does not, however, share Kay's fear of trees or her despair; as she surveys Kay's yard, where the elder tree once stood, she says: "What a plain little yard. . . . I couldn't live without my trees; they give me hope."

Although Flo and Gordon reconcile with the understanding that Sweetie will have living quarters of her own, Campion follows the consequences of dysfunction and mental illness until the end. Louis finds the remains of the uprooted elder tree and, stunned by the extent of Kay's abnormality, leaves. In a fit of outrageous behavior, Sweetie climbs up into her old treehouse, strips naked, paints her body black, and refuses to come down. Tragically, yet predictably, the treehouse collapses under her weight, and Sweetie falls to her death, almost killing Gordon and injuring Flo. Symbolically, the position or role created for Sweetie by her father has denied her self-expression, authentic communication, and any sense of her own identity, and is not only inadequate for growth as an individual, but is life-killing. But, as the film is essentially Kay's story, she is the one who rushes to Sweetie after she falls and, despite a lifetime of bitterness and antagonism, attempts to save her. Kay's lips are smeared with Sweetie's blood as she frantically tries to resuscitate her. Gordon and Flo, who stand idly by and stare at the events, exhibit vague symptoms of relief. At the interment, Kay notes that "Trees never leave you alone. . . . They had to saw the tree roots off before they could get the coffin down," emphasizing graphically the persistence of family ties and the difficulty of trying to break free of them.

In the final scene, Gordon wanders under the tree and remembers Sweetie as a child, mechanically performing and singing "Love Me With All Your Heart," and continues to cling to a vision of his creation. Interestingly, Flo does not attend Sweetie's funeral and is not seen again following Sweetie's death. Kay is reunited with Louis, and they attempt to rebuild their relationship. Within the symbolic framework of the film, only after Sweetie has died does Kay have the freedom to become herself.

One of the more striking aspects of the film is its frame composition. Intrigued by taking risks and showing an eccentric story rather than just telling one, Campion and her cinematographer, Sally Bongers, focused on the frame to highlight the dramatic situation and reflect the characters' emotion (Ciment, 1989, 41). Characters are shot on opposite sides of the frame, or appear to be clinging to one side of the frame, indicating their alienation from each other. At the same time, their faces are bathed in soft light, reflecting Campion's sympathy for her characters. This works particularly well with the drab sets, which, through framing and lighting, avoids mere depictions of sordid reality. Some shots are remarkably effective in their off-beat ability to communicate: the swimming scene in the country in which Flo and Kay, with only their heads visible, come to believe they can "begin again"; the fortune teller's groaning, demented son, who according to his mother, "will never know love . . . but he's sick with it"; as Sweetie falls from the tree, Campion's camera is on a large spool of water hose that unwinds uncontrollably; the scene in the cemetery with the tracking shot along the hedges, past the tree in the wind that appears to be breathing, to Sweetie's grave.

Following *Sweetie*, Campion began *An Angel at My Table*, based on the three autobiographical volumes of *To the Island*, *An Angel at My Table*, and *The Envoy from Mirror City*, all written in the early 1980s, detail her growing up in a poor, rural family in the South Island of New Zealand. A plump girl with wild, frizzy, red hair and bad teeth, Frame tried to find solace from her loneliness and shyness through writing poetry. After the accidental drowning deaths of two of her sisters and her suicide attempt, she was advised to enter a mental institution and "rest." During her eight years there, she was misdiagnosed as schizophrenic and was subjected to more than 200 electroshock treatments. "I'm not committed to niceness. I'm committed to seeing what's there," said Jane Campion (Williamson 9).

Because of its length, *An Angel at My Table* was essentially made for a three-part television series. It was a huge undertaking for Campion, requiring the casting of 140 speaking parts and three different actresses to play Janet Frame from childhood to adult. Campion went back to New Zealand for filming in order to make every detail authentic and perfect. Whereas *Sweetie* called for dramatic risk-taking, experimental technique and a focus on dark, complex, and somewhat inaccessible emotions, Campion wanted, in *An Angel at My Table*, to speak the language of the heart in telling a simple intimate story and establish a strong connection with the audience. Campion had been drawn early in her life to Frame because she was an abandoned, troubled, yet strong person who desperately needed a way to express herself. Campion and her cinematographer, Laura Jones, concentrated upon creating a softness around Frame to reinforce the intimacy of the story, even using filters to mute the intensity of contrasts in the New Zealand light into more mellow, golden colors. As continuity was also important in presenting Frame's life evolving over a period of thirty years,

Campion uses suggestions rather than specific discourse to help the audience understand Frame's descent into depression and provides a fluid narrative with smooth transitions that maintain connections between the three time periods.

Familiar themes emerge in this film that continue on in films to come: Campion's preoccupation with creativity, artistic turmoil, solitude of the artist, the oppression of women in a patriarchal society, and the compulsion to find a means of self-expression. Also prominent in this film (as in *Sweetie*) is an exploration of madness or the line between madness and eccentricity. But, as Sweetie was in need of institutional help, Frame was not at the beginning of her incarceration, but seemed to degenerate because of her treatment. She was not schizophrenic. She suffered from painful shyness, impoverishment, and loneliness, and as a consequence of never finding any relationships as comforting as those with her sisters, she was an outsider in most social situations.

Campion's repetitive scenes of lush, green, beautiful New Zealand landscape contrast Frame's expansive vision with her own crushing limitations. Her incarceration, which threatens to erase her creativity and imagination, shows the horror of life without it: Frame clutches her little bag containing a volume of Shakespeare in a desperate effort not to be swallowed up by the madness; Frame's degeneration is depicted graphically, from the shock treatments, each one of which Frame recalled as the equivalent of the fear of execution, to the squalid day room that served as punishment for trouble makers; and the unsettling shots of silent, lobotomized women, wearing scarves and wandering or sitting in the sunshine. When Frame was released from the mental institution and, through her literary grant, traveled to Europe, she finally gained access to the world of history, books, and culture she had dreamed of. Once again, Campion expands the landscape, showing the grandeur of European cities and the possibilities for self-expression there, but ultimately contrasts it with Frame's own personal difficulty in sustaining a personal relationship.

The Piano, a work in progress for five years, was released in 1993. It is the film almost universally recognized as Campion's masterpiece; it won the *Palme d'Or* at Cannes and went on to win numerous awards in Australia, England, Canada and the United States. After rendering faithfully on film an autobiography that she admired immensely, Campion, in *The Piano*, returned to her own specific interests. She herself wrote the script, which details the arrival of mail-order bride, Ada McGrath (Holly Hunter), along with her daughter, Flora (Anna Paquin), and her beloved piano to the wild New Zealand coast to marry a man she had never seen, in an arrangement made by her father. The time period of Ada's venture from Scotland to the primitive world of the bush is the 1850s—the same time that Campion's ancestors, European colonials, arrived in New Zealand and began settling the Maori ancestral lands. As she belongs to a colonial culture, Campion had long envisioned writing and directing a film that would be invested with her own twentieth-century point of view of the nineteenth century.

Campion had been fascinated with the bush since her childhood when she and her family frequently hiked there, and its claustrophobic, impenetrable darkness seemed the perfect atmosphere for her film about characters who experience love and passion for the first time. A great admirer of nineteenth-century novels, particularly Gothic novels and especially those by the Bronte sisters, Campion saw the New Zealand bush as a counterpart of Emily Bronte's wild, windswept moor of *Wuthering Heights* and its clear association with the darker aspects of human nature. The romanticism that Campion sought in her film was not the "pretty" side, but the dark side, the "feeling of terror in the spectator when faced with the power of natural elements" (Bourguignon and Ciment, 1993, 107).

The Maori inhabitants of the dark, mysterious landscape provide a sharp contrast with the European colonials. Alisdair Stewart (Sam Neill), Ada's husband, like many of the colonials, seems uncomfortable with the thick proliferation of vegetation and proceeds to clear it. He is identified through the film with the slash-and-burn practice evident in the area surrounding his house, the fence he is building, and his ever-present ax. His actions suggest a less harmonious relationship with nature; in fact, his attempts to control it indicate an uneasiness with his own nature, specifically with regard to his repressed, puritanical approach to sexuality. George Baines (Harvey Keitel), on the other hand, who appears to exist between the Maori and the whites, is actually neither. He has apparently lived in New Zealand for a long time and, although he has learned Maori and functions as an interpreter between the natives and Stewart, he is still an outsider, a loner. Significantly, Baines, unlike Stewart, is able to communicate with Ada. His half-finished tribal markings indicate, perhaps, an earlier desire to become Maori that has been abandoned.

Ada has attempted to control her own nature through her will. A mute who has not spoken since she was a child, she now speaks through sign language to her daughter, Flora, who announces her mother's wishes. Campion emphasizes the closeness of the two as they caress one another, whisper, laugh, and play. The world into which Ada has retreated in her muteness is also a secret world of art where the piano is her means of expressing her passion and longing. Stewart's callous refusal to transport Ada's piano to his farm, thus abandoning it on the beach, brings forth Ada's intense determination to thwart Stewart's ultimatum. In turning to Baines, who senses her love for the piano, she begins the first step of her symbolic journey out of loneliness, alienation, and passion in that it suggests her sexuality, though encased in Edwardian clothes and layers of crinoline, is being awakened by the power of nature in a primitive land.

It is the piano and the intrusion of that instrument of cultivation into the wild, primitive land that is the catalyst for the powerful feelings exhibited by each character. Ada's love for the piano means no more to Stewart than do the Maori ancestral burial grounds; they both exist for his disposal. Baines, however, becomes fascinated with her passion for her piano, and following the deal he strikes with Stewart and Ada to rescue the piano in return for piano lessons, he sets about trying to find a way into her secret world and its passions. Despite the fact that Ada does not speak and Baines frequently resorts to monologues, they understand one another instinctively. As for Flora, the piano lessons initiate a shift in her mother's attention away from her and toward Baines, and out of jealousy and resentment, she betrays her mother to Stewart. Stewart, who witnesses Ada's passion for Baines through the cracks in the cabin walls, attempts to rape her and imprisons her in his house. When she tries to see Baines again, Stewart cuts off her finger with his ax, much as he would eliminate the fertile vegetation of the bush in his empire building and affirm the repressed ethics of the Europeans.

As Ada, along with Baines and Flora, leaves the bush, the piano once again plays a major role in Ada's symbolic journey. On the boat, Ada gives instructions to throw the piano overboard. As it descends into the dark, silent sea, her foot becomes entangled in the rope which drags her down with the piano. Underwater, her will chooses life, as she frees herself from the rope and ascends from death and the depths of life above the surface. In Ada's symbolic drowning, she leaves the piano in the silence of the sea, no longer needing the piano to speak for her, and is reborn as a liberated person with a voice of her own.

Campion's interest in women who go on journeys and discover themselves continues in *The Portrait of a Lady*, based on Henry James's novel of the same name. Long one of Campion's favorite books, *Portrait* proved a difficult book to film inasmuch as James's first chapters are concerned with conversations about marriage, and James's characteristic methods are not filmable. Campion says that upon rereading the novel, she understood that she was only going to shoot the "story of *Portrait* ... interpreted by [her], with some of the original dialogue" (Ciment 178). Campion's aims were "to make the situations physical, develop the sexual elements that were only suggested, [and] give Isabel fantasies" (Ciment 178). She chose to relate Isabel's quest with that of modern females, seen at the film's beginning lounging in the grass and talking in voiceover about their views and experiences. Also, she filmed Isabel in the grasp of a sexual fantasy involving her three suitors and herself to suggest that Isabel, as she "affronts her destiny," will be guided by eroticism. Campion views Isabel, who speaks of freedom, exploration, or perhaps starting a career, as really searching for passion, and unlike Ada, who is liberated by her sexuality—though at a terrible cost—becomes enslaved because of it.

Although Campion explores the darker aspects of James's novel, she begins with a depiction of Isabel similar to his. Isabel (Nicole Kidman), a beautiful, poor, yet spirited girl, is taken by her wealthy aunt to Europe when her father dies. Arriving at Gardencourt in England, the estate of her uncle, Mr. Touchett, and his son, Ralph, she is pursued by Lord Warburton, a bachelor nobleman, whom she turns down, claiming allegiance to her independence and freedom. Isabel, arrogant and naïve, seems to be convinced that she deserves better than Lord Warburton in her great journey toward knowledge and exploration. Her uncle Touchett (John Gielgud) dies, leaving her at the behest of Ralph (Martin Donovan), who is impressed with her refusal of Warburton, a fortune to assist her in discovering her potential. But her potential is to be discovered in ways Isabel had never dreamed of. Betrayed by her friend Madame Merle (Barbara Hershey), Isabel becomes the target of a plot hatched by Merle and Gilbert Osmond (John Malkovich), Merle's former lover and father of her child, to be ensnared for her money.

Unlike everyone else, who could see Osmond's perversity and smallness, Isabel, who has rebuffed numerous sterling suitors, is totally charmed by his attention and believes herself to be in love with him. When Osmond says to Isabel, "I'm absolutely in love with you," and gives her a lover's kiss, her need for physical contact overpowers her intelligence and she succumbs to his manipulation. During the course of their marriage, she bears a son who dies and becomes the victim of her husband's cruelty, domination, and usurpation of her fortune. She receives word that Ralph Touchett is dying, and though forbidden by Osmond to return to England, Isabel, who has just learned the real truth about their marriage, defies her husband and goes to Ralph's deathbed. She confesses her mistakes, her misery, and her poverty to him and, after his death, debates whether to return to Italy or pursue her own direction, ending the film on a note of indecision.

While James suggests that Isabel returns to Italy not necessarily to Osmond but for her friendship with Pansy, the daughter of Madame Merle and Osmond, Campion hints that these events in Isabel's life may have propelled her to her potential. Does Isabel have the experience and character now, despite her poverty, to reject Osmond and continue with her own journey? Campion is content not to indicate, but to show Isabel hurrying up the path between the two trees—as her first film scene with Lord Warburton occurred beneath trees—and pause at the door to reflect. Campion's themes in this film, aside from her interest in sex as the great leveler, explore the idea of women unwittingly "finding" themselves through painful experiences and becoming human (Abramowitz 188).

The techniques employed by Campion throughout the film, though characteristically imaginative and daring, were thought by some to be inconsistent with James's narrative. The soggy English weather is more significant for Campion than is the fine weather in Florence, Italy. Many shots of life in the English mansion—of dogs, of servants, of roaring fires, of rain pounding on the windowpanes—underscore the emotional balance of life in England as opposed to beautiful, sensuous Tuscany, a land of death for Isabel. Also, after her devastating existence in Florence, she returns to Gardencourt for another death and another decision to be made under the trees—suggesting England as a touchstone for her ambitions. All the turning points of her life—including Isabel and Madame Merle getting acquainted in their walk around the house and gardens under parasols in the rain—have occurred there. Rather than focusing on landscape, many of Campion's shots in *Portrait* are close-ups of faces and teary eyes that reflect the emotional wrenching that is explored throughout the film. In addition to the sexual fantasy scene, the scenes following Osmond's proclamation, "I am absolutely in love with you," replay that instant in Isabel's mind as she sees and hears him say it repeatedly throughout her year-long trip. In fact, lima beans on a plate intone his words, and the trip she so anticipated is represented as a montage of places in a short black-and-white film whose main function is to prepare Isabel for the main event: her marriage and life with Osmond.

Campion's fourth film, *Holy Smoke*, based on a novel of the same name written by sisters Anna and Jane Campion, concerns an Australian woman, Ruth (Kate Winslet), who while on vacation in India falls under the spell of guru Baba and becomes convinced she has found her true path. Fearing manipulation, her family conspires to bring her home through deception and, subsequently, hires a "cult exiter" specialist, P. J. Waters (Harvey Keitel), to carry out her deprogramming. Waters takes Ruth to a "half-way hut" in the Australian outback for three days, during which time the roles are reversed as the powerful becomes powerless and, conversely, the powerless emerges victorious.

Again, familiar themes emerge: the oppressiveness of dysfunctional families, the search for spirituality or meaning in the tawdry grotesquesness of life, and battles between men and women hinging on liberating or humiliating effects of eroticism. Despite the comedic aspects of Ruth's enlightenment, abetted by Campion's hilarious depiction of her third-eye inner vision, the film considers an alternative belief system. Ruth's move toward Indian mysticism seems more understandable when the audience views her monotonous house in a huge middle-class subdivision in Sans Souci, Sydney, and meets her largely unpleasant family, who has effected her return to Australia by telling her falsely that her father is dying. Her siblings leave her no choice but to follow Waters's deprogramming. Ruth is offended immediately by Waters's dyed hair, black attire, cowboy boots, and his macho behavior: in two hundred deprogramming efforts, he has never failed. On the second day of the program, she seduces Waters, and by the third, she has reduced his powerful advantage over her to a whimper. Reeling from her cruelty and taunts, he writes "Be Kind" on her forehead, causing her to loathe herself for her own behavior. Having ferreted out his insecurities, she dresses him in a red dress, smears red lipstick on him, and sets off across the outback wearing books tied to her feet—he had taken her shoes—with him in pursuit. Waters soon abandons the truck, following her on foot, a ridiculous figure in his red dress and wearing one boot. Eventually, they are discovered by her family, whom Ruth astounds by holding Waters compassionately on the return trip—hallucinating, dehydrated, his body bruised and his will broken.

One year later, according to postcards they exchange, Waters has married and is the father of twins; Ruth and her mother are working in India. Having been deprogrammed from his earlier arrogant, macho, superior position, Waters is now presumably capable of the give-and-take alliance a successful marriage requires. Ruth and her mother, whose husband ran off with his teenage girlfriend and their child, are content to pursue enlightenment in India.

Campion's most recent film, *In the Cut*, based on Susanna Moore's novel of the same name is a venture into noir genre in the shape of a thriller that yielded mostly negative, disappointed reviews despite a smallish amount of quite positive ones. Intended for Nicole Kidman, who begged off during her divorce from Tom Cruise, the role of Frannie is played instead by Meg Ryan, who, by all accounts, desired to change her image from pert, comedic heroine to gritty, serious actress by way of the sex-obsessed, ambiguous English teacher character in this film. Frannie, a poetically minded person collects slang words and phrases for a book she intends to write. Posted throughout her apartment are bits of paper bearing notations she has found impressive, for example, "I want to do to you what Spring does to the cherry trees." Also, she carries a small notebook in which to jot down gleanings from overheard conversations, store fronts, and ads on the bus. Frannie and her half-sister, Pauline (Jennifer Jason Leigh), who lives above a strip club, console one another in their loneliness and the absence of men in their lives. Pauline's obsession with a married doctor has led her to make eleven appointments with him in one week—a practice he has ordered her to stop. Frannie is stalked by her ex-boyfriend (Kevin Bacon), an unbalanced medical student whose only companion is his small, hairless dog.

The film begins on a note of confusion, when Frannie awakens from a dream of her mother and father ice skating, sees the shower of blooms in the breeze from her window, and thinks it is snowing. This scene establishes a misinterpretation that is crucial to the narrative's development. Later that day, Frannie meets an African American student who passes on new slang phrases to her. Excusing herself in search of a downstairs bathroom, she inadvertently discovers a woman with blue fingernails giving oral sex to a man with a 3-of-clubs tattoo on his forearm. A few days later, Frannie is visited by a NYC policeman, Giovanni Molloy (Mark Ruffalo), who is investigating the murder and "disarticulation" (the word fascinates Frannie) of a woman who lived in the same building and "part of whose body" was found in the garden outside Frannie's window.

Frannie and Molloy begin a steamy, sexual relationship; she notices a 3-of-clubs tattoo on his arm and fears that he is the killer. As their relationship continues, a second woman is found murdered, and then a third—Pauline, Frannie's sister. At this point, Frannie is convinced Molloy is the guilty party, despite his explanation that the tattoo is a mark used by members of a club. She handcuffs Molloy to the bed, exits the apartment and is picked up by Molloy's partner, Rodriguez, who takes her to a lighthouse, where he plans to kill her. During a terrible struggle, she kills him, walks back to her apartment, lies down beside Molloy and places her head on his shoulder.

Issues of trust, of course, pervade the film, as well as Frannie's inability to interpret Molloy's tenderness and sexual passion rightly. In retrospect, the signs that targeted Rodriguez were there all along: indications of repressed homosexuality in his behavior toward Frannie; immature behavior; past history of violence toward his wife; and the fact that he and Molloy celebrated their first big bust as cops by getting themselves tattooed. Pauline's desperation for a man to love prompted her to invite the wrong man into her apartment, whereas Molloy's ability to please Frannie sexually failed to connect with Frannie as it should have. What all this has to do with Frannie's love of slang is not clear; neither is the connection between her sex-obsessed repression and her fear of Molloy.

LENI RIEFENSTAHL

The controversial German film director known to the world as Leni Riefenstahl was born Helene Berta Amalie Riefenstahl in Berlin on August 22, 1902, to Bertha and Alfred Riefenstahl, owner of a plumbing firm. Determining early in her life to become a dancer, she was educated at the Kunstakademie in Berlin and then studied Russian ballet and modern dance; by 1920, she was an accomplished dancer touring in Germany, Switzerland, and Czechoslovakia.

When she suffered an injury and was forced to give up dancing, she became interested in the films of Arnold Fanck, geologist and director who demonstrated his passion for mountain climbing in documentary and feature films, and began the popular mountain film genre in Germany. Riefenstahl met Fanck, convinced him to offer her a role in his next film, *The Holy Mountain* (1926), which was so well received that she decided to remain in motion pictures. During the next seven years, she made five more films with Fanck: *The Great Leap* (1927), *The White Hell of Piz Palu* (1929), *Storms Over Mont Blanc* (1930), *The White Frenzy* (1931), and *S. O. S. Iceberg* (1933). These adventure films were action-filled, with Riefenstahl frequently the only woman in a company of rugged men exposed to the dangers of high mountains and the ocean's depth. She learned to ski and climb, but most important, she learned everything possible about camera work, editing, and directing.

In 1932, having borrowed many members of Fanck's production crew, Riefenstahl directed her own mountain film, *The Blue Light*. Based on a mountain legend, the romantic, mystical motion picture featured Riefenstahl herself as Yunta, a partly civilized idealistic Italian girl, who climbs rugged mountains to admire concealed crystals that emit a magical blue light but cause climbers to fall to their deaths. A German painter who falls in love with Yunta seeks to make her wealthy; he opens a new trail up in the mountains, enabling the villagers to exploit the crystals, and at the same time unwittingly removes the magic power that drew Yunta to them. Disheartened by the misuse of the crystals, she falls in the abyss. The film was an outstanding success. Riefenstahl's youthful romanticism and beautiful cinematography received awards and praise both at both home and abroad. Its mysticism, a continuation of traditional German filmmaking and German expressionism, achieved through chiaroscuro and shadow, artistically expresses the conflict of ideals and reality so prominent in the film—and attracted the attention of Adolf Hitler. Hitler, who had recently come to power, asked Riefenstahl to film the 1933 Nazi party rally in Nuremberg; that film, *Victory of Faith* (1933), has been lost, but Riefenstahl's film of the 1934 rally, *Triumph of the Will*, also commissioned by Hitler, is considered a monumental propaganda film and the film that, as a glorification of Hitler and Nazi Ideals, eventually destroyed her career as a director. The film won The German Film Prize for 1935 and the International Grand Prix at the 1937 Paris World Exhibition. Riefenstahl's next film, *Day of Freedom: Our Armed Forces* (1935), was a short film shot to appease the German Armed Forces, who had received very little coverage in the earlier film. Riefenstahl was then assigned to film the 1936 Olympic Games in Germany; *Olympia* was released in 1938 in two parts—Part I, *Festival of Nations* and Part II, *Festival of Beauty*—and was lauded widely as an art form. Riefenstahl's *Lowlands*, based on an eighteenth-century Spanish opera, pursued feverishly as an antidote to war horrors, came to a halt in 1944. Recurring illness, the deaths of her father and brother, and her marriage to Peter Jacob, a decorated major in the German army (after which Hitler had her placed under constant surveillance), all weighed heavily upon her. Known as "Hitler's Film Goddess," she was arrested and imprisoned after the war but was released and absolved in 1948 and in 1952 by the Allied commission of any collaborative action that warranted official action. In 1951 she reedited *The Blue Light* (released in 1952) and in 1954 she completed *Lowlands*, but she was unable to revive her film career and was ostracized by the film community. In 1956, Riefenstahl traveled to Africa and began *Black Cargo*, a color documentary on the slave trade that was not completed. Over the next fifteen years, she wrote three screenplays in Spain, toured Germany with the film *Olympia*, completed a remake of *The Blue Light* with two English screenwriters, made numerous trips to Africa, and published a volume of photographs, *The Last of the Nuba* (1968). She was commissioned by the *London Times* to photograph the 1972 Olympic Games in Munich and, in 1974, while attending the Film Festival in Telluride, Colorado, she was picketed by anti-Nazi groups. Returning to her interest in the Sudanese, she took up scuba diving in 1975, and published another volume of photography, *People of Kau* (1976). She began to focus on underwater coral life photography, and published *Coral Garden* in 1976. When Riefenstahl was 91, German director Ray Mueller released his film biography of her entitled *The Wonderful, Horrible Life of Leni Riefenstahl* (1993), coincendentally the same year the English translation of her autobiography, *Leni Riefenstahl: A Biography*, was published. In 2002, the year she was 100, she released a new film, *Underwater Impressions*, forty-five minutes culled from hours of deep-sea diving, and was feted with birthday celebrations and a retrospective of her work. She died in her sleep on September 8, 2003, at her home in Poecking, Germany, at the age of 101.

Riefenstahl's reputation as a film director is tainted by her association with Hitler and the Nazi Party, and the documentary she claims to have made only for aesthetic purposes was funded, equipped, staffed, and distributed by the Nazi Party. Almost universally vilified for her role in the propaganda effort to manipulate the emotions of German men and women, turning them toward solid support of Hitler and the Nazi Party, Riefenstahl has also been widely praised for her artistic techniques in *Triumph of the Will*. And although her justifications for having made the film are questionable, if not incredible, she established new benchmarks in cinematography and editing for the documentary that are worthy of observation and discussion.

Riefenstahl was asked to film the 6th Party Congress in Nuremberg, Germany, September 4–10, 1934, and was given cameras, equipment, and a crew of 172 people. The events to be filmed were primarily marches, speeches, rallies, in both day and night sequences, Hitler's arrival by plane and the tent camp soldiers performing their morning rituals as the city awakens. But her real task was to depict Hitler as Germany's heroic visionary who had unified all Germany, both geographically as well as ideologically, and was poised to lead the country into a glorious future. Accordingly, in Riefenstahl's opening scene, the little plane that brings him to Nuremberg is seen emerging from the clouds as Germany's savior descends from the heavens and is welcomed ecstatically by the populace. His slow progression in an open car to his hotel furnishes even more opportunities to suggest his eminence: a beautiful child offers him a garland of flowers, a cat stops licking itself to gaze at him, and sunlight glints off his upraised hand almost as a token of his divinity.

Her first real challenge lay in presenting Hitler as an attractive, forceful leader, which was accomplished through ingenious camera work that meticulously photographed him from below looking up, making him look taller and more imposing, and refrained from showing him alongside others who dwarfed him or made him appear insignificant. Early in the morning following his arrival, Riefenstahl's cameras take viewers on a tour of the city, of the Pegnitz River and the tent camps, where soldiers arise, eat, and play games. Next, we see a large group of Germans, dressed in regional costumes representing various geographical areas, who parade before Hitler demonstrating their support of him. At the first party congress, Deputy Rudolph Hess welcomes all the participants and introduces eleven other speakers, whose lengthy comments have been edited by Riefenstahl to a brief statement of each official's message. Following this, Hitler attends the Service Rally, where workers dignify manual labor by carrying shovels rather than weapons and they too, as representatives of their own regions, pledge allegiance to Hitler. The emphasis on unity continues as Hitler observes a flag ceremony that, aiming to connect the living with the dead, honors those who died in battle. At night, the storm troopers gather for a rally followed by a fireworks display.

On the next day, a youth rally was held in a huge arena, followed by an address by Hitler. Other events of the day were a lengthy military parade through Nuremberg, an outdoor rally and another speech by Hitler, who was surrounded by flags and standards, and later, a review of troops. On the succeeding day, an impressive war memorial ceremony was observed, followed by a lengthy parade of troops, coordinated for a show of strength. The agenda for the last night was a night congress in a huge indoor auditorium with a procession of flags and standards, climaxed by a lengthy speech by Hitler. The event ends with Deputy Hess declaring, "The party is Hitler, but Hitler is Germany, just as Germany is Hitler."

In a 1972 interview for the British Broadcasting Corporation, Riefenstahl recalled working eighteen hours a day in the cutting room for five months trying to make the film "interesting." Unconcerned with presenting chronological accuracy on the screen, she searched for an intuitive means of connecting events and impressions and, through editing, was able to achieve a pattern of rhythm and movement that transformed sixty-five hours of footage into two captivating hours of film. Riefenstahl relied on her ballet training to shape the film artistically, using her own sensibility to record the speeches at the time they were delivered, adding the crowd sounds, cheers, and music in the studio. A great many viewers felt that the most compelling element in the film was Herbert Windt's music, which was actually conducted in orchestra by Riefenstahl in order to synchronize it with the variable speeds of footage. Windt's music was of great variety, extending from

Wagnerian (Richard Wagner was the favorite composer of Hitler and also many party officials) and neo-Wagnerian themes to German folksongs, patriotic march music, and party anthems, which proved as potent for the psyche of German viewers as the portrayal of Hitler and the events of the congress itself (Berg-Pan 101).

In addition to rhythm, the guiding principle for Riefenstahl was movement, accomplished not only through editing but also creative camera work. First of all, she alternated scenes, moving from night to day and back again, from marches to rallies, and from storm troopers to Hitler youth. During Hitler's speeches, the camera never stops, traveling from various flattering low-angle shots of him, or his profile, always in close proximity to the swastika, iron cross, or the eagle (the party's symbol and his personal emblem), usually banked by an array of flags and standards, to shots of party officials and high-angle sweeping shots of throngs of supporters, slowing occasionally to catch low-angle shots of adoring troops. In military reviews, designed to display Germany's might to the world, cameras placed at strategic points show marching troops from assorted perspectives, intercut with Hitler's approval, and, in the case of the lengthy parade through Nuremberg, the privileged positions of the camera also revel in the architecture of the historic city as natives line the streets and seem to invite Hitler and his regime to flow into the city's history.

One of Riefenstahl's strong points is her filming of large groups of people, particularly in the camera movement from Hitler to the masses at the rallies or to the soldiers passing in review, not only for diversity's sake, but to emphasize one of the Nazi party's themes—the individual merging with the group. At the Hitler youth rally, the low-angle cameras linger meaningfully on enthusiastic and devoted fair-haired young men and children as an indication of the Aryan type of "supermen" the party sought to continue in its ideals. The famous panoramic shot of Hitler, SS Chief Heinrich Himmler and SA Chief Victor Lutzke moving as tiny figures between awe-inspiring formations of silent troops lined in precise rows, to the War Memorial for the laying of the ceremonial wreath in honor of Germany's fallen heroes, attests to Riefenstahl's unforgettable artistic skill and emotional impact in the integration of individuals and masses. During the parade of the flags, they were filmed slightly out of focus to give the appearance of individual flags streaming together. And, in the final congress, the huge gathering of people at the night meeting, amidst light and shadows and surrounded by countless eagles, iron crosses, and swastikas, cheering passionately for Hitler's final oration, furnishes an eerie finality to the film's conclusion.

As Riefenstahl, at Hitler's behest, had presented a deceptive view of a unified, powerful Germany in *Triumph of the Will* in 1936, she began, again at Hitler's request, to depict, untruly, Germany as a strong, unified country respectful of human equality in the Olympic Games. Actually, several athletes from Austria and France refused to compete in view of the inhuman treatment of Jewish persons in Germany. And, despite the fact that Hitler was forced by the president of the Olympic Committee to remove obscene anti-Semitic signs from the road leading to Olympic Village and include Jewish athletes on the German teams or forfeit both the Winter and Summer Olympics, Riefenstahl set about in *Olympia* to blend propaganda with art in a celebration of the beauty of athletic competition. *Olympia* was also designed to promote world harmony at the same time that Hitler, secretly planning war, had marched into the Rhineland (as a test) in defiance of the Locarno Treaty, which listed Germany's concessions to France following World War I, one of which was that the Rhineland must remain demilitarized (Berg-Pan 137–38). Hoping to impress the world, Hitler and the Nazi party had placed at Riefenstahl's disposal enormous resources, both financial and human. She had insisted that the film be produced by her company, to which Hitler agreed, suppressing the fact that Riefenstahl's company was merely a front for the Nazi party, and leading the Olympics Committee to believe that she was making this film all on her own. Primarily concerned with making the film according to her artistic vision, Riefenstahl began working sixteen-hour days while the party officials took care of the paper work.

While Riefenstahl's first interest in the film was the sports, which she had always enjoyed, numerous problems existed in the filming of sports. First, sporting events were considered unfit for accomplished filmmakers and relegated generally to newsreel cameramen. Second, the light sensitivity of film was limited, which, in turn, limited the depth of field. Activities involving constant movement, diving in water, leaping high in the air or throwing the javelin were nearly impossible for the camera to follow. Also, the Amateur Athletic Federation was emphatic that cameramen were not to interfere with the athletes, requiring them to remain a certain distance from the field.

Skilfull and inventive, Riefenstahl began to develop new camera techniques. To film the hundred-yard dash, she determined she needed a camera on rails beside the track to operate at a variable speed—always just ahead of the runner. Since no noise from the camera or from the rails could be allowed, and since there existed at that time no zoom lenses, engineers developed a camera whose whirring sound was barely audible even for close-ups. To reconstruct the movement of a horse and rider in competition, Riefenstahl used an automatic camera that would be placed on a bag filled with feathers situated on the saddle of another horse. She also placed small automatic cameras in baskets, attached to balloons and released to drift over the stadium as they captured small portions of the events. Also, she planned an overhead shot of the opening ceremony from the airship Hindenburg, summoned to be over the stadium at the exact minute, but the effort was unsuccessful because of rain. In addition, Riefenstahl had a special camera adapted for filming underwater that would allow her cameraman to dive alongside the Olympic diver, filming him as they descended into the water, then often changing the lens at the bottom of the pool. For filming above the water, she affixed a small camera on the side of a rubber raft, which could be propelled alongside the swimmer (Infeld 123–24).

With regard to the finished product, Riefenstahl reached the same decision she had with *Triumph of the Will*—to ignore chronological events and follow her artistic sense of movement and rhythm. She was of the opinion that sports films were dull and she, clearly, did not want hers to be dull. As one interested in form above content, Riefenstahl thought the beauty of the form should incite interest in the content, and her duty as director was to alternate the sound and image to produce total impact on the audience.

Having shot over one million feet of film, Riefenstahl was faced with editing the footage into two films not to exceed two hours each. Part 1, *Olympia Festival of Nations*, dwells on the competitive spirit, whereas Part 2, *Festival of Beauty*, accents the beauty of the human body, both demonstrating Riefenstahl's artistic beliefs. The prologue, filmed in Greece, was aimed at establishing a link between the Olympic Games in ancient Greece and those in 1936 Berlin; also, through its photography of classical ruins and sculptures in Greece, the prologue began the theme of beauty carried over into the Berlin Olympics by way of Riefenstahl's worship of the human body. Shots of nude women dancing in forests and exercising on a beach announced her artistic appreciation of beautiful bodies. Most fascinated by the male physique, however, Riefenstahl had captured every move of the runners carrying the torch from Greece to Germany; and as the last one, a slender young Nordic German, entered the stadium to light the Olympic flame, she created an unforgettable cinematic experience in filming that event. At the track-and-field competition, Riefenstahl was captivated by Jesse Owens, the black athlete from the United States, whose expressive face and strong slender body was so admired by her that she devoted much film footage to shots of him. When the photogenic Owens captured the medals for the hundred-meter dash, the running broad jump and the two-hundred-meter dash (setting a new record), Riefenstahl seemed justified in selecting him as the prime athlete in these events. Typically, Hitler flew into a rage and refused to be photographed with Owens, leaving her film as the only evidence of Germany's goodwill at the Olympic Games. Despite Hitler's unbridled delight with Germany's wins, drawing censure from the Olympic Committee, Riefenstahl shows little interest in winners, delighting only in the grace and beauty of the human body.

Much footage in Part 1 was also lavished on the grueling twenty-six-mile marathon race, specifically on Kitei Son, who entered under the flag of Japan and triumphed over fifty-five other runners to win. Always avoiding straight reporting, Riefenstahl shot the small, thin, bowlegged runner by accentuating his pace by showing the passing scenery in the background, his body in relief against the sky and surrounding fields, and by showing him in silhouette. After the victory of Son, who joined Owens, both of whom were living proof of the fallacy of Hitler's racial theory, Riefenstahl filmed the pole vaulters until dark, at which time she focused on the empty stadium, ringed with flags and the Olympic flame blazing.

Part 2, *Festival of Beauty*, less organized than Part 1, concentrates largely on team sports—athletes lounging in chairs, young women practicing gymnastics, low-angle shots of male gymnasts on parallel bars filmed in slow motion against the sky. Winners of contests are rarely mentioned in this section, as Riefenstahl overlooks the competition to create beautiful forms. Her famous diving sequence shows anonymous bodies flying into the sky and dipping into the water, the camera tarrying over a diver's maneuvers, slowing the motion so he appears to be flying. Soon, Riefenstahl underexposes the bodies, and we see silhouettes against the cloudy sky as they propel themselves with complex precision. Part 2 comes to an end abruptly, with shots of various flags and the Olympic bell, and then fadeout.

Riefenstahl worked eighteen months meticulously editing the footage for its premiere on Hitler's birthday, April 20, 1938. *Olympia* received excellent reviews in Germany, but since the world had begun to see Hitler as a monster, international reviewers were very critical. Reviews in the United States, while generally favorable, concluded the film was not only an interesting factual account of the 1936 Olympic Games but an outstanding artistic documentary as well as propaganda for the Nazis.

AGNES VARDA

The future "Grandmother of the New Wave" was born May 30, 1928, in Ixelles, Belgium, to Eugene Jean, an engineer, and Christiane Pasquet Varda. Amazingly unaware of the world of cinema, Varda studied art history at the Ecole du Louvre. As she was interested in a more creative career, she studied photography in night classes and after qualifying as a photographer worked for ten years (1951–1961) as official photographer at the Theatre National Populaire in Paris. Established during the years after the end of German occupation, it aimed to attract large groups of people to a vibrant theater. Varda's progression from still photography to cinema seems almost inevitable at this time, considering her concern with the passage of time and the struggle of life against it.

At the Theatre National Populaire, Varda met actors who would play roles in her first film, made with a small inheritance and the encouragement of friends. *La Pointe Courte* (1954), named for a fishing village outside Sete, and whose fishermen play themselves, was well received by the critics writing for the magazine *Cahiers du Cinema* under the editorship of the legendary realist spokesman, Andre Bazin. During the eight years following the completion of *La Pointe Courte*, Varda continued her work in photography and filmed experimental, short films. For the French Tourist Office, she made *O Saisons, o chateaux*, a documentary of castle footage intercut with shots of fashion models posing as exotic birds; also for the French Tourist office, in 1958 she directed *Du cote de la cote*, another documentary focusing on the French Riviera. Later in this same year, Varda finished a documentary, *L'Opera Mouffe*, in which a pregnant woman surveys a poor Paris neighborhood, focusing on everyday occurrences on a market street, particularly food, couples strolling, individuals shopping, and groups of inebriated people.

In 1962, Varda returned to the feature-length film with *Cleo From 5 to 7*, in which a young woman awaits the results of her medical tests for cancer. This well-received film was followed by *Salut les cubains* (1964), a documentary containing various photographs Varda had made of Cubans and their activities; she combined about 1500 hundred of these photographs into a film of continuous still pictures. For the film, she was awarded the Bronze Lion at the 1964 Venice Film Festival. Varda's next film, *Le bonheur* (Happiness), an experimentally pictorial film, received in 1965 the Silver Bear from the Berlin Film Festival, the Prix Louis Delluc in France, and the David O. Selznick Award in America. Varda followed this accomplishment with *Les Creatures*, in which she used tinted footage to add to the emotions within the film, and two political films—*Loin du Vietnam* (Far From Vietnam), containing various criticisms of America's involvement in Vietnam, and *Black Panthers*, a documentary sympathetically portraying the activists of the radical Black Panther organization. For this film, she was awarded the first prize from the Oberhausen Film Festival.

Varda's first English-language film, *Lions Love*, finished in 1969 and, sporting characteristics of an improvised underground film, garnered mixed reviews. She then made *Daguerrotypes* (1975), a documentary concerning a two-block area on a street in Paris named Daguerre, in honor of the nineteenth-century French painter and photographer who invented the daguerrotype. Varda's camera seeks out the details of the lives of those people who live and work in this small area, and in doing so also pays them a tribute. Following this documentary, Varda turned to a feature film and one with clear feminist concerns—*L'Une chante l'autre pas*—released in the United States as *One Sings, The Other Doesn't*. The story of two women who remain friends through fifteen years of struggles to survive was applauded for its content and also for its film techniques. In 1981, in Los Angeles, where she had negotiated a contract with EMI Studios for a project that stalled and was eventually forsaken, Varda made *Mur Murs* (*Mural Murals*). On a very small budget, she shot footage of various murals as well as conducted interviews with many of the artists. She also made *Documenteur*, an observation of Los Angeles from a French woman in a strange country.

One of Varda's most applauded films, *Sans toit ni loi* (*Without Roof or Law*) (1986), released in the United States as *Vagabond*, another pictorial film of a teenager's last days during a journey through the French countryside, assumes a documentary-like perspective. The grim narrative, supplied by people she had met in her strange meanderings, arrives at no explanation for the girl's behavior, and Varda treats the girl's emotional and social problems in a matter-of-fact tone. For *Vagabond*, Varda was awarded the Venice Film Festival's golden Lion and France's prestigious Prix Melies.

Sandrine Bonnaire, who played the teenager, was awarded a Cesar (a European Oscar) for best actress. During this productive decade, Varda also directed *Jane B par Agnes V*.

The loss of her husband, French director Jacques Demy, in 1990 has imbued Varda's work throughout the 1990s. *Jacquot de Nantes* (1991), a tribute to Demy, attempts through his memories as he had told her of them to recreate his past. In addition to Jacquot, she released *L'Univers de Jacques Demy* (*The Universe of*

Jacques Demy) in 1993, and in 1994, *Les 101 Nuits* (*The Hundred and One Nights*), a celebration of the centenary of cinema.

In 1955, the year that Varda released *La Pointe Courte*, French cinema was undergoing a crisis, as the younger filmmakers were struggling to free themselves from the big-budget productions of the studio system that had continued from prewar cinema. The most significant stylistic influences upon the younger generation of filmmakers came from the French documentary trends in the fifties and from the films of independent filmmakers outside the studio system. The *Nouvelle vague*, or New Wave, as the young filmmakers and their films came to be called, initiated radically new techniques, essentially designed to answer questions of film authorship and to infuse new life into a stagnant cinema. In 1951, a prestigious journal, *Cahiers du cinema* (literally "cinema notebooks"), had been founded by French film theorists Andre Bazin and Jacques Coniol-Valcroze, who gathered around them young critics who were to become the directors of the New Wave. The Cinema Notebooks favored the use of mise-en-scene, as opposed to montage, and emphasized the long take and in-depth composition that denoted a creation of mood and atmosphere through camera placement and movement. The dominant position of New Wave filmmakers is that film should call attention to itself and its unique language which emphasizes cinematic devices of which only film is capable. The Cinema Notebooks also advocated a "policy of authors," the idea that the film distinctly mirrors the director's "signature"—his or her preoccupations, themes, or techniques. The knowledgeable French critics of the New Wave, who had devoted years to watching American films, discerned evidence of personal expression in the works of certain American film directors, including Orson Welles, Alfred Hitchcock, John Ford, and Howard Hawks.

Although Varda's first film, the documentary, *La Pointe Courte*, earned little money at French box offices, critics noted its pictorial composition and documentary-like narrative. Not one of the core group of critics who contributed to the Cinema Notebooks, Varda nevertheless articulated their common concerns in this film that anticipated the New Wave that was to flourish in the 1960s. Also, the originality of her photography and her use of color, light, and structure produce images that achieve narrative content through their relative relationship to one another and to the geographical location. In *La Pointe Courte*, the small struggling fishing village of the same name is the backdrop against which a young couple walk on the beaches and discuss their failing marriage. Each shot is structured to emphasize the progress being made in their discussions through the visual juxtaposition of one to the other and to their surroundings (Smith 20). Varda's film rejects traditional editing techniques, developing instead two storylines, with the story of the couple playing against the second storyline, which details the life of the village in a semi-documentary manner.

Varda's preoccupation with people and places that has come to characterize her films (Smith 61) issues from a long-standing belief that "place has a profound effect on character and perception" (Smith 60). In a 1961 interview, Varda said, "I believe that people are made not only of the places they were brought up, but of those they love. I believe the environment lives in us, directs us"(Cinema 61, S91). *Cleo From 5 to 7*, her first feature film, details two hours in the life of a beautiful pop singer who awaits the results of her biopsy. The two-hour film, whose reel time approximates real time, is divided into two parts: the first, wherein Cleo sees a tarot reader with a disturbing message, returns home to her spacious flat, is visited by her lover, and later, begins a rehearsal. Throughout this first half, we see Cleo, surrounded by mirrors, gazing at herself, admiring her own beauty while thinking of the ugliness of death, and continuing to see herself as others see her. Neither her secretary nor her lover takes her illness seriously; her insensitive manager ironically gives her a new song to rehearse that suggests her own situation. At this point, she rips off her elaborate blonde wig, bemoans her "doll" face, abruptly ends the rehearsal, and exits. Part two of the film details Cleo's second walk through Paris streets as a contrast with her walk in part one. She wears dark glasses, hoping to remain unrecognized and at the same time suggesting a more sobering look at the images in her environment. To emphasize the change, Varda's camera allows the audience to see the images that reflect Cleo's internal change, specifically depicting Cleo within the Paris mise-en-scene and not, as in the first half of the film, merely following Cleo. As she observes people in the street and changes from "woman seen to a woman seeing" (Lewis 229), her fear of dying compels her to look outside herself to the lives of others. Wandering through a bar, Cleo pays attention to various individuals there and listens to bits of conversation. She visits an old friend, Dorothee, who earns money while modeling nude for art students and ponders the dissimilarity in their perceptions of such actions. When she meets Antoine, a soldier on leave from the Algerian war, she finds him interesting and realizes that her outlook has changed.

Cleo's new perception of herself, seen in her perception of her surroundings that the audience sees through her eyes, is developed throughout the film in a literary manner Varda refers to as "cinecriture," or cinewriting. Having coined the term herself, Varda uses it not to indicate the work of the scriptwriter, but of the filmmaker: A well-written film is also well filmed, the actors are well chosen, so are the locations. The cutting, the movement, the points of view, the rhythm of filming, and editing have been felt and considered in a way a writer chooses the depth of meaning of sentences, the type of words, number of adverbs, paragraphs, asides, chapters which advance the story or break the flow, etc. In writing it's called style. In the cinema, style is cinecriture (Smith 14).

Varda's next feature film, *Le bonheur*, tells the story of a happily married couple through repeated images of family togetherness that suggest happiness. Visually stunning, her first color film, denoting a strong interest in color, shows every image bathed in brilliant light and color combinations that, along with Mozart's music on the soundtrack, depicts a stylized representation of marriage. Of the film, Varda has said, "I tried, with a very simple subject, to do Impressionist painting" (Lewis 233). The film pictorially tells the story of a man, happily married, who falls in love with a postal clerk in another town, and conducts an extramarital affair with her for a time. He confides his happiness to his wife, who before long is found drowned, and his mistress replaces the wife in the images of family happiness. Through the Impressionist pictorial images of family happiness, Varda presents clichés of happiness, without any real character insight or depth, any visible conflict or struggle—those wherein the individuals are interchangeable as she appears to suggest that the clichés of happiness may constitute happiness.

One Sings, the Other Doesn't, an influential film set in the time period just following the 1976 legalization of abortion in France and during an intense period of feminine consciousness raising, reflects Varda's concerns as it renders the political activity of two women in the women's movement. The narrative follows the friendship between Pauline, a rebellious teenage school girl who calls herself Apple, and Suzanne, a downtrodden mother of two and mistress of Jerome, a suicidal artist. Apple extracts money from her parents under false pretenses for Suzanne's abortion and later provides emotional support for Suzanne when Jerome hangs himself. Suzanne and her children take refuge at her parents' farm, where with great difficulty she acquires secretarial skills and eventually goes to work at a Family Planning Clinic. More outgoing and dynamic than Suzanne, Apple becomes a songwriter and singer who challenges various audiences as a spokesperson for the Female Condition. The two women, whose personalities lead them to separate contributions to the movement, correspond with each other largely by postcards for a period of ten years. At a demonstration outside the courtroom trial of four women accused of procuring an abortion for the daughter of one of them—which actually occurred in 1972—Suzanne and Apple are reunited.

While the film extols the friendship and devotion of two women committed to the women's moment and one another, it continues for Varda an exploration she had begun earlier in films that seeks to discern the identities of women. Cleo From 5 to 7 clearly shows Cleo progressing from a woman who sees herself as her male managers see her to a woman who begins to see her world and her situation in it authentically. In 1975, when Varda was asked to prepare an eight-minute film for television on the subject, "What it means to be a woman," she centered her issues on women's bodies and the contradictions involved in ways of looking at them. In One Sings, the Other Doesn't, Varda addresses not only "what it means to be a woman but what it means to be a feminist" (Smith 107). Many of the challenges Apple tosses to her audience reflecting her experience of being a woman come about as a result of her meeting Jerome, Suzanne's lover. Jerome, who insists that he photographs the "truth" in women, exhibits his pictures of women and all, including Suzanne, seem tired and sad. As he deems Apple unfit for photography because he could not "get through" to her, and rejects the image she projects for the one he wants to coerce from her, Apple responds, "It feels as if I'm not a real woman." She proceeds from this juncture to develop and construct an identity with which she is comfortable and project it throughout the remainder of the film. The idea of a male-constructed image of a woman as a victim is targeted by

Varda in the character of Jerome, who contends that because Apple insists upon projecting her own image, she is not what he wants.

Apple's self-image is put to the test in regard to her relationship with Darius, an Iranian whom she marries following a career setback and accompanies to Iran. There, Darius, her seemingly liberated husband, seems to shift back to the role of traditional, repressive husband—a position Apple refuses to accept. Soon after their return to France, Apple gives birth to their son, whom Darius intends to take back to Iran. At their departure, Apple is again pregnant and in a few months gives birth to a daughter she dotes upon. Suzanne marries her colleague at the Family Planning Center, and both women are content with their lives.

Vagabond (*Sans toit ni loi*), perceived by critics at its release in 1985 as Varda's masterpiece, begins with the death of Mona, whose body is found frozen in a ditch, and proceeds to reconstruct her identity through the flashbacks of people who met her during the last weeks of her life. A female narrator begins speaking as Mona's corpse is placed in a body bag, and police investigators, who take measurements and record statistics, determine, despite wine stains upon her body and nearby objects, that she died of natural causes. The narrative voice that announces a determination to inquire into the life of Mona indicates another documentary-like film that is ambiguously tied to certain real-life events. The film itself is known to have partially originated from a meeting Varda herself had with a person named Settina, and its original conception leaned more toward a general film about young homeless persons.

The people who encounter Mona during the last days of her life know her only through their own subjective perceptions of her; consequently, the film reflects their preoccupations and shows very little about Mona. Throughout the film, we see Mona, who, upon being asked what she does, replies, "I move," and we witness her compulsive moving away from people and relationships, beyond social bonds, and ultimately to her own death. While the narrator insists that "no traces were found" that would link Mona to family or a life before her wandering, the film actually portrays traces of Mona left on those who had known her. Smith divides these people according to gender, contending that roughly, "there are two different ways of seeing Mona" (Smith 118). Most of the men view her as a potential sexual or romantic partner according to the image they have of a woman in her predicament. The goatherd, who offers her a place to live and work, and Asouna, the Tunisian vineyard worker with "kind eyes" is forced to withdraw his offer to her of a place to live and work because of his fellow Moroccans. Of the women, Yolande sees in Mona and her sleeping boyfriend an image of the closeness she desires but cannot attain with her own boyfriend, Paolo; while Mrs. Landier, a kind of patroness, seems to find in Mona what she fears in herself. All who come to know Mona, whether on a shallow level as with the men or as the women, who reach a level of frustration from Mona's "refusal to conform" to their views of her, eventually reject her (Smith 126).

Interestingly, *Vagabond* bears certain resemblances to Orson Welles' Citizen Kane, in that both films concentrate upon a search for a character's identity that involves a reconstruction of the character based upon the impressions of those persons who knew the character in question. And, while the meaning of "rosebud" in Citizen Kane, presumed to provide a key to Kane's identity, is eventually divulged to the audience but not Thompson, the reporter/detective, the attempt at the reconstruction of Mona, according to those individuals who had encountered her during her last days, reflects the impossibility of knowing Mona, except subjectively, and the inevitable absence of any knowledge of her identity.

Exempting the cinetracts and documentaries made following this important film, the next significant film Varda made is The Gleaners and I (2000), an intriguing documentary about gleaners, both ancient and modern, and their current status in French society. Varda sports a digital video camera, newly purchased and focused on capturing her images that make a personal statement about her own artistic and aesthetic gleaning of images, and the aging hands that have "little time left." Awarded the Melies Prize for Best French Film of 2000 by the French Union of French Critics, The Gleaners and I seems, at first, a continued effort to bridge the gap between feature film and documentary. But it may be more specifically seen to mark a return by Varda to the documentary format of her early years in the New Wave; in fact, Varda herself relished the idea of making this film as a way to get back to the early short films and to film herself—in other words, getting involved as a filmmaker (Anderson).

Early on in the filming, Varda became convinced that she had no statement to make, because the film entails "meeting real people and discovering with them what they express about the subject, building the subject through real people" (Anderson). In her homage to the tradition of gleaning, the ancient tradition of women picking up scraps of food after a harvest, as memorialized in the painting by nineteenth-century French Jean Francois Millet, Varda extends the "humble gesture of picking things up from the painter ground" into contemporary French society to gypsies who glean potato fields, to those who pick grapes left in vineyards to rot, to individuals who salvage refuse from garbage, to those who make art projects from recycled goods. All of Varda's people speak of their lives and their economic situations. One of her most interesting persons is Francois, who rails at the enormous waste in the country and boasts that he has lived "one hundred percent from garbage" for the last ten years, never buying anything, finding food and clothing in the street. Another is a chef, who cannot afford to buy spices and seasonings, and is compelled to search the fields for useful herbs. Yet another, an individual with a Master of Arts degree, comes to the city early every morning to gather fruit and produce from the street, retiring to his home that evening to his private school, where he teaches foreigners to read and write French, free of charge. In her film, Varda meets, films, and talks with individuals whose livelihood depends upon gleaning, and others, mostly men, who, in a land of waste, glean for principle's sake. Because those she met freely and honestly spoke of themselves while she gleaned images and emotions from them for her film, she included images and emotions from herself. The shots of her hair and her hands that play with the trucks indicate her advancing years and establish her own perception of her aging, bringing subjectivity to an objective documentary in the manner of many of her documentaries throughout the nearly fifty years of her work. *Cleo From 5 to 7* incorporates both subjectivity and objectivity in the way Varda employs time, and in *Vagabond*, in the purely subjective responses to Mona that provide no objective insight into Mona's identity. Varda insists this film reflects the relationship she wants with filming: "editing, meeting people, giving the film shape, a specific shape, in which both the objective and subjective are present" (Anderson). For Varda, merging society's facts with her own feelings about the facts include specific organizational objectives that do not end with the completion of the film. She then takes the film to festivals and various cities, showing it "to peasants, in villages and other places," who love it because "it deals with something they know" (Anderson).

LINA WERTMULLER

Born Arcangela Felice Assunta Wertmuller von Elgg Spanol von Braueich on August 14, 1928, in Rome, Italy, to Federico, a lawyer, and Maria Santa Maria Wertmuller, Lina Wertmuller was interested in film from an early age. Her father encouraged her to study law, but in successive Catholic schools, she found the first principles of her catechism loathsome. She quarreled with priests and nuns about the idea of God's creation of humanity and its endowment with free will, knowing (as HE is omniscient) that the many who will stray from the good path will fall into hell, an already constructed eternal misery. She felt so strongly about this point that she broke with the Church.

She enrolled in the Academy of Theatre in Rome and following her graduation in 1951, she traveled all over Italy for a year with Maria Signorelli's puppet troupe. For the next ten years, she labored as an actress, stage manager, set designer, publicist, and writer for theater, radio, and television. During this time, she collaborated with the exceptional writing team of Garinei and Giovannini writing musical comedies for the Italian television. For many years, she worked with them on more than a dozen shows while continuing to work in television and theatre and when she began making films. Of the two plays she wrote for the stage, one of them—*Two and Two Are No Longer Four* (1968)—a very successful production, brought to Wertmuller talented partners for a lifetime. Directed by Franco Zeffirelli, the play displayed the detailed art work of Enrico Job, whom Wertmuller has since married and who is now art director on all her films, and Giancarlo Giannini, one of the finest stage actors in Italy, who has since become her leading male actor. Flora Mastroianni, Wertmuller's friend from convent school days and wife of actor Marcello Mastroianni, introduced Wertmuller to Federico Fellini, who was so impressed with her that he asked her to become his assistant on $8\frac{1}{2}$ in 1962. Using some of Fellini's crew, she directed her first feature film, *I basilischi* (*The Lizards*), in 1963. Wertmuller's films that followed are controversial, to say the least, as the viewing public as well as critics have interpreted them in radically inconsistent ways.

Ferlita insists that her "protagonist is always the common man, a citizen of the third world that every society, even the most developed, nourishes in its midst" (111). Her topics—honor, survival and sex—are presented essentially through the Italian comic film tradition that tends to unite humor with a cynicism that indicates a desperate need "to survive in the face of overwhelming obstacles" (*Italian Cinema* 145). Often through grotesque comedy, Wertmueller posits capitalist against proletariat, though concealed by allegory and sex, where characters must choose between honor and mere survival. To make matters more confusing, the tone of her films shifts unexpectedly from brutal to funny to heart-wrenching at any moment, keeping viewers off balance.

Although Wertmuller has written screenplays for and directed about thirty films, four films from the middle period of her work are considered by many critics to be the most appealing. With *The Seduction of Mimi* (1972), Wertmuller achieved fame internationally in her depiction of Mimi (Giancarlo Giannini), a poor Sicilian laborer who defies his frigid wife, the government, and the Mafia to support a Communist candidate in an election. Losing his job, he goes north to Turin, finds work in a metals factory, joins the Communist Party, and falls in love with Fiore (Mariangela Melato). Before long, he is transferred back home and discovers that his wife, Rosalia, has attempted to shed the repressive Sicilian values by venturing out in the world, finding an industrial job, having an affair with a married man, and becoming pregnant. Mimi holds on to Fiore, their child, and Rosalia, but as much as he craves sexual freedom, he cannot allow the same independence to his wife. Consequently, he reverts to the traditional Sicilian vendetta: convinced that his wife has betrayed him, he forces himself to sleep with Amalia, whose husband is the father of his wife's child, and she too becomes pregnant. Mimi confronts Amalia's husband, who is shot by a Mafia thug, but Mimi is convicted of the crime and is sent to prison. At his release, he is compelled to support both Rosalia and Amalia and all their children by working for the very Mafia he once tried to escape.

One of Wertmuller's enduring themes—the inability of ideological change to affect deeply ingrained behavior patterns—appears in *The Seduction of Mimi*, whose title describes the political seduction of Mimi, who modernizes his political views but cannot escape his "outdated code of masculine honor" (Landy 356). In the development of the connections between sex and politics, Wertmuller uses the traditional grotesque comedy, much in the manner of her mentor Federico Fellini, in that the authority figures are comically depicted with moles on their faces, and the romance between Mimi and Fiore is carried out through mime and music from Verdi's opera, *La Traviata*. Controversial scenes in the film include the bizarre fish-eye lens shot of Mimi's seduction of the hugely obese Amalia, an action that results from Mimi's absurd efforts to reclaim his honor.

Love and Anarchy (1973) notes the contradictions between love and politics when they unite. Tunin (Giancarlo Gianinni) is a person who has been

"radicalized" by having witnessed the brutal murder of his friend and goes to
Rome to assassinate Mussolini. Once there, he goes to the meet with Salome, a
prostitute who has been cultivating a professional relationship with Spatoletto,
chief of Mussolini's secret service. In the bordello, which for Wertmuller, represents Italy, Tunin meets and falls in love with Tripolina, who, in an effort to
save his life, does not wake him on the appointed day. Maddened by having
overslept, he shoots at a platoon of police and is captured, tortured, and murdered
in prison by Spatoletto's henchmen. Wertmuller's comments upon the demands
made upon Tunin by love and politics, as suggested in the title, reflect ironically
upon the macho image associated with Spatoletto (and Mussolini) and the com-
plexities within the brothel/Italy, implying that neither love nor anarchy can lead
to the end of Fascism in Italy. *Swept Away by an Unusual Destiny in the Blue Sea
of August* (1975) depicts two individuals trapped on a desert island far from civilization and its restrictive or delimiting influences. In Wertmuller's film, Raffaella
(Mariangela Melato), a haughty, pampered Northern Italian woman is marooned
on a deserted island with Gennarino (Giancarlo Giannini), a sexist, Communist
Sicilian sailor who, as a Southern Italian, sees women merely as sexual objects.
Raffaella, convinced of her superiority to Gennarino, her servant on the tropical
cruise, berates and insults him, and demands that he accompany her on a short
trip in less than favorable weather. They become lost from the ship and, drifting
aimlessly, end up on a deserted island, where she, attempting to reestablish her
preeminence, discovers quickly that he is acutely aware that she cannot survive
without him.

No other Wertmuller film has caused more heated debates than *Swept Away*.
Women in large numbers have deplored what they perceive as her offensive representation of women in the film. In the state of nature outside society, Gennarino,
stronger and more skilled in survival, and Raffaella reverse places as she becomes
subordinate to him, and eventually comes to totally accept his curses, blows, and
total domination of her. Gennarino falls in love with her, desiring to return to
society to test Raffaella's love, while she, though dodging rescuers, knows that
their love affair could flourish only beyond social barriers. True enough, after
their rescue, Raffaella reverts to her original behavior, and prefers her husband to
Gennarino—proving, according to Wertmuller, "that social class always determines the outcome of personal relationships" (Landy 61). Wertmuller's primary
interest here is political, rather than sexual. Insisting that her allegory "places a
man in the role of the exploited class and a woman in the role of the exploiting
class, while feminist critics would prefer to see all men of whatever class as ex-
ploiters of all women" (Landy 363), it seems to go without saying that Wertmuller,
though interested in the political aspects and implications of the film, was clearly
aware of its contents as an assurance of a large audience. But it was with *Seven
Beauties* (1976) that Wertmuller directed a film that has been hailed by many as
a masterpiece. Employing her famous tragic-comic tone, she goes far beyond class
relationships into the concentration camps of World War II and moral issues
of survival. Through the use of flashbacks, the film's narrative involves a dandy

whose nickname is "Pasqualino Seven Beauties" (Giancarlo Gianinni) who lives off the labors of his seven, plump sisters, one of whom dances in a music hall and becomes a prostitute. Pasqualino believes, much like Mimi, that to preserve his "honor" he must kill the man who enticed her into a life of dishonor. After the deed is accomplished through a series of serio-comic actions, he is arrested, tried, and eventually ends up in an asylum, where he rapes another patient. Compelled to join the army, he deserts, is soon captured by the Nazis and committed to a concentration camp. There, he seduces the female commandant, who then forces him to kill his friend in order to save his own life.

Seven Beauties follows Wertmuller's thematic and stylistic patterns in that its nonlinear, flashback-laden narrative tracing Pasqualino's path from his crime of honor in Naples to the scene of German mass extermination in the death camp ultimately suggests a parallel between the two. Pasqualino's antics as a Neapolitan dandy revolted by his sister's vulgarity, his absurd dismemberment of the body of her pimp, and his theft of food from a German farmhouse, following his desertion from the army, are all measured comically against his dehumanized situation in the death camp. Some critics lamented Wertmuller's mixture of comic and tragic inflections, claiming that she implied an "equation of petty crime and mass murder" (Landy 363), but Marcia Landy maintains that only through the mixture of tragic and comic could Wertmuller convince viewers of the state to which Pasqualino has been reduced (363).

Wertmuller's depiction of a man whose instincts for survival at whatever cost contains, along with a flair for comedy and satire that reflects Fellini's influence, many of her thematic concerns of other films: the vain, chauvinistic Neapolitan who hangs on to an antiquated sense of "honor," the complications that arise from a combination of sex and politics, and the relentless inclusion of cruelty, which Wermulller maintains resides inherently in human nature, and should be depicted. Despite the fact that Wertmuller clearly indicates that Pasqualino's survival is not worth the price he pays, other characters manifest beliefs that seem to rate the approval of the director. Prisoners who refuse to submit to the Nazi regime and are killed are depicted heroically; the anarchist who believes in "man in disorder" (Landy 363); Pasqualino's friend who understands Italy's implicit responsibility in the Holocaust in its alliance with Germany are all placed on a level above the Neapolitan, who sees his sexual prowess as his salvation. And, when Pasqualino returns home and discovers that all his sisters, as well as his young fiancée, have become prostitutes in order to survive, he realizes that their actions mirror his own. Our final view of him is of someone a bit confused, pondering life's priorities and trying to understand the significance of the recent events in his life.

5

Newcomers

SOFIA COPPOLA

Born May 14, 1971, in New York to Francis Ford and Eleanor Coppola, Sofia Carmina Coppola spent most of her childhood in Napa Valley, California, where her parents owned a vineyard. Because of her father's directorial fame and her mother's interest in documentary filmmaking, she seemed almost destined to take up film directing at some point. Sofia made her acting debut shortly after her birth as the infant in the baptism scene at the end of Coppola's acclaimed film *The Godfather*. She and her brothers, Gian Carlo and Roman, frequently accompanied their father to locations where he was filming, most notably the Philippines, during his agonized production of *Apocalypse Now*, in 1976–1979. Using the name "Domino," she also had bit parts in her father's early 1980s films— *The Outsiders*, *Rumble Fish*, and *The Cotton Club*. On Memorial Day weekend in 1986, Sofia's brother Gian Carlo was killed in a boating accident in Maryland.

In 1989, Sofia and her father wrote a segment "Life Without Zoe" for Woody Allen's 1989 trilogy, *New York Stories*, a collaboration between Allen, Coppola, and Martin Scorsese. While directing his next film, *The Godfather III*, Coppola cast Sofia in a role intended for Winona Ryder, who had unexpectedly withdrawn from the film because of illness. Critics screamed noisily. Thereafter, Sofia avoided taking classes at the Californa Institute of the Arts, and cohosted a 1993 cable TV show, *Hi-Octane*, with her friend Zoe Cassavetes, daughter of legendary director/actor John Cassavetes.

She became a photographer and worked for *French Vogue* and *Allure*. Frustrated with her life because she felt creatively stifled, she began, with a friend from the primary grades, a clothing company, Milk Fed, which became a huge success in Tokyo, allowing her financial freedom. Eventually, Sofia's interest in music and fashion took her back to film. Through her music friends, she met her husband,

Spike Jonze, and became acquainted with Jeffrey Eugenides' novel *The Virgin Suicides*. Drawn to the story of five sisters in an affluent suburb who commit suicide one by one, and hearing that a screenplay was being written to include additions of sex and violence to the narrative, Sofia quietly began writing a screenplay of her own. She eventually became the director of the film, and the result was an acclaimed first effort. During Sofia's frequent trips to Tokyo with her business partner, she conceived an idea for a screenplay about two lonely Americans who meet in the Park-Hyatt hotel bar and develop a close friendship. The film this screenplay became, *Lost in Translation* (2003), received glowing reviews as well as awards from the New York Critics Award for best director, and the Academy Award for best screenplay.

When Sofia Coppola read *The Virgin Suicides* she immediately wanted to re-create the story on film in order to draw on the innocence and sweetness she found in the book, and all the while try to visually reproduce the elegance of Eugenides' writing. Coppola retains much of the spirit of the book about the boys and their view of the girls through her skillful creation of ethereal images that define first love. As the story of the radiant but doomed Lisbon sisters evolves from the memory of a group of now-grown men who, after twenty-five years, are still pondering the mystery of the girls' taking of their own lives, Coppola bathes the screen with dreamy memories of an idealized past. Adolescence revisited—the 1970s neighborhood setting, the girls' austere parents, and the girls' descent into despair is viewed through the eyes of the men who were adolescents at that time, and is presented through their unrealistic, soft-focus recollections. The film's setting, Detroit's Grosse Pointe area, its dying trees marked for extinction, suggests a decaying suburbia that becomes the crucible wherein all the participants in the action are tested as they proceed toward the shattering event. The "first one to go"—in the words of the narrator, Giovanni Ribisi, whose words echo the collective memory of the boys—is the youngest, Cecilia, whose failed suicide prompts the girls' parents to invite the boys over for a social gathering in the den. Abruptly, she excuses herself, goes upstairs and throws herself out the window, impaling herself upon the fence beneath it, and initiating a pattern of renewed restriction and frustrating the boys' efforts to learn more about the girls. Heartthrob Trip Fontaine wangles the parents' consent to take lovely fourteen-year-old Lux to the school prom, and selects eager escorts (the boys) for the other sisters as well. But when Trip leaves Lux asleep and she misses curfew, the girls are removed from school and secluded in the house. Forced to burn her favorite albums, Lux surreptitiously begins to seek other outlets—namely, wantonly meeting delivery boys at night on her roof—all of which is observed by the boys, whose telescope and binoculars are trained on the Lisbon house searching for clues of the girls' existence.

Eventually, the boys phone the girls and transmit musical greetings with Todd Rundgren's "Hello, It's Me"; the girls answer from their hi-fi with Gilbert O'Sullivan's "Alone Again (Naturally)." The boys send more music to the girls, who respond with Carole King's "So Far Away"—plaintive messages of solitary longing wafting across the airwaves. Soon after, the four Lisbon girls take their own lives, leaving the boys frozen in time with their adolescent perceptions of the girls.

The description of the girls is actually the boys' imaginings of their lives that envision them as prisoners of their unreasonably conservative parents—an intolerable situation that leads to the girls' suicides. The boys, who understand nothing about the girls—for that matter, neither do the viewers—are themselves victims of their feverish, adolescent longings. Early on in the film, one of the boys, a guest in the Lisbon home, is seen in the girls' bathroom, furtively searching for clues to the secrets of the lovely creatures. He sniffs a lipstick tube and immediately a rapturous vision of Lux's smiling face appears in a halo of blonde hair and sunshine. Similar slow-motion images of the luminous, smiling, mysterious girls occur throughout the film, reinforcing the fact that the girls are silent, and their story is narrated by neighborhood boys who have only conjectures for the tragedies that befall the girls. They do not know the reason for Cecilia's suicide, which haunts her family and friends; they haven't the faintest glimpse into Lux's own perception of herself. Yet, it is their memories of the strange, doomed girls and the role they played in the boys' own loss of innocence that make them unable to reconcile that crucial episode in their adolescence and prevent the memories' encroachment into their present life. As adults, they continue to lament that the girls were unfathomable—suggesting that all females are, and hinting at less than ideal relationships with their wives—and to retain the sense of the "oddly shaped emptiness" that engulfed them when the girls died.

Coppola's acclaimed second feature film, *Lost in Translation*, a small, personal film about two Americans who meet in Tokyo and become close friends, earned her an Academy Award nomination as director. Only the third woman, and the youngest, to receive this honor (the other two being Jane Campion and Lina Wertmuller), Coppola wrote the screenplay for Bill Murray, who plays a middle-aged actor who comes to Tokyo to film a whisky commercial for $2 million. Jet-lagged and unable to sleep, Bob Harris (Murray) frequents the hotel bar and there meets Charlotte (Scarlett Johannson), a recent Yale graduate who has accompanied her workaholic photographer husband to Tokyo. A sensitive young philosophy major, Charlotte, also sleepless and lonely in her husband's absence, explores the city's exotic culture but is disappointed to not "feel" anything.

Charlotte, married for two years and "stuck" about what to do with her life, finds herself attracted to Bob Harris, married 25 years and alienated from his wife, who, throughout the film, is an irritating voice on the phone or an insistent fax message. Bob and Charlotte spend a great deal of time together drinking, watching Japanese television late at night, prowling karaoke bars, strip bars, talking, enjoying each other's company as neither appears to enjoy that of their spouse, and discovering they are kindred souls. Amid the loneliness and isolation of the neon-drenched city, the man in mid-life crisis and the young woman who seems to have little in common with her husband, sense a deep connection between the two of them and come to love each other. She asks if life gets easier (he says yes), and if marriage gets easier (he indicates no), and he speaks of the changes and joys that children bring—each understanding the poles of experience (or lack thereof) from which they speak. The relationship, which remains platonic, is a still point in an aimless, undirected world that both share, but return to their lives.

Both of Coppola's films are personal films that require courage to make in that they go against the Hollywood grain and could expose the director of such films to harsh criticism if they fail. Coppola excels at providing meticulous details that contribute to the creation of mood and states of being and at providing emotional buildups within the narrative. *Lost in Translation* features much ironic humor, notably in the hilarious scenes of Bob Harris's skirmishes with the Japanese language and Charlotte's lack of sympathy for the strident, non-stop-talking American model/actress who is a guest at the Park-Hyatt Hotel.

KIMBERLY PEIRCE

Born September 8, 1969, in Harrisburg, Pennsylvania, of Jewish and Italian descent, Kimberly Peirce was the child of fifteen-year-old parents who divorced. Much of Peirce's life was spent moving around. After graduating from Miami Sunset High School in Florida, she lived for a time in Puerto Rico before moving to Chicago. She studied at the University of Chicago until she ran out of money, whereupon she moved to Kobe, Japan, where she worked as an English instructor and model. She toured Southeast Asia taking photographs, but she sustained injuries in a motorcycle accident in Thailand and was forced to spend time in recovery. Withdrawing her saved earnings from the bank, she stashed it in her sock and flew back to the United States.

With enough money to complete her degree at the University of Chicago, Peirce re-enrolled, earning a BA in English and Japanese literature. From there, she went to Columbia University Film School, making her debut film (in 16 mm), *The Last Good Breath* (1993), an acclaimed film that made numerous appearances at film festivals. The following year, Peirce was involved in the making of two short films, *Greetings From Africa* and *Miss Ruby's House*. While preparing her thesis on a Civil War spy story about a woman masquerading as a man, Peirce read an article in *The Village Voice* about Brandon Teena, the girl who became a boy and was murdered by two of his friends, and immediately switched her thesis to a film about the brutal murder. Peirce began intensive research on the event, went to Falls City, Nebraska, attended the trial of the two men accused of the murder and spoke with law enforcement officers and others. In 1995, she made a short film about Brandon that was nominated for the university's Princess Grace Award and won an Astrea Production Grant that supplied enough money to begin production of a full-length feature. The film, called at that time *Take It Like a Man* and coscripted by Peirce (with Andy Bienen), was chosen in 1997 for the

Sundance Institute Film Laboratory's workshop and released in 1999 to awards and controversy.

Much like Sofia Coppola, who chose to make a film about something she knew, Peirce was initially drawn to the story of Brandon Teena because to her, it was about a strong, courageous girl with a passionate desire to reinvent herself and find family and love in the process. Peirce's own years of drifting and searching for a satisfying identity perhaps boosted an attraction for someone willing to risk everything for that kind of fulfillment. Peirce spent months preparing for this film because of her approach to the narrative. She drew upon her own perspective for numerous characterizations in the film: for Tom and John, Brandon's friends who turn on him and kill him, she remembered the escapades of her father and his brothers, which could change them from sympathetic to unsympathetic. It was very important to her that the audience love Tom and John before they see their violence and hate them. Her interviews with Lana convinced her that the real story in the film is not the crime but the love story, and most important, she felt the need for audiences to understand Brandon. Peirce made *Boys Don't Cry* in 1999.

Brandon Teena (Hilary Swank) is a girl from Lincoln, Nebraska, who wants to be a boy and do things she thinks boys do, including drinking, fighting, horsing around, dating girls, getting married, and living happily. During the opening credits, we see her as a girl in trouble with the law, and then being transformed into a boy—hair cut, breasts bound, and a sock stuffed in his pants. She moves to Falls City, Nebraska, a notoriously red-neck area, where people with sexual crises are not treated kindly. She makes friends with John, Tom, and Lana (Chloe Sevigny), and becomes part of Lana's family. All goes well until Brandon and Lana fall in love, whereupon all the love the family had for him suddenly turns into unbelievable rage and violence. John and Tom strip, beat, and rape Brandon and demand silence from him about the incident. Not unexpectedly, Brandon's injuries require medical attention, necessitating a trip to the hospital, which, in turn, involves the police. John and Tom find Brandon hiding in an old farmhouse and kill him.

Understandably, the film offers no real answers, but raises a number of questions, many of them unresolvable. Aside from the threats to the manhood of John and Tom, the rape of Brandon that presumably restored the balance of power to the masculine side, how were they threatened? Moreover, what does it mean to be a man? Is gender fixed? Upon learning that Brandon was merely passing as a man, Lana's mother, who had previously been motherly toward him, grew angry and vicious, heaping insults and threats upon him and throwing him out. The character Lana, who had evidence from the beginning that Brandon was a female, continued to love him despite the heinous behavior of her family and friends. Through Lana, Peirce suggests the fact that gender and desire are not as fixed as presumed, and through Lana's inability to situate Brandon as either male or female within a fixed culture, raises questions about shifting identity that arise from a deep need that is unfulfilled by culture.

PATTY JENKINS

Born in 1971, Patty Jenkins, the daughter of a fighter pilot, had lived all over the world by the time she was six years old. Most of her growing-up years were spent in Lawrence, Kansas, after which her family moved to England and back to Washington, DC. While in Kansas, she had studied painting and had pursued art and music, but was still uncertain what she wanted to do. Because money was scarce, she was interested in attending college at Cooper Union in New York, an institution whose tuition was free to students who were admitted. Her first job, at age fourteen, was a summer internship working on the Allen Ginsburg and William H. Burroughs beat documentary, *The River City Reunion*. After enrolling in Cooper Union College to study painting, she became interested in film and produced a series of short films that were premiered to enthusiastic audiences. Following her graduation from college, she became a Union First Assistant Camera person and began working on, during the next five years, hundreds of commercials, music videos, and films. She was admitted to the American Film Institute's Director's program, making two short films—*Just Drive* (2001) and *Velocity Rules*, also in 2001, an eighteen-minute thesis film that was featured at the AFI Fest in 2001. That same year, *Velocity Rules* won in the short film category at the Telluride Indiefest.

After her graduation from AFI, Jenkins became interested in making a low-budget serial-killer crime film about Aileen Wuornos, a former prostitute on death row in Florida for the murder of seven men. Wuornos, on death row for 12 years, had been found guilty and sentenced to death in 1990, when Jenkins, a freshman in college, had followed her sensational trial. In 2002, when Jenkins was planning to make a serial-killer film, she talked with Wuornos by phone and became convinced not to exploit Wuornos in the film, but attempt to reveal her humanity. As Wuornos had demanded to be executed, Governor Jeb Bush complied and scheduled her execution to take place in four weeks. Therefore, while Jenkins's research into court records, transcripts, written materials, and Nick Broomfield's two documentaries on Wuornos was extensive and painstaking, the personal information to be gathered from Wuornos herself was indeed limited.

Meanwhile, Jenkins had written the script, and was searching for money for its development into a film. Her producer, whom she had met at AFI, secured financing for the film; she had also convinced Charlize Theron, a gorgeous former model from South Africa, who resembled Wuornos very little, to play the lead. While the film was in pre-production, Wuornos was executed. The night before her execution, Jenkins talked with Wuornos and her best friend from Michigan who was in Florida with Wuornos about gaining access to the hundreds of letters Wuornos wrote to her friend over a period of 12 years. Almost unbelievably, Wuornos agreed. *Monster* was made in 2003.

Armed with Wuornos's soul-baring comments to her lifelong friend, Jenkins began shooting on a twenty-eight-day schedule in Florida in some of the exact places that Wuornos and the love of her life, lesbian Selby Wall (Christina Ricci), had frequented, as well as quite possibly some of the same roads off the interstate that Wuornos had withdrawn with johns and murdered them. Jenkins's goal was to humanize Wuornos but not sympathize with her. Realizing that sympathy for a character in film usually implies the character is innocent, Jenkins withstood numerous criticisms of her perspective in *Monster*, but remained adamant in her approach. The fact that the film was conceived not as a crime drama but as a love story adds further evidence of humanization in that Selby—the waif, evicted from her home by her parents because she kissed another girl in church, who desperately needs love, and for whose financial benefit many of the johns were murdered by Wuornos—ultimately betrays Wuornos, testifying against her in court.

Jenkins's depiction of the first murder of the john whose background included rape charges and convictions is exceedingly brutal as Wuornos, after being raped and tortured horribly, summons the strength to overpower him and shoot him. Beyond this murder, others were of johns far less threatening to Wuornos, some merely the victims of robbery and the last one who merely stopped to help her. Jenkins received criticism from families of the murdered men, upset because she had not presented their side of the story and also because she had seemed to present a motivation for the murders that was modified from Wuornos's final statement about her reasons for committing them.

KASI LEMMONS

Despite the fact that both Patty Jenkins and Kasi Lemmons have no large body of work, both directors have achieved such impressive first efforts that they should be examined. Whereas Patty Jenkins's controversial film focused upon a subject she had followed for years, Lemmons achieved notoriety because she, an African American actress, wrote a script about family life that she cared about deeply. But despite Lemmons's opportunity and her film's acclaim, she is only one of a very few black women making feature films at this time. Since Julie Dash's *Daughters of the Dust*, there has been Leslie Harris's *Just Another Girl on the IRT* (1993), about a cheeky slum girl whose plans for her life are dashed when she becomes pregnant (a winner of the special jury prize at the Sundance Film Festival). Darnell Martin's *I Like it Like That* (1994), focusing upon the highs and lows of an interracial marriage between a black woman and a Latino, is the only film by a black woman director that was allowed to be made in a studio; and Lemmons, whose stunning success with *Eve's Bayou* was not repeated with her second film, *The Caveman's Valentine* (2001), a critical and commercial failure. Why black women directors encounter such difficulties in making films is the subject of much speculation, much of which centers on their desire to create alternative depictions of black women—meaning those not traditionally used in studio films.

Lemmons was born February 24, 1961, in St. Louis, Missouri, the child of a poet/psychotherapist mother and a father who taught biology. When Lemmons was eight, her parents divorced, and she and her mother and two sisters moved to Newton, Massachusetts, a suburb of Boston. In her youth, Lemmons performed with the Boston Youth Theater, and after graduation from high school she enrolled in New York University's Tisch School of the Arts. She transferred to the University of California at Los Angeles in order to expand her education beyond acting, but returned to New York to enter the New School of Social Research and make documentary films. She made a short film, *Fall From Grace*, in 1990, about homeless people in New York, but returned to acting. She continued a series of acting roles begun with Spike Lee's *School Daze* (1988), including Jonathan Demme's *Silence of the Lambs* (1991), and Bernard Rose's *Candyman* (1992). The roles that came Lemmons's way left her with little sense of artistic fulfillment, and out of this sense of frustration came her first script, written with no expectation of it ever being filmed. She eventually showed it to her husband, actor Vondie Curtis Hall, who encouraged her to look for a producer.

But, although Lemmons found a producer for *Eve's Bayou*, convinced Samuel L. Jackson, her friend from *School Daze*, to play the male lead (Dr. Louis Batiste) and also assume the role of coproducer, and signed other impressive actors and actresses on as members of the cast, still no one wanted to direct the film. She decided to take on the film's direction herself. Lemmons, who had not been reared in the Deep South, anchored her script with knowledge of it gathered from her father and mother who had grown up there, and from spending summers with her grandmother in Alabama. Written over a three-month period, her narrative injects Gothic narrative into family drama in the story of ten-year-old Eve (Jurnee Smollett) and her well-to-do family: Dr. Batiste, father; Roz (Lynn Whitfield), mother; Mozelle (Debbi Morgan), Batiste's sister; the Batistes' fourteen-year-old daughter, Cisely, and nine-year-old son, Poe.

However, the story is not about African Americans but, as Lemmons suggests, a story of universal significance. Going beyond the roles of black women in film beyond the traditional servant, trouble maker or "ho" in the Hollywood depictions, Lemmons wrote and filmed a drama of a black, almost all-female family, whose existence is owed to miscegenation, and whose pain seems to radiate from people who love with too much passion and intensity. The story is told by Eve, who begins her retrospective of the summer when the family's lives began to disintegrate by noting that "Memory is a selection of images ... some elusive, some printed indelibly on the brain. The summer I killed my father, I was ten years old." Although Eve's narration primarily concerns discovering her father's infidelity and its effects upon the entire family, she becomes close friends with her dad's sister, Aunt Mozelle, a psychic whose abilities failed to foresee the early deaths of the three men she had loved. Eve quietly observes Mozelle "see" and disclose hitherto concealed information to her clients concerning missing money or people, eventually coming to realize that she has the "touch" as well.

Strong characterization in Lemmons's film emphasizes the power of female bonding and indefinable connections between family members. When Eve related witnessing her father's sexual encounter to Cisely, who vehemently denied that it happened, Eve had no knowledge that the love Cisely had for her father was beyond what a daughter's love should be. Enveloped in jealousy, incest, voodoo, and spiritual yearnings, Eve's story relates more than she understands: her beloved father, an attentive husband and exceptional provider, loves his wife and family but is a hopeless philanderer; her aunt Mozelle confesses that she and her brother, Louis, are much alike in that they are both compelled to continue love affairs until they end in tragedy; Cisely's description of her father's attempt to molest her is shown to be neither true nor false but, like most of the other interconnections within the film, unknowable.

The cinematography in the film about the disintegration of a family informs the story with mystery, sultry eroticism, and passion that the bayou scenery transmits to the characters and events. Shadows, haze, and snakes gliding on the water portend unknowable depths of human nature or anything beyond the pretense of the present. The visions of Moselle and, later, Eve, that are represented as "second sight" are shown through computer-generated black-and-white depictions of psychic truth that conflicts with the bayou-influenced events involving the characters. Yet, these visions emanate from the close connections between characters and fuel the ambiguities throughout the narrative. Lemmons's film was not perceived as an African American film, in that its perception of the mysteries of human relationships is so universal that it attracted more of a white audience than black.

Lemmons's second film, *Caveman's Valentine*, fell victim to the sophomore jinx common to many new directors whose first film is hailed as impressive and masterful. Also primarily a vehicle for Samuel L. Jackson, *Caveman's Valentine*, the story of a strange homeless man whose effort to solve a murder mystery involves unexplained ambiguities surrounding him that include moth seraphs that emerge from dancers and forceful rays that are emitted from the Chrysler Building, home of his imaginary arch enemy. His more rational side reflects on his previous life as a musician and composer from Julliard School of Music, and events in the film revive his passion for music. He begins a new composition. Adapted from the Edgar Award–winning novel by George Dawes Green, the film failed to translate the intricate ambiguities of the script into a coherent film; and although Lemmons' distinctive presence as a director is evident, the film's reviews were scathing, and the film was deemed a failure.

$$\Longrightarrow 6 \Longleftarrow$$

Actresses Turned Directors

ANJELICA HUSTON

The second child of legendary director John Huston and his fourth wife, Enrica Soma, Huston was born on July 8, 1951, in Los Angeles, California. When she was small, her father moved the family to St. Clerans, a huge estate in County Galway, Ireland, where she and her brother, Tony, enjoyed riding horses and writing and performing their own plays for visitors. When she was eleven, her parents separated and she was taken by her mother to live in London and attend a private school. Anjelica was miserable; she did not understand why her parents separated, and she was tall and skinny and thought herself very unattractive.

In 1968, John Huston cast fifteen-year-old Anjelica in the film *A Walk With Love and Death*, which dealt with teenagers in medieval France. The unpleasant experience of making the film (she hated the part, she had trouble with her lines, she thought she looked ugly) continued into the unkind reviews and the failure of the film at the box office. The following year, at age sixteen, Anjelica was devastated by the death of her mother, age thirty-nine, in an automobile accident.

Anjelica changed directions and went into modeling. Photographs of Anjelica in Ireland by famed photographer Richard Avedon filled thirty pages in *Vogue*. She continued to agonize because she thought she was ugly. In 1973, Anjelica attended a party at the home of Jack Nicholson, with whom she fell in love, and was with, off and on, for seventeen years. She gave up modeling, moving in with him, eventually enrolling in acting lessons to help her get back into films. In 1982, she was hit head-on by a drunk driver, requiring six hours of facial surgery.

After she recuperated, she began to take small parts in television, and was offered the lead in *Ice Pirates*, a fun romp that increased her confidence. The producer of *Ice Pirates*, John Foreman, offered her a part in his next film, *Prizzi's Honor*, which was eventually directed by Anjelica's father, John Huston, and starred Jack Nicholson. She won an Oscar for her portrayal of Maerose, and has been in demand for roles since then. Since then, she has acted in thirty-nine films and, in 1996, ventured into directing.

Anjelica's directorial debut was *Bastard Out of Carolina*, based on Dorothy Allison's semi-autobiographical novel of 1992 about generations of white-trash and their lifestyle of drinking, fighting, and taking care of family. The film was made as an original film for Ted Turner's network, but Turner reneged on the deal when he viewed the shocking contents in the film, which was picked up by Showtime. The film opens with Anney (Jennifer Jason Leigh) being taken to the hospital for the birth of her child. Her sister and brother are on their way to the hospital, Anney lying in the back seat. The truck plows into the rear of a vehicle in front of them, and Anney flies through the windshield. All survive, and born that night is the novel's narrator, Bone, whose tininess is memorialized in her name. Bone's mother, Anney, is determined to erase the "bastard" designation from her child's birth certificate by finding a good husband. She meets Lyle Parsons (Dermot Mulroney) and marries him, but he is killed before the birth of his daughter. She eventually meets Glen (Ron Eldard), a friend of her brother and an alienated son of a rich man, whom she marries. On the night Anney is in the hospital for the birth of their child (who is stillborn), Glen, waiting in the parking lot, invites Bone (Jena Malone) to the front seat of the car, where he places her on his lap and abuses her sexually.

The shocking, painful scene is indicative of the entire film, which is essentially about Anney and her desperate search for love as a means of legitimizing her daughter, Bone. Disappointed that his child died, Glen then loses his job and the family is thrust into poverty. For reasons not altogether clear—perhaps resentment, anger, or some perverse attraction to her—he beats Bone, once so badly she has a stay in the hospital. Anney's family learns of Glen's mistreatment of Bone, whereupon two of Anney's brothers beat him up. Later, Glen pleads with Anney to come back, but when she asks Bone to come too, saying, "I wouldn't ask you to come if I didn't know it was safe," Bone refuses. Knowing Anney will not return without Bone, Glen beats Bone viciously, breaking her arm and raping her. Anney finally realizes she has betrayed Bone, who goes to live with Anney's sister.

Bastard Out of Carolina is extremely hard to watch because of Huston's grim, realistic depiction of brutal child abuse. No Hollywood glossiness here, her film is a courageous look at the outrageous treatment of an eleven-year-old child, made even more outrageous by the mother's repeated forgiveness of her husband because she desperately needs to be loved. Huston utilizes country music throughout to reflect Anney's emotional state as well as to provide a social backdrop for the narrative. Huston emphasizes Anney's poverty as we see her working as a waitress and in a scene where she feeds her children ketchup on crackers because there is nothing else.

Huston's second film, *Agnes Browne* (1996), is far less controversial than her first one. Based on *The Mammy*, the 1994 best-seller spun off by Irish comic

Brendan O'Carroll from *Mrs. Browne's Boys*, his successful radio series. Huston directs herself in the title role of Mrs. Browne, a working-class street vendor and mother of six boys and a daughter. The film begins on the day Browne's husband dies, soon after which Browne heads for the government office to request her widow's pension. As progress in a bureaucracy is glacially slow, she borrows money from the ruthless local loan shark, Mr. Billy, to pay for her husband's funeral. Browne's best friend, Marion (Marion O'Dwyer), whose vending stall is next to Browne's, encourages her to date a French baker who has shown an interest. But, the film shows a darker side in that Browne's nine-year-old son is ensnared by Mr. Billy, who lends him money to buy Browne a new dress to wear on her date, and Marion is diagnosed with cancer.

The film features an episodic narrative, suggestive of a serial story. Set in 1967 in Dublin, Huston's film focuses on the Irish working class and its pluck, humor, and grit. Browne tells her seven children, ages two to fourteen, "We're Brownes. We stick together." But, besides keeping the family together, the film's main emphasis is on the bonding of women. We see the joking women at the market, the camaraderie of her friends who come to help Browne prepare for her date, the close friendship of Browne and Marion, and their hilarious, bawdy humor away from men. Chuckling about sex, Browne says, "Seven children I've had, and no organisms to show for it." The two women share jokes, songs, and laughs, and lusty stories and provide support and encouragement for one another.

Huston's third film, *Riding the Bus With My Sister* (2005), featured Rosie O'Donnell as Beth Simon and Andie MacDowell as Rachel Simon, author of the book on which this is based. Beth, who has severe developmental deficiencies (mental retardation), has developed a lifestyle of riding the bus around all day. She has a little family of friends on the bus. Rachel is a busy writer whose relationship with her sister has grown distant. One day Beth challenges Rachel to ride with her on the bus for a year, and Rachel accepts. She discovers the richness of the life her sister leads, and writes a book about their adventures together. The film had deeply influenced Huston in that she has become devoted to raising awareness about the mentally handicapped.

PENNY MARSHALL

Carole Penny Marscharelli, the youngest of three children, was born on October 15, 1942, to Anthony W. and Marjorie Irene Marscharelli in New York. Her father, an industrial filmmaker, and her mother, a dance teacher, lived in a middle-class ethnic Bronx neighborhood, where Penny spent much time in her mother's dance studio. The family changed its last name to Marshall during Penny's youth, and Marshall, an accomplished dancer, felt she was unattractive and chose to hang out with friends and make fun of herself through comedy. In 1956, her mother's dance troupe, The Marshalettes, appeared on *Ted Mack Amateur Hour* and won, earning them a spot on *The Jackie Gleason Show*. After graduating from high school and seemingly uninterested in show business, Marshall enrolled in the University of New Mexico at Albuquerque. There she met and married Michael Henry, a football player, in her sophomore year; she bore a daughter, Tracy, and found herself divorced. Reluctant to return home, she phoned her brother, Garry Marshall, a television writer-producer, who invited her to come to Hollywood and encouraged her to audition for television shows. In a repertory group, she met another Bronx native, Rob Reiner, who landed the role of Meathead in *All in the Family*. In 1971, she and Reiner were married as his career took off and hers faltered. After a string of small parts in various television programs, Marshall and Cindy Williams (through Garry Marshall's efforts) secured primary roles in *Laverne and Shirley*, a spin-off of *Happy Days*.

Marshall's first directorial efforts began in the last days of *Laverne and Shirley* when she assumed the helm for a few episodes. Despite her newly found appreciation for directing, she did not get an opportunity until 1986, when she was drafted as a replacement director of Whoopi Goldberg in *Jumpin' Jack Flash*. Featuring Goldberg as a bank employee who becomes enmeshed in international undercover work when her computer picks up signals from a British spy in Russia, the film suffers from a weak script and unutilized ensemble characters. Before *Jumpin' Jack Flash* was completed, director James Brooks gave Marshall the script for her first feature film, *Big* (1988), which, upon release, won for Tom Hanks best actor awards from Golden Globe and L.A. Film Critics in 1989. *Big* was followed up with a drama, *Awakenings* (1990), based on the true story of Dr. Oliver Sacks, from his book of the same name, and won awards for its primary actors, Robert De Niro and Robin Williams. In 1992, Marshall directed *A League of Their Own*, a story of the Rockford Peaches, a team in the All-American Girls Professional Baseball League, and their coach, played by Tom Hanks. After these three impressive films, Marshall then directed *Renaissance Man* (1994), featuring Danny DeVito as an unemployed ad man who is hired to teach Army recruits Shakespeare; *The Preacher's Wife* (1996), a remake of Henry Koster's 1947 film *The Bishop's Wife*; and *Riding in Cars With Boys* (2001), based on a memoir by Beverly Donofrio.

The charge that Marshall had ridden to success and fame on the coattails of her brother and father, who were the producers of *Laverne and Shirley*, were met by Marshall, who countered that because Hollywood is an industry, certainly sons and daughters of successful people grow into it. But the best response to that charge is to be found in Marshall's first feature film. *Big* concentrates upon a twelve-year-old boy who is humiliated at a carnival in the presence of an older, taller, very pretty teenage girl (with whom he is smitten), and wishes he were big. He makes the wish to Zoltar, a strange type of wishing machine which belches out a card assuring him his wish will be granted. The next morning, Josh has become a thirty-year-old man (Tom Hanks), who terrifies his mother and ends up fleeing into New York City accompanied by his friend, who helps him rent a room in a pimp and prostitute-infested hotel. He finds a job as a computer person in a toy factory and endears himself to the owner (Robert Loggia) through his great interest in toys from a kid's perspective. He also meets Susan (Elizabeth

Perkins), an aggressive, cynical fellow employee with whom he has a romance. However, Josh misses his family and friends, and through the help of his friend, finds another Zoltar, who grants his wish to be small again.

Perhaps her own painful adolescence inclined Marshall to this story, as it deals with the agonies of growing up that must be endured. Josh, who has begun to notice girls, is aware that the one he likes makes him seem to be a child, and the magic that changes him and creates dilemmas is treated by Marshall delicately. Josh's innocence is emphasized throughout his foray into the adult world, beginning with the horrid St. James Hotel, where the television violence Josh is watching matches the discord in the hotel and the street. Josh cries for home and mom. He manages to escape the vicious company politics through his genuine knowledge of what kids want in toys, which eventually results in a promotion that places him above the nasty worker (John Heard) who sought to do him in. One of the most interesting aspects of Marshall's film is her sly suggestion that there's actually little difference in grown men and kids, especially from the standpoint of play. Despite the fact that Susan cynically sets out to seduce Josh, she is soon seduced by his childlike playing, for example, jumping on his trampoline; sleeping in his bunk bed, while he's on "top" in the top bunk; enjoying the carnival. When their romance progresses to Josh's first sexual encounter, Marshall is tactful and tender in her depiction of Josh's first experience. When Susan, a sexually savvy person, is asked by an old boyfriend what she sees in Josh, she ironically replies that "He's grown up."

Marshall's emphasis upon helping the audience empathize with Josh, as a conflicted person, or a similar situation that human beings can relate with continues on into *Awakenings* (1990), her second film effort. This dramatic film, based on the stories of Oliver Sacks concerns some survivors of the encephalitis epidemic that occurred in the United States in 1926. A group of catatonic patients in a Bronx hospital, who have slept for as long as 30 years were given L-dopa by Dr. Sacks and awakened dramatically, but as the medication was not a cure, the patients became more immune to the dosage and soon began to return to their cataleptic state. In the film, Robin Williams plays Dr. Malcolm Sayer (Sacks), a doctor who had spent most of his life in research but has accepted the position of physician in the Bronx hospital in 1969. Sayer finds out about L-dopa, a new drug designed for Parkinson's disease victims, but he believes those stricken by encephalitis might benefit from it also. He is permitted by hospital administration to use the drug experimentally on one patient, Leonard Lowe (Robert De Niro), whose mother continues to visit him every day in the hospital.

The early part of the film shows Leonard as a child when he was losing his ability to write or control his hand. From this time to when he was placed in the hospital, a period of nine years, he spends in his room reading. Leonard is an intelligent, perceptive, well-read individual whose awakening is marked by a spelled reference to a poem by the German poet Rainier Maria Rilke and, therefore, marks his return as one with more pathos than the others, because we know more about him. With Leonard's success, money is raised to fund medication for the others, who enjoy equal success and confusion in a world so changed over the better part of three decades. When the others go dancing to celebrate their return to life, Leonard has lunch with an attractive girl, whom he looks forward to seeing again. But the film is also about Dr. Sayer and his relationships with other people; having spent years researching earthworms, he believes he is not "very good" with people. The transformation of emotionally blocked Sayer to developing a friendship with Leonard is an inspiring part of the film's call to live life to the fullest. Sayer is the only champion of the ghost-like encephalitic patients, challenging the hospital administration to provide aggressive treatment for them. His devoted nurse, Eleanor Costello (Julie Kavner), is his chief supporter who is interested in having a relationship with him, who only in the final scene responds to her. Eleanor also comforts him in his remorse and guilt for "cruelly" bringing the patients back to life, and then slowly losing them again forever; she reminds him that "life is given and taken away for all of us."

While *Awakenings* did not match *Big*'s success at the box office, it was a popular film that offered audiences uplifting sentiment about "the importance of friendship and family" (from an address by Dr. Sayer), the zest for life displayed by the revived patients throughout the summer months of their "rebirth," and not least by their heartbreaking return to their frozen states. The film raises questions about the limits of consciousness, the inadequacies of medical science and the decision-making process determining who is to be chosen for experimental drugs.

Marshall's fourth film, *A League of Their Own*, also based on true events, concentrates on the Rockford Peaches, one of four initial girls' baseball teams in the United States. Fearing that World War II would decimate the major league teams, thereby collapsing major league ballparks, Philip Wrigley, owner of Wrigley Field, home of the Chicago Cubs, dispatched scouts to find suitable young women to play softball or baseball in the event that major league play were seriously threatened. Women were found, and the All American Girls Professional Baseball League was formed in 1943. Intended to exist only until the men came home from war, the league flourished and continued on until 1954.

Marshall's cast for the film is Tom Hanks, playing Jimmy Dugan, a washed-up alcoholic former home-run king who has "sunk" to coaching girls; Geena Davis, as Dottie Hinson; and Lori Petty as Dottie's low-esteem sister, Kit, who came along because Dottie refused to join the team without her; and other teammates played by Madonna, Rosie O'Donnell, and Megan Cavanaugh. The film is commercially made to appeal to mainstream audiences and provide interesting portrayals of female athletes, friendship, rivalry, and looks at the status of the girl baseball players. Before they were allowed to play, the girls were required to attend charm school to learn poise and good manners, and they were forced to wear skirts during play. Other particulars of interest are the girls' quality of play (they are facing the Racine Belles in the championship), Coach Dugan's warming to his girls and becoming interested in their game, the rivalry between sisters Dottie and Kit, and the raunchiness of Madonna's character.

But, while the film is an enjoyable entertainment and, like *Big*, earned over $100 million at the box office, most critics were harsh and biting in their evaluation of it. Criticisms ranged from deploring the condescending attitude toward women in the film, to the absence of any real baseball being played to Marshall's playing to easy laughs rather than taking a risk and elevating the film to more than just entertainment.

Marshall followed this film with *Renaissance Man*, featuring Danny DeVito as a fired ad man, Bill Rago, whose desperation for a job leads him to accept a position with the Army teaching next-to-hopeless underachieving recruits. DeVito does not want to teach, does not like Army khaki, and only becomes interested when he reads his students' biographies and is appalled at their backgrounds. At this point, he realizes that if he fails, they will be tossed back into their hopeless lives and, at that point, he begins to read Hamlet. A semi-autobiographical script, *Renaissance Man* is an uplifting story of Rago, who, unable to reach his students, finds that *Hamlet* with its madness, suicide, incest, and murder speaks to their own abysmal situations in ways they can understand. Consequently, Rago gains the respect of the recruits, who become sufficiently enlightened to remain in the army, and Rago achieves success.

The Preacher's Wife, Marshall's sixth film, is a remake of Henry Koster's film about an Episcopalian bishop whose prayers for money to build a new church are answered by an angel sent down to earth to solve the problem. Nearly fifty years later, Marshall's new version, a Christmas film backed by Disney, is light, inspirational family fare about the Reverend Henry Biggs (Courtney B. Vance), whose church is in dire need of material and spiritual guidance. His church is about to be gobbled up by a greedy developer, many of his congregation are in financial need, and his marriage is in trouble. His devoted wife, Julia, portrayed by Whitney Houston, leads the choir and suffers with her husband about the state of affairs. Angel Dudley (Denzel Washington), out of the blue, falls into a snow bank, sent from heaven as an answer to the couple's prayers. He and Julia become attracted to each other, but in an uplifting film about faith, passion takes a back seat to spiritual fulfillment. That the film has a largely African American cast adds a new dimension that is a delight to audiences seeking African American characters without criminal tendencies. The film is essentially a tribute to Houston's voice and Washington's charm.

Marshall's most recent film, *Riding in Cars With Boys*, is based on the 1990 Beverly Donofrio memoir of the same name, but with broad changes in the script. As Marshall herself gave birth to a child and married and divorced at an early age, she may well have been drawn in this film to the hazards of raising a child alone when the mother is little more than a child herself. Drew Barrymore, a child star who had her own childhood difficulties, plays Bev, whose father (James Woods) is the Wallington, Connecticut, chief of police and her mother (Lorraine Bracco), is unsympathetic to any of Bev's problems. The film traces Bev's life from 1965 to 1986 that includes a teenage pregnancy and marriage at the age of fifteen to a sweet but dim boy named Ray (Steve Zahn) whose occupation as carpet installer is made more difficult by his being a junkie. Bev's best friend, Fay (Brittany Murphy), also becomes pregnant and gets married. Much of the film depicts the two friends raising their children together; they both wanted girls, but Bev's child is a boy named Jason (ultimately played by Adam Garcia), who grows up to fall in love with Fay's daughter, Amelia. But the primary conflict—among so many—is that Bev's dream to go to NYU and become a writer is put on hold because of her situation. Through the years, she blames her parents for not being able to talk with them; her husband for his inability to support her dream; and her son, Jason, for just being there. Her son grows up without his father, whose heroin addiction leads to his leaving the home, and he leads a controlled, emotionally frustrated, resentful life. Years after Ray leaves and Jason is a student at NYU, we see Bev in 1986 at age 36. She has written her book and is traveling in a car with Jason, age 21, to see Ray, whose signature is necessary for a release from liability for the material in the book.

BARBRA STREISAND

The second child of Diana and Emanuel Streisand, Barbara Joan Streisand, was born on April 24, 1942, in Brooklyn, New York. Her father was the son of Austro-Hungarian immigrants, and her mother, Ida (Diana) Rosen, was the daughter of Russian immigrants. Shortly after Barbara's first birthday, Emanuel died, leaving her mother grief stricken and financially unstable. Diana worked as a secretary to raise Barbara and her older brother, Sheldon. In 1949, Diana married Louis Kind, a businessman sixteen years her senior, and gave birth, two years later, to another daughter, Roslyn.

Barbara, who had long retreated to a fantasy world to escape her own life, began to pursue singing. Graduating from Erasmus High School at sixteen, she left home to follow her theatrical ambitions. While living with friends and working menial jobs, Barbara won a talent contest in Greenwich Village. She dropped the second "a" from Barbara, becoming Barbra and began her first professional position for $125 a week at a nightclub, the Bon Soir, in September 1960. Barbra's stage debut in New York in 1961, *Another Evening With Harry Stoones*, was followed by *I Can Get It For You Wholesale*, in 1962. While working in this musical, Barbra met Elliot Gould and they became a couple, marrying on September 13, 1963. The year 1963 was a breakthrough year for Barbra, who remained for the rest of the decade the top-selling female album artist. In 1964, Barbra opened in *Funny Girl* at the Winter Garden Theater, and her career continued to escalate. In 1967, she gave birth to Jason Emanuel Gould, and she and Gould divorced in 1971.

Beginning with the film version of *Funny Girl* (1968), Barbra has acted in fourteen films: *Hello, Dolly!* (1969); *The Owl and the Pussycat* (1970); *On a Clear Day You Can See Forever* (1970); *What's Up Doc?* (1972); *Up the Sandbox* (1972); *The Way We Were* (1973); *For Pete's Sake* (1974); *Funny Lady* (1975); *A Star Is*

Born (1976); The Main Event (1979); All Night Long (1981); Nuts (1987); and Meet the Fockers (2004).

During the making of The Main Event, Streisand, who disliked the film, vowed to make Yentl, the short story written by Isaac Bashevis Singer, into film. Barbra's obsession with the story of a young Jewish girl who, forbidden to study the Talmud, disguises herself as a boy who gets caught up in romantic difficulties, had begun in 1968. Through the years, Streisand had wrestled with the wanting to bring the story to film, but was afraid to assume the control necessary to accomplish it (Nickens and Swenson 161). Twelve films later, she finally accepted the challenge and began her search for financing. Having been turned down by Orion, Warner Brothers, Columbia, and Paramount, Streisand's film was picked up by United Artists, who guaranteed her a $14.5 million budget, but forced her to give up director's approval of final cut. The film was also to be shot entirely on location in Czechoslovakia.

Yentl (1983) is the story of a father's only daughter who, because of her female status, is forbidden to study the Talmud. Rather than insist she learn to cook and sew, her father secretly teaches her the Talmud. When he dies, women who guess the truth about her studies, descend upon her to put her in her place as a woman. She cuts her hair, dons her father's clothes and glasses, changes her name to Anshel, and moves to another town. She is admitted to a yeshiva, where she meets Avigdor (Mandy Patinkin), with whom she falls in love. He loves Hadass, who cannot marry him because of his brother's suicide. Anshel marries Hadass to allow Avigdor to remain in town. Conflicts uncovered on the wedding night are eventually overcome allowing Hadass and Avigdor to marry and Yentl to leave Eastern Europe for the United States.

As little as Streisand, at age 40, actually looks like a seventeen-year-old boy, she plays the part convincingly. But it was the film's innovative use of music that scored exceptionally well with the audience. While only Streisand sings and, until the film's end, sings alone, her songs are seen as soliloquies that she only sings when she's alone, for example the prayer to her dead father, "Papa, Can You Hear Me?" Music is integrated into various scenes and is heard rising above the dialogue to acquaint the audience with Yentl's thoughts and feelings. The film's music was awarded an Oscar.

Streisand fell in love with The Prince of Tides, the novel by Pat Conroy, as she read it, and was surprised to discover that Robert Redford, her costar in The Way We Were, was also interested in it. Redford relinquished the property to her, and as soon as she was given the go-ahead signal from MGM/UA, she began to work on making the nearly 600 pages that span decades and generations into a viable script. The story is of Tom Wingo (Nick Nolte), an unemployed English teacher and coach on the South Carolina coast, who learns of his twin sister's attempted suicide (not the first time) and goes to New York to meet with her psychiatrist, Dr. Susan Lowenstein (Barbra Streisand). There, he too becomes Dr. Lowenstein's patient, as he invokes the past to uncover his and his sister's childhood abuse. Both Tom and Dr. Lowenstein are unhappily married, and they become romantically involved—each providing the other strength for forgiveness and healing. Tom helps his sister and himself accept the past; he also parts with Dr. Lowenstein to return to his wife and children, for whom he feels a renewed commitment.

Despite criticism by psychiatric organizations about Dr. Lowenstein's affair with her patient, audiences responded to the emotion displayed in the film, and it was a box office success. Streisand was bitterly disappointed not to win an Oscar for the film, but it remains probably the best film she has directed.

Streisand's third film, *The Mirror Has Two Faces* (1996) is based on a 1958 French film, *Le Miroir a Deux Faces*, in which the female lead undergoes cosmetic surgery for her transformation. Streisand is more interested in the heroine of her romantic comedy, who is transformed by her love for a man. The story involves Rose Morgan (Streisand), a somewhat dumpy professor of romantic literature at Columbia University, who, convinced of her unattractiveness, believes she can never have a romantic affair. She lives with her mother (Lauren Bacall), who was and still is beautiful. Her sister (Mimi Rogers) answers an ad placed by Gregory Larkin (Jeff Bridges), a math professor at Columbia who wants a companion for a platonic relationship. After a few dates, Gregory proposes and Rose accepts, hoping passion will appear after the marriage. When she attempts to seduce him sometime after the wedding, he leaves. Crushed, she loses weight, exercises and applies makeup. Ironically, Gregory preferred the old Rose to the new one.

Issues that appear in this film have apparently been quite real for Streisand— the relationships between mother and daughter, the fraud of appearances, and the transformation from ugly duckling to swan. Many critics see this film as a vanity piece by Streisand that validates her attractiveness and desirability, specifically in view of the fact that she never looks as frumpy as the script implies she is. The fact that Streisand directs herself in films that appear to be spectacles of herself causes some critics to suggest that she needs a different director.

ELAINE MAY

Elaine May was born on April 21, 1932, in Philadelphia, Pennsylvania, to theater director Jack Berlin and the actress Jeannie Berlin. May attended the University of Chicago, and having occasionally acted with her father in the Yiddish theater he operated, she joined the Compass Players, a forerunner of the Second City Troupe. In Chicago, she met and joined Mike Nichols as a deadpan comic duo who took their improvisational material to cabaret, television, and Broadway. After working together three years, they parted company in 1961.

In the sixties, May devoted her attention to playwriting. Her most successful play was the one-act *Adaptation*. She also performed on radio and made comedy albums. Her directorial debut, *A New Leaf* (1971), was based on Jack Ritchie's story, "The Green Heart." In this film, for which she wrote the script, directed, and acted in, Henry Graham (Walter Matthau) is an aging playboy who awakes one morning to discover he has no more of his inheritance left. Having squandered it through financing his ridiculously spendthrift lifestyle, his options now are suicide or marriage to a wealthy woman. Work, to him, is out of the question. He meets Henrietta (May), who, though disgustingly wealthy, is a college professor of botany who dreams of discovering a new species of fern. Henry and Henrietta get married, to the horror of her lawyer and trustee Harry (Jack Weston), who has been systematically bleeding her estate dry for years. The film essentially follows the efforts of Harry to kill Henrietta for her money; and, of course, when the time is finally right, he finds he cannot do it. "Damn, damn, damn, *damn*," he says. "Nothing *ever* works out the way it's supposed to!"

This film is not the script that May gave to the studio, reportedly a 180-minute black comedy that the studio shortened and turned into a strange romantic comedy. May sued the studio to remove her affiliation from it and petitioned a judge to prevent the release of the film. Neither of those events occurred. Ironically, the film, as it is, was loved by its audience and is considered a classic.

May's film has drawn various responses from critics. Vincent Canby of the *New York Times* says the film "shares with the great screwball comedies of the Depression an almost childlike appreciation of money" (March 12, 1971). The film was perceived as controversial by feminists, who noted the reversal of the character leads in that Henrietta is wealthy and intelligent and Henry is sizing her up as a potential mate. Barbara Quart laments that May's "derogatory images of the women themselves . . . [move one] to pain, embarrassment, and sympathy simultaneously" (Women Directors 40).

Quart's charge about May's depiction of women carries over into May's second film, *The Heartbreak Kid* (1972). Written by Neil Simon from a story by Bruce Jay Friedman, "A Change of Plan," the film firmly established May as a mainstream director. The story is of Lenny Cantrow (Charles Grodin), an upwardly mobile, ex-Marine, sporting goods salesman, who meets Lila Kolodny (Jeanne Berlin, May's daughter), and after a short time, Lila, a twenty-two-year-old virgin and Lenny get married in a traditional Jewish wedding. On their drive to Florida for their honeymoon, Lenny begins to find her singing voice and her eating habits annoying. In Miami Beach, Lila gets badly sunburned the first day and must stay indoors. Alone on the beach, he meets Kelly (Cybill Shepherd), a shallow blonde beauty from Minnesota, and falls for her charms. After three days of seeing Kelly, Lenny announces to his bride that he wants a divorce. He agrees to give her everything, and soon he is in Minnesota pursuing Kelly. Kelly's father (Eddie Albert) has a great dislike for Lenny and offers him $25,000 to go away. Lenny persists, and the film, as it begins with a Jewish wedding, ends with a Protestant wedding.

May's film, struggling to remain a comedy, suggests the real reason for marriage is not love, but lust. The reason Lenny marries Lila, it seems, is because she had resisted his attempts to seduce her and had saved herself for marriage. On their wedding night, Lenny finds her talking through it all and eating candy bars in bed irksome but pretends otherwise. May also shows Lenny following

Kelly to Minnesota, consumed with lust, and entering into a marriage apparently destined for conflict. The most sympathetic character is Lila, whose cinematic predicament is viewed by some feminists as May's shameful treatment of her daughter. However, it seems that May's sympathies do not really lie with the male characters in her first two films, as she appears to be giving them room to hang themselves.

May's first two films set standards that she was never able to meet in her films again. Her third film, *Mikey and Nicky* (1976), set in the streets of Philadelphia, is the story of two longtime friends trying to dodge a hitman. John Cassevetes as Nicky, a down-and-out alcoholic gangster, is being shuttled about by Mikey (Peter Falk) to avoid the hitman (Ned Beatty). Mikey looks after his friend, tends to his ulcer and attempts to soothe his anxieties. But in this dark comedy, Mikey is also spiteful and allows the stings of former slights to induce him to turn his friend over to those who want to kill him. Unaware of his betrayal, Nicky inadvertently outfoxes the would-be assassin at every turn.

May's love of improvisation led her to insist on allowing her actors space for improvising also. Working with Cassavetes, whose own approach to film depended "more on the actors' personalities than on predetermined scripts and camera technique" (Levy 105), May, too, wanted to explore the emotional truths of her characters. As the friends move from one location to another, they speak of threads of their lives from childhood through marriage and gangster activities. Nicky suspects Mikey may have fingered him, but is also painfully aware that Mikey is the only friend he has. Caught in the intense tangle of their thirty-year friendship interspersed with fond memories and bitterness, the two men find themselves reopening old wounds. As a result of wanting to let these two inventive actors explore themselves as much as possible with the male bonding theme, May found herself with an over-long rambling film on which she labored more than a year to edit into a semblance of the original script. Consequently, Paramount Studios released the unfinished film without May's approval.

May then turned to scriptwriting, coscripting along with Warren Beatty the immensely popular *Heaven Can Wait* (1978), a rewrite of Alexander Hall's 1941 film *Here Comes Mr. Jordan*. She then became a script doctor, one of a small group of writers who are paid handsome fees by studios to do uncredited work on a script. She worked on scripts for *Reds* (1981), written and directed by Warren Beatty; *Tootsie* (1982), directed by Sydney Pollock; and *Labyrinth* (1986), written and directed by Jim Henson.

In 1987, after an absence of nine years, May took up directing again with *Ishtar*, which became a monumental economic disaster. The film features Warren Beatty and Dustin Hoffman as two terribly untalented singers, Rogers and Clarke, who, unable to find any gigs in New York, sign up for a run at Chez Casablanca, a night-club in Morocco. On their way, they get sidetracked in the neighboring mythical country of Ishtar, whose government has been set up by the U.S. Government. Fearing a leftist revolution, the CIA agent (Charles Grodin) hires Clarke as a CIA spy, and a revolutionary representative (Isabelle Adjani) hires Rogers to spy.

Difficulties involving the actors and the absence of plot were noted, but most of the blame fell on May. Her typical extended sketch narrative was seen as lacking any real plot, and she also was charged with mismanagement. She has made no films since then. She has, however, collaborated with Mike Nichols on *The Birdcage* (1996), by writing the screenplay for his direction and again with Nichols on *Primary Colors*, for which she wrote the screenplay from Joe Klein's novel.

Conclusion

The women directors in this volume account for a very small percent of the total number of directors who have attempted, achieved, or rejected mainstream designation within the time span covered here. And of the twenty-nine women, diversity is not necessarily the ruling principle, as all but two directors considered are white. Dash and Lemmons are African Americans, who, despite having made critically acclaimed and successful first films, have suffered diminishing returns since then. In addition to the efforts of both to shed the stereotypical perception of black women in Hollywood, both women utilize complex, nontraditional narratives that express their own identity but, ironically, may partially explain their failure to appeal to mainstream audiences.

Despite exerting more control over their films, woman independent filmmakers often endure enormous difficulties with funding and frequently lack distribution. All attest to the fact that it is much harder to get second and third films started than the first. Even Barbara Kopple, who earned an Oscar for her first film, found most financial doors closed to her on her second try for funding. Lizzie Borden, whose controversial views, along with the specific social and ethnic concerns of Dash, Savoca, and Anders, were stymied by the corporate opinion that their limited appeal to viewers would not begin to recoup an allotted budget, and have been shuttled into television. Spheeris, financially comfortable from a brief, successful foray into mainstream, personally financed her most recent documentary.

The few women directors who, however fleetingly, found themselves successful in mainstream, which equates profits with talent, have felt the sting of rejection when they have attempted to tweak the rigid formula that has granted them success—and failed. After a lifetime in the movies, Ida Lupino fulfilled a dream to direct a comedy; the public, accustomed to her taut, suspense-filled narratives, was disappointed. Nora Ephron, whose own misery fed most of her narratives, was deemed strident and unentertaining when she wandered from the delightful fantasy of light romantic comedy into material from her own life (and, most important, failed to make money); as a result, she has made no successful films since 1998. Amy Heckerling's failures were those that ventured too far from comedy. Mimi Leder tired of special effects and tried a film of her own choosing that faltered at the box office; and Kathryn Bigelow, whose films exhibit an ingenious blend of style and content, has not made a film in years.

While the increase in popularity of independent films benefits women directors to some extent, their future is not altogether promising, as history and culture work inevitably against them. Perhaps the primary benefit of this volume comes through sampling the many excellent films of these women directors and realizing the great wealth of stories about women's lives and experiences that remain untold.

Filmography

Dorothy Arzner

Christopher Strong. RKO Pictures, 1933.
Craig's Wife. Columbia Pictures, 1936.
Dance, Girl, Dance. RKO Pictures, 1940.

Ida Lupino

Not Wanted. Emerald Productions, 1949.
Never Fear. Filmmakers, 1950.
Outrage. Filmmakers, 1950.
Hard, Fast and Beautiful. Filmmakers, 1951.
The Hitch-Hiker. Filmmakers, 1953.
The Bigamist. Filmmakers, 1953.
The Trouble With Angels. Columbia Pictures, 1966.

Nora Ephron

This Is My Life. 20th Century-Fox. 1992.
Sleepless in Seattle. Sony Pictures, 1993.
Mixed Nuts. Sony Pictures, 1994.
Michael. Alphaville Pictures, 1996.
You've Got Mail. Warner Brothers, 1998.
Lucky Numbers. Paramount, 2000.
Bewitched. Sony Pictures, 2005.

Nancy Meyers

The Parent Trap. Disney, 1998.
What Women Want. Paramount, 2000..
Something's Gotta Give. Columbia, 2003.

Amy Heckerling

Fast Times at Ridgemont High. Universal, 1981.
Johnny Dangerously. 20th Century-Fox, 1982.
National Lampoon's European Vacation. Warner,1984.
Look Who's Talking. Sony Pictures, 1989.
Look Who's Talking Too. Sony Pictures, 1990.
Clueless. Paramount, 1995.
Loser. Sony Pictures, 2000.

Martha Coolidge

Old-Fashioned Woman. Films Inc., 1974.
Not a Pretty Picture. Coolidge Productions, 1976.
Valley Girl. MGM, 1985.
Real Genius. Sony Pictures, 1985.
Rambling Rose. Live/Artisan, 1991.
Lost in Yonkers. Sony Pictures, 1993.
Angie. Caravan,1994.
Three Wishes. HBO, 1995.
Out to Sea. 20th Century-Fox, 1997.
Introducing Dorothy Dandridge. HBO, 1999.
If These Walls Could Talk. HBO, 2000.
The Prince and Me. Paramount, 2004.

Kathryn Bigelow

The Loveless. Pioneer Films, 1982.
Near Dark. F/M, 1987.
Blue Steel. MGM, 1990.
Point Break. 20th Century-Fox, 1991.
Strange Days. 20th Century-Fox, 1995
The Weight of Water. Lions Gate, 2000.
K-19: The Widowmaker. Paramount, 2002.

Mimi Leder

The Peacemaker. Dreamworks, 1997.
Deep Impact. Paramount, 1998.
Pay It Forward. Warner Brothers, 2000.

Maya Deren

Meshes of the Afternoon. Mystic Fire Video,1990.
At Land. Mystic Fire Video, 1990.
A Study in Choreography for Camera. Mystic Fire Video, 1990.
Ritual in Transfigured Time. Mystic Fire Video, 1990.

Lizzie Borden

Born in Flames. First Run Features, 1983.
Working Girls. Anchor Bay, 1987.
Love Crimes. Miramax, 1992.

Mary Harron

I Shot Andy Warhol. MGM, 1996.
American Psycho. Universal, 1999.
The Notorious Bettie Page. HBO, 2006.

Julie Dash

Illusions. AFI Independent Filmmakers Program, 1982.
Daughters of the Dust. Kino International, 1992.
The Rosa Parks Story. CBS, 2002.

Nancy Savoca

True Love. Forward Films, 1989.
Dogfight. Warner Brothers,1991.
Household Saints. Sony Pictures, 1993.
If These Walls Could Talk. HBO, 1996.
24 Hour Woman. Lions Gate, 1999.
Dirt. Canned Pictures, Inc., 2003.

Allison Anders

Gas Food Lodging. Sony Pictures, 1992.
Mi Vida Loca. Channel 4 Films, 1993.
Grace of My Heart. Universal, 1996.
Sugar Town. Channel 4 Films, 1999.
Things Behind the Sun. Showtime Entertainment, 2001.

Penelope Spheeris

The Decline of Western Civilization. Part 1. Spheeris Films Inc., 1981.
The Decline of Western Civilization. Part 2. New Line Cinema, 1988.
The Decline of Western Civilization. Part 3. Spheeris Films Inc., 1998.
Suburbia. Warner Brothers, 1983.
The Boys Next Door. Anchor Bay, 1985.
Hollywood Vice Squad. First Look Studios, 1986.
Dudes. Lions Gate, 1987.
Thunder and Mud. Sony Pictures, 1988.
Wayne's World. Paramount, 1992.
The Beverly Hillbillies. 20th Century-Fox, 1993.
The Little Rascals. Universal, 1994.
Black Sheep. Paramount, 1996.
We Sold Our Souls to Rock and Roll. Divine Pictures, 2001.
The Kid and I. The Kid & I Productions LLC, 2005.

Barbara Kopple

Harlan County, U.S.A. Cabin Creek Films, 1976.
American Dream. Cabin Creek Films, 1991.
Fallen Champ: The Untold Story of Mike Tyson. Cabin Creek Films, 1994.
A Century of Women: Work and Family (codirector). Cabin Creek Films, 1994.
A Century of Women: Sexuality and Social Justice. Turner Entertainment, 1994.
Wild Man Blues. New Line Cinema, 1997.
A Conversation with Gregory Peck. NBC, 1999.
My Generation. Cabin Creek Films, 2000.
The Hamptons. PBS, 2002.

Gillian Armstrong

My Brilliant Career. New South Wales Film Corp., 1979.
14's Good, 18's Better. Australian Film Commission, 1980.
Mrs. Soffel. MGM, 1984.
High Tide. Tri-Star, 1987.
Bingo, Bridesmaids and Braces. Film Australia Pty. Ltd. 1988.
The Last Days of Chez Nous. Australian Film Commission, 1992.
Little Women. Columbia Pictures, 1994.
Not 14 Again. Beyond Films, 1996.
Oscar and Lucinda. AFFC, 1997.
Charlotte Gray. Film Four, 2001.

Jane Campion

Sweetie. New South Wales Film Corp., 1989.
An Angel at My Table. Australian Broadcasting Corp., 1990.
The Piano. CiBy 2000, 1993.
Portrait of a Lady. PolyGram, 1996.
Holy Smoke. Miramax, 1999.
In the Cut. Pathe, 2001.

Leni Riefenstahl

Triumph of the Will. Leni Riefenstahl-Produktion, 1935.
Olympia. Olympia Films, 1938.

Agnes Varda

La Pointe Courte. Cini-Tamaris, 1954.
Cleo From 5 to 7. Cini-Tamaris, 1962.
Le bonheur (Happiness). Parc Film, 1965.
One Sings, The Other Doesn't. Cini-Tamaris, 1977.
Vagabond. Channel 4 Films, 1986.
The Gleaners and I. C.N.D.P., 2001.

Lina Wertmuller

The Seduction of Mimi. European International Film, 1972.
Love and Anarchy. Fox Lorber, 1973.
Swept Away. Koch Lorber, 1975.
Seven Beauties. Koch Lorber, 1976.

Sofia Coppola

The Virgin Suicides. Paramount, 1999.
Lost in Translation. Universal Studios, 2003.

Kimberly Peirce

Boys Don't Cry. 20th Century-Fox, 1999.

Patty Jenkins

Monster. Sony Pictures, 2003.

Kasi Lemmons

Eve's Bayou. Lions Gate, 1987.
Caveman's Valentine. Universal Studios, 2001.

Anjelica Huston

Bastard Out of Carolina. Fox Lorber, 1996.
Agnes Browne. PolyGram, 2000.
Riding the Bus With My Sister. Hallmark, 2005.

Penny Marshall

Big. 20th Century-Fox, 1988.
Awakenings. Sony Pictures, 1990.
A League of Their Own. Sony Pictures, 1992.
Renaissance Man. Disney, 1994.
The Preacher's Wife. Buena Vista Home Entertainment, 1996.
Riding in Cars With Boys. Sony Pictures, 2001.

Barbra Streisand

Yentl. Barwood Films, 1983.
The Prince of Tides. Barwood Films, 1991.
The Mirror Has Two Faces. Barwood Films, 1996.

Elaine May

A New Leaf. Aries Productions, 1971.
The Heartbreak Kid. Palomar Pictures Corp., 1972,
Mikey and Nicky. Paramount, 1976.
Ishtar. Columbia, 1987.

Bibliography

Abramowitz, Rachel. "Jane Campion," in *Jane Campion: Interviews*, edited by Virginia Wright Wexman.

Aldama, Frederick Luis. *Postethnic Narrative Criticism: Magicorealism in Oscar "Zeta" Acosta, Ana Castillo, Julie Dash, Hanif Kureishi, and Salman Rushdie*. Austin: University of Texas Press, 2003.

Allen, Michael. *Contemporary U.S. Cinema*. New York: Longman, 2003.

"Amy Heckerling on Underage Actors, Full-Frontal Nudity and Other Fast Times." http://www.eonline.com/Features/Live/Film School 2000/Heckerling.

Anderson, Melissa. "The Modest Gesture of a Filmmaker: An Interview with Agnes Varda." *Cineaste*, Fall 2001.

Armes, Roy. *French Cinema*. New York: Oxford University Press, 1985.

Arzner, Dorothy. "Interview with Dorothy Arzner." Interview by Gerald Peary and Karyn Kay in *The Work of Dorothy Arzner: Towards a Feminist Cinema*, edited by Claire Johnston, 1975.

"Barbara Kopple." *Seattle Arts and Lectures*. http://www.lectures.org/kopple.html.

Berardinelli, James. "The Decline of Western Civilization: Part III." http://movie-reviews.colossus.net/movies/d/decline3.html.

Berardinelli, James. "The Peacemaker." http://moviereviews.colossus.net/movies/p/Peacemaker/html.

Berg-Pan, Renata. *Leni Riefenstahl*. Boston: Twayne Publishers, 1980.

Bobrow, Emily. "Penelope's World: Spheeris Returns with Third Punk Doc." *Indiewire:People*. http://www.indiewire.com/people/int_Spheeris_Penel_000711.html.

Bondanella, Peter. *Italian Cinema: From Neorealism to the Present* (3rd edition). New York: Continuum International Publishing Group, 2001.

Bourguignon, Thomas, and Michel Ciment. "Interview with Jane Campion: More Barbarian Than Aesthete," in *Jane Campion: Interviews*, edited by Virginia Wright Wexman.

Brakhage, Stan. *Film at Wit's End: Eight Avant-Garde Filmmakers*. Kingston, NY: McPherson & Company, 1989.

Brooks, Peter. *The Melodramatic Imagination: Balzac, Henry James, Melodrama and The Mode of Excess*. New Haven, CT: Yale University Press, 1976.

Campion, Jane. "Interview." *Sydney Morning Herald*, July 5, 1989. Reprinted in *Jane Campion Interviews*, edited by Virginia Wright Wexman.

Campion, Jane and Virginia Wright Wexman, eds *Jane Campion: Interviews*. Oxford: University of Mississippi Press, 1999.

Canby, Vincent. "A New Leaf." *New York Times*, March 12, 1071.

Cheshire, Ellen. *The Pocket Essential Jane Campion*. London: Pocket Essentials, 2002.

Ciment, Michel. "Two Interviews with Jane Campion," in *Jane Campion Interviews*, edited by Virginia Wright Wexman.

Clark, Veve A., Millicent Hodson, and Catrina Neiman. *The Legend of Maya Deren*. Vol 1 (Part 1 and 2). New York: Anthology of Film Archives, 1988.

Cohen, Richard. "High-School Confidential." *Rolling Stone*, September 7, 1995, 53.

Cole, Janis, and Holly Dale. *Calling the Shots: Profiles of Women Filmmakers*. Kingston, Ontario: Quarry Press, 1993.

Collins, Felicity. *The Films of Gillian Armstrong*. Victoria, Queensland: Australian Film Institute; 1999.

Corrigan, Timothy and Patricia White. *The Film Experience: An Introduction*. Boston: Bedford/St. Martin's, 2004.

Crown, Lawrence. *Penny Marshall: An Unauthorized Biography*. Riverside, California: Renaissance Books, 1999.

Cunha, Tom. "Barbara Kopple Shadows Woody Allen, Jazz Musician." *The Director's Chair Interviews*. http://industrycentral.net/director_interviews/ BK01. HTM.

Dargis, Manohla. "Naughty and Nice: Bettie Page Beyond the Va-Voom." *New York Times*, April 14, 2006.

Dash, Julie. *Daughters of the Dust: The Making of an African American Woman's Film*. New York: The New Press, 1992.

Denby, David. *New York*. March 26, 1990. 77.

Deren, Maya. "A Letter to James Card." April 19, 1955, in *Women and the Cinema: A Critical Anthology*, edited by Karyn Kay and Gerald Peary.

Deren, Maya. "Cinematography: The Creative Use of Reality," *Daedalus* (Winter 1960), 154–155.

De Vries, Hilary. "Curtain Call: Writer, Director and Now Playwright Nora Ephron Enters a New Stage with *Imaginary Friends*." *W*, December 2002 31(12), 194.

Donati, William. *Ida Lupino: A Biography*. Lexington: University of Kentucky Press, 1996.

Ferlita, Ernest and John R. May. *The Parables of Lina Wertmuller*. New York: Paulist Press, 1977.

Fischer, Lucy. *A History of the American Avant-Garde Cinema: A Film Exhibition Organized by the American Federation of Arts*. New York: American Federation of Arts, 1976.

Flitterman-Lewis, Sandy. *To Desire Differently: Feminism and the French Cinema*. Urbana: University of Illinois Press, 1990.

Geller, Theresa L. "Dorothy Arzner." *Senses of Cinema*. http://www.senses of cinema.com/.

Georgakas, Dan. "Ida Lupino: Doing It Her Way." *Cineaste*, Summer 2000, 25(3).

Gerosa, Melina. "Ephron, Symbolist." *Entertainment Weekly*, July 9, 1993, 33, n178.

Guerrero, ed. *Framing Blackness: The African American Image in Film*. Philadelphia: Temple University Press, 1993.

Hall, John. "Interview with Barbara Kopple." *Latent Image*. http://www.pages.emerson. edu/organizations/fas/latent_image/issues/1992-04/kopple.htm.

Haskell, Molly. *From Reverence to Rape: The Treatment of Women in the Movies*. New York: Holt, Rinehart and Winston, 1974.

Heck-Rabi, Louise. *Women Filmmakers: A Critical Reception*. Lanham, MD: The Scarecrow Press, 1984.

Hejnar, Mark. "The Next Decline: A Conversation with Penelope Spheeris about *The Decline of Western Civilization Part III*. *Fringecore Magazine*. http://www.fringecore. com/magazine/m8-5.htm.

Henshaw, Richard. "Women Directors: 150 Filmographies." *Film Comment* 8 (Nov.Dec. 1972), p. 34.

Hillier, Jim, ed. *American Independent Cinema: A Sight and Sound Reader*. London: British Film Institute, 2001.

———. *The New Hollywood*. New York: Continuum, 1992.

Holleran, Scott. "Rose Queen: An Interview with Martha Coolidge," *Box Office Mojo*. http://www.boxofficemojo.com/features/?id=14248 page num=28p=htm.

Hollywood Reporter, September 12, 1936, 3.

Infield, Glenn B. *Leni Riefenstahl: The Fallen Film Goddess*. New York: Thomas Y. Crowell Company, 1976.

Jacobson, Sarah. "Here comes 'the Sun'; Allison Anders Out of the Past." *Indiewire*. http://www.indiewire.com/people/int_Anders_Allison_010817.html

Jameson, Frederic. "Postmodernism and Consumer Society," in *The Anti-Aesthetic: Essays on Postmodern Culture*, edited by Hal Foster. Port Townsend, Washington: Bay Press, 1983.

Jayamanne, Laleen, ed. *Kiss Me Deadly: Feminism and Cinema For the Moment*. Sydney: Power Publications, 1995.

Jermyn, Deborah and Sean Redmond, eds. *The Cinema of Kathryn Bigelow: Hollywood Transgressor*. London: Wallflower Press, 2003.

Johnston, Claire, ed. *The Work of Dorothy Arzner: Towards a Feminist Cinema*. London: British Film Institute, 1975.

Kael, Pauline. *Deeper Into Movies*. Boston: Little, Brown, 1972.

Kay, Karyn and Gerald Peary. *Women and the Cinema: A Critical Anthology*. New York: E, P, Dutton, 1977.

Kuhn, Annette, ed. *Queen of the B's: Ida Lupino Behind the Camera*. Westport: Greenwood Press, 1995.

Landy, Marcia. *Italian Film*. Cambridge, U.K.: University of Cambridge Press, 2000.

Lane, Christina. *Feminist Hollywood: From Born in Flames to Point Break*. Detroit: Wayne State University Press, 2000.

Levy, Emanuel. *A Cinema of Outsiders: The Rise of the American Independent Film*. New York: New York University Press, 1999.

Levy, Emanuel. "French Cinema's Continuous Creativity." http://www.emanuellevy.com/ printpage.php?article ID=1474.

Lewis, Jon, ed. *The New American Cinema*. Durham, NC: Duke University Press, 1998.

Lucia, Cynthia. "Redefining Female Sexuality in the Cinema: An Interview with Lizzie Borden." *Cineaste*, (Feb. 1993), 19(2–3), 6–10.

Marcus, Millicent. *Italian Film in the Light of Neorealism*. Princeton, NJ: Princeton University Press, 1986.

Margulies, Lee. "Tribute—1975." *Action* 10, 2 (March/April 1975), 18.

Maslin, Janet. "Film View; Penelope Spheeris Finds the Heart of Rock." *New York Times*, June 26, 1988.

Maslin, Janet. "The Cold War is Back, Nuclear Bombs and All." *New York Times*, September 26, 1977.

Mayne, Judith. *The Woman at the Keyhole: Feminism and Women's Cinema*. Bloomington, IN: Indiana University Press, 1990.

————. *Directed by Dorothy Arzner*. Bloomington, IN: Indiana University Press, 1999.

McCaughey, Martha and Neal King, eds. *Reel Knockouts: Violent Women in the Movies*. Austin: University of Texas Press, 2001.

McCreadie, Marsha. *The Women Who Write the Movies*. New York: Carol Publishing Group, 1994.

Mercurio, James P. "Contemporary Melodrama: Interview with Allison Anders." *Creative Screenwriting* 3.4 (1996): 25–28.

Motion Picture Daily, September 12, 1936, 2.

Nesselson, Lisa. "A Conversation with Gregory Peck." *Variety*. November 15, 1999, 377(11) 91.

Never Fear. Directed by Ida Lupino. Emerald Productions, Inc. 1950.

Newsweek, August 1, 1949, 64.

Nichols, Bill, ed. *Maya Deren and the American Avant-Garde*. Berkeley, CA: University of California Press, 2001.

"No Future: Andrea Sperling talks with Penelope Spheeris about *The Decline of Western Civilization Part III*." *Filmmaker*. http://www.filmmakermagazine.com/Winter1998/nofuture.php.

Onstad, Katrina. "Tales From the Front: A Conversation with Documentarian Barbara Kopple." http://www.cbc.ca/arts/film/Kopple.html.

Patterson, Troy. "What a Beach: Documentarian Barbara Kopple Reveals the Sociological Shenanigans of a Ritzy Summer Enclave in The Hamptons." *Weekly, May 31, 2002, 1656, 24.Entertainment*.

Polan, Dana B. *Jane Campion*. London: British Film Institute, 2002.

Porton, Richard. *Film and the Anarchist Imagination*. London: Verso, 1999.

Quart, Barbara Koenig. *Women Directors: The Emergence of a New Cinema*. New York: Praeger, 1988.

Rabinovitch, Lauren. *Points of Resistance: Power and Politics in the New York Avant-Garde Cinema 1943–1971*. Urbana and Chicago: University of Illinois Press, 1991.

Ransley, Hannah. "Kathryn Bigelow", Yoram Allon, Del Cullen & Hannah Patterson, eds. *Contemporary North American Film Directors: A Wallflower Critical Guide* (2nd edition). London: Wallflower Press, 2002.

Redding, Judith M. and Victoria A. Brownworth. *Film Fatales: Independent Women Directors*. Seattle: Seal Press, 1997.

Rich, B. Ruby. *Chick Flicks: Theories and Memories of the Feminist Film Movement*. Durham, NC: Duke University Press, 1998.

Robson, Jocelyn, and Beverley Zalcock. *Girls' Own Stories: Australian and New Zealand Women's Films*. London: Scarlet Press, 1997.

Rosen, Marjorie. *Popcorn Venus: Women, Movies and the American Dream*. New York: Coward, McCann and Geoghegan, 1973.

Rosenfeld, Paul. "Reconcilable Differences Series: The Rites of Hollywood." *Los Angeles Times*, July 12, 1987, 4.

Rosenthal, Alan. *The Documentary Conscience : A Casebook in Filmmaking*. Berkeley, CA: University of California Press, 1980.

Savlov, Marc. "Interview with SXSW Honoree Penelope Spheeris," *Serious Rock and Roll Anthropology*. http://www.austinchronicle.com/issues/dispatch/2001-03-09/screens_feature.html.

Seger, Linda. *When Women Call The Shots: The Developing Power and Influence of Women in Television and Film.* New York: Henry Holt and Company, 1996.

Scheib, Ronnie. "Ida Lupino," *American Directors II,* Jean-Pierre Coursodon and Pierre Sauvage, eds. New York: McGraw-Hill Book Company, 1983.

"She Made it: Mimi Leder, Television Director, Producer." *The Museum of Television And Radio.* http://www.shemadeit.org/meet/biography.aspx?m=38.

Simon, Scott. "A Conversation With Documentarian Barbara Kopple," NPR Weekend Edition, June 19, 2004.

Sitney, P. Adams. *Visionary Film: The American Avant-Garde.* New York: Oxford University Press, 1979.

———, ed. *Film Culture Reader.* New York: Praeger, 1970.

Slide, Anthony. *Early Women Directors.* Cranbury, NJ: A.S. Barnes and Co., Inc., 1977.

———. *The Silent Feminists: America's First Women Directors.* Lanham, MD: The Scarecrow Press, Inc., 1996.

Smith, Alison. *Agnes Varda.* Manchester, U.K.: Manchester University Press, 1998.

Smith, Gavin. "'Momentum and Design': Interview with Kathryn Bigelow." In *The Cinema of Kathryn Bigelow*, by Deborah Jermyn, and Sean Redmond, eds. Spicer, Andrew. *Film Noir.* New York: Longman, 2002.

St. Johns, Adela Rogers. "Get Me Dorothy Arzner," *Silver Screen*, IV(2), December 1933, 24.

T.M.P. *New York Times Film Reviews.* July 25, 1949, 11(4).

Tasker, Yvonne. *Working Girls: Gender and Sexuality in Popular Cinema.* London: Routledge, 1998.

Taylor, Charles. "Sapocalypse Now." http://www.salon.com/ent/movies/reviews/1998/05/07 review.hmtl? CP.

Taylor, Charles. "*The Peacemaker* Makes Casualties of George Clooney and Nicole Kidman." http://www.salon.com/Sept97/entertainment/peace 970926.html

Thompson, Kristin and David Bordwell. *Film History: An Introduction.* New York: McGraw-Hill, Inc., 1994.

Time, October 12, 1936, 32.

Varda, Agnes and Melissa Anderson. "The Modest Gesture of the Filmmaker: An Interview with Agnes Varda. *Cineaste*, Fall 2001, 26(4), 24.

Webb, Veronica. "Big bad Bigelow—film director Kathryn Bigelow—Director Profile—Interview," November, 1995. http://www.findarticles.com/p/articles/mi_m1285/is_n11_v25ai_17632982/print

Williamson, Kristin. "The New Filmmakers," in *Jane Campion: Interviews*, edited by Virginia Wright Wexman.

Winokur, L.A. "Barbara Kopple." *Progressive*, November 92, 56 11.

Wood, Jennifer M. "Free Love, Commercialism and Violence: Oscar-Winning Documentarian Barbara Kopple explores Three Generations of Woodstock," *Moviemaker*. http://www.moviemaker.com/issues/43/documentary.htm.

Wood, Robin. *Hollywood from Vietnam to Reagan.* New York: Columbia University Press, 1986.

"Young Man with a Gun," *Time*, January 22, 1951, 19–20.

Index

Abu Ghraib, 59
Action and special effects, 44–45, 46–47, 48–50
Adams, Brooke, 75
Adjani, Isabelle, 150
African-American film, 67–71; 137–138
Akins, Zoe, 3
Albert, Eddie, 149
Alcott, Bronson, 98
Alcott, Louisa May, 94, 98
Alda, Alan, 21
Allegory, 127–129
Allen, Woody, 88, 89, 130
Allende, Isabel, 73
Alley, Kirstie, 24
Allison, Dorothy, 140
Altman, Robert, 29, 78
American Film Institute (AFI), 22, 47, 66, 135
American Graffiti (1973), 23
Anders, Allison: childhood and early life, 74; education, 74; directing, 74–78; awards, 74–75. Films: *Gas Food Lodging*, 74, 75–76; *Mi Vida Loca*, 76–77; *Grace of My Heart*, 77; *Sugar Town*, 77–78; *Things Behind the Sun*, 78
Anders, Devon, 74
Anders, Tiffany, 74
Anderson, Elizabeth, 37
Angelou, Maya, 88

Anger, Kenneth, 42
Another Evening With Harry Stoones (1961), 146
Antonioni, Michelangelo, 93
Arch, Jeff, 16
Argo, Victor, 72
Arlen, Alice, 15, 16
Arnold, Tom, 83
Armstrong, Gillian: early life, 93; education, 93–94; directing, 94; awards, 93–94; Films: *One Hundred a Day*, 94; *The Singer and the Dancer*, 94; *Smokes and Lollies*, 94; *14's Good: 18's Better*, 94; *Bingo, Bridesmaids and Braces*, 94; *Not 14 Again*, 94; *My Brilliant Career*, 94–95; *Mrs. Soffel*, 95–96; *High Tide*, 96–97; *The Last Days of Chez Nous*, 97–98; *Little Women*, 98–99; *Oscar and Lucinda*, 99–100; *Charlotte Gray*, 101
Aronson, Letty, 88
Arzner, Dorothy: early education, 2; early studio work, 2; directing, 2–7, Films: *Fashions For Women*, 2; *Ten Modern Commandments*, 2; *Get Your Man*, 2; *Manhattan Cocktail*, 2; *The Wild Party*, 2; *Sarah and Son*, 2; *Anybody's Woman*, 2; *Paramount on Parade* (a sequence) 2; *Honor Among Lovers*, 2; *Working Girls*, 2; *Merrily We Go to Hell*, 2; *Christopher Strong*, 2, 3–4; *Nana*, 2; *Craig's Wife*, 2,

About the Author

MARY G. HURD is Director of Film Studies at East Tennessee State University. She has been a contributor to major reference works from Oxford University Press and Salem Press.